Ivan Reid is senior lecturer in education at the University of Leeds. He previously taught at the universities of Bradford and Liverpool, Edge Hill College of Education, both comprehensive and secondary modern schools. He has written several books, a large number of articles and is an editor of the *British Journal of Sociology of Education* and *Research in Education*.

Also by Ivan Reid

Sociological Perspectives on School and Education
*(Open Books 1978)*

Sociology and Teacher Education
*(with Eileen Wormald, ATCDE 1974)*

Sunday Schools; a suitable case for treatment
*(Chester House 1980)*

Social Class Differences in Britain
2nd Edition. *(Blackwell 1981)*

Sex Differences in Britain
*(with Eileen Wormald, Blackwell 1982)*

Teachers, Computers and the Classroom
*(with James Rushton, Manchester University Press 1985)*

Ivan Reid

# THE SOCIOLOGY OF SCHOOL AND EDUCATION

Fontana Press

First published in 1986 by Fontana Paperbacks
8 Grafton Street, London W1X 3LA

Copyright © Ivan Reid 1986

Fontana Press is an imprint of
Fontana Paperbacks, part of
the Collins Publishing Group

Set in Linotron Garamond
Made and printed in Great Britain by
William Collins Sons & Co. Ltd, Glasgow

This book is dedicated to the memory of my grandparents and parents-in-law.

# Contents

List of Tables

# 8 Education, Occupation and Mobility

## 10 Appendices

# Tables

# 1

# Foreword – A Reader's Guide

## 1.1 About this book

The sociology of education is an exciting, vital and useful field of knowledge for all those interested in, or practising, education. This foreword shares with readers something of the author's aims in writing the book, outlines its contents and suggests ways in which it can be used.

The discipline of sociology of education in Britain is both extensive and complex. It is extensive in terms of its subject matter and research, and complex in its range of approaches. The major aim of this book is to present the discipline, at an introductory level, as a particular approach to educational phenomena. It attempts to come to grips with the reality of the sociology of education in a straightforward way. At the same time, it neither avoids current concerns within the discipline nor a recognition of the limitations of the subject.

The sociology of education is a subject of importance for everyone interested in schooling and education in our society. So this book is addressed to students of education in the fullest sense. By definition, all its readers will have experienced schooling, and the majority are or will be involved professionally in education. More specifically, the book is aimed to be of direct benefit to those engaged in initial and in-service courses of teacher education (BEds, PGCEs, diplomas and masters degrees), together with non-award bearing courses – both those on the course and in subsequent practice. Thus it sets out to show how the discipline contributes to our understanding of educational phenomena, rather than merely forming a part of the body of knowledge called sociology. To be useful, the sociology of education must be good sociology, but even more importantly, it must be relevant to the practice of education.

There are two aspects of textbooks in the field which consistently annoy involved readers – the over-use of material from other cultures, and statements or research which appear so naive about educational/social reality as to suggest the reader's experience to be superior to that of the sociologist. In order to avoid these, I have used British material wherever possible and attempted to avoid furthering educational naivety (ever a danger) by pointing out when it occurs.

Textbooks often veer between two extremes. Some are full of fine-sounding over-generalizations which leave readers wondering how these relate to reality. Others can be extensive bibliographies where readers have difficulty in seeing the wood for the trees. This book adopts a course between the two. I have selected essential topics, so as to allow, in a relatively small volume, for the fairly extensive display of the work of sociologists of education. I hope this will give readers as deep a familiarity with the literature and ideas of the discipline as might be expected. Extensive referencing will point readers towards further literature and knowledge.

One unfortunate outcome of the timetables imposed by educational establishments on students is that disciplines become defined as a set of topics. Consequently, textbooks tend to be used for specific and limited purposes rather than read as a whole. In the circumstances this is a natural and legitimate use, which the design of this book will contribute to. At the same time, such a segmented approach can lead to compartmentalization. One mark of the good student – probably only because of its rarity – is the ability to relate relevant material from one topic to the treatment of another. There are good reasons for treating the content of this book as a whole. First, it is designed to be an overall introduction to the discipline. Second, and more important, there are very definite inter-relationships between the topics presented. For example, you cannot fully understand what goes on in a classroom without taking account of other factors, such as the nature of the institution of which it is part, and the structure of the educational and social systems in which it operates.

## 1.2 Reader's aids

In order to achieve comprehensive treatment of topics, identify relationships between different topics and avoid over-duplication of material, extensive in-text referencing is used. In the body of the book chapters are referred to simply by number, and each major sub-section by a further number; hence this section is 1.2. Further sub-sections are referred to by letters and roman numerals. A full listing of the titles of all sections and sub-sections is found in the Contents List on p. 7. Further and detailed cross-referencing is contained in 12, the Subject Index.

This book contains a good deal of quantative research data, much of it presented in tables, a full listing of which is at p. 13. Details of the definitions of social class and educational qualifications used in reported research are provided in 10.1 and 10.2. To save space and take account of the growing number and use of acronyms and abbreviations – many of which are more familiar than the full title – these have been used throughout the text and a key provided at 10.1.

Finally, in view of the growing number of collections of readings (readers) in the sociology of education, many of which reproduce material from journals, other sources and each other, there is cross-referencing in 11 (Bibliography and Author Index) to any listed readers. This should assist access to these sources.

## 1.3 Routes through the book

The presentation, assimilation and use of a body of knowledge is never straightforward or predictable. Textbook writers can only partly anticipate the needs and demands of their readers. The order of presentation of the discipline here derives from my experience in teaching the sociology of education (and sustaining interest in it), with some heed given to the syllabuses in teacher education and sociology. In the end, though, a compromise has to be struck between these and the many constraints of a textbook. So the map which follows provides, for those who need it, an outline of how they may read or use this volume.

The obvious, straightforward route is from 2 to 9. This exposes readers initially to a consideration of the uniqueness of the approach of sociology of education to educational phenomena, reviews the variety of approaches it employs and something of the development, academic and social environment and purpose of the discipline (2). In 3, 4 and 5, readers are taken into the familiar worlds of school and classroom and shown the enormity of the task of describing schools and classrooms and examine the nature of the sociology of the school (3), of schools as social institutions and the cultures found in them (4) and the more intimate consideration derived from the participants' – pupils' and teachers' – viewpoints, their interaction and negotiation (5). Much of the content of 2 to 5 points to an intimate relationship between what goes on in schools and society outside. In 6, differentiation in school and classroom and its correspondence with differentiation in society is explored, a discussion which provides a bridge between the sociology of the school and that of education. The ways in which educational achievement are related to social class, sex and ethnic groups are the major concern of 7, which also looks at possible explanations for these relationships. In 8 we look at how education is related to occupation and income, its economic role and the part it plays in social mobility (movement between social classes) and at some of the explanatory theories. Finally, 9 takes up the question of the extent to which education reproduces the existing social structure, serves the interests of state or dominant class(es), and the extent to which education and its participants are independent of the social, economic and political contexts in which they operate. Some guidance is offered on the limitations and usefulness of the sociology of education to educational practice.

For some, a more attractive route will be to start with the familiar – schools and classrooms (4 and 5) – which will lead them on to the wider aspects of education and society (6 to 8) and then to see how and where the interpretative views were provided – the sociology of education (2 and 9). A further route begins with the role and relationships of education and society (7 and 8) which leads back into differentiation in the two sites (6), and school and classroom (3 to 5), to arrive at an exploration of the discipline (2 and 9).

While the three routes outlined above are the most direct, they do not exhaust the possibilities. Using 12, thematic routes are easy to find and allow for the rapid assimilation of what the book has to say on particular topics. It is the author's hope that whatever route is chosen by readers, their exploration will be fruitful and lead them well beyond the confines of this volume into the less constrained and extremely fertile fields which lie beyond it, as indicated by the references and bibliography.

## 1.4 Acknowledgements

I have always been impressed with the saying that within each teacher there was a textbook on what they taught. So my first gratitude goes to all those who sustained my audacious venture into a second textbook and in particular to Pat, Diane and Helen who gave their usual unsurpassable family support, with occasional and healthy lack of interest.

As I pointed out in my first textbook, in the sociology of education, one is struck by how little of what one writes can really be called one's own and consequently the considerable debt owed to others. Wherever possible this has been formally acknowledged by reference, but here it is generally and genuinely professed. I trust that those who look in vain for mention or full discussion of their work will appreciate the constraints of a textbook and the premise from which this one is written.

What insights into the discipline I have would not have been attained without the continual challenge of my students, mainly at the Universities of Bradford and Leeds and at Edge Hill College of Education, whose unique combination of enthusiasm and scepticism, friendship and 'chalk-face' experience I have greatly enjoyed. Many colleagues have similarly contributed and I am particularly grateful to those who have helped to create the space necessary for sustained bouts of research and writing. I am especially grateful to Sylvia Vallance who not only typed parts of the manuscript but whose cheerfulness and efficiency helped me to maintain my administrative role within the School of Education, University of Leeds.

I am also grateful to Patrick Taylor of Open Books for releasing me from my contract and thus enabling me to undertake a new textbook rather than a second edition. I was delighted to re- establish a publishing relationship with Helen Fraser, whose advice and encouragement have been extremely helpful. My work has benefited too from the often unsung talents of sub-editing supplied in this case by Ariane Goodman.

Notwithstanding my indebtedness to those mentioned and not mentioned above, I unreservedly claim all the book's shortcomings for myself.

The author and publisher would like to thank the following for permission to use or reproduce data or diagrams presented in this book: Basil Blackwell, Oxford, and authors for data from Price and Bain, (1976); the editor of *Centre for Educational Sociology Collaborative Research Newsletter* for a diagram from Burnhill, (1981); the Controller of Her Majesty's Stationery Office for Crown Copyright data from: *Education for All* (1985); *Education Statistics for the United Kingdom* (1984); *General Household Survey 1982* (1984); *Higher Education* (1963); *Statistics of Education* (1964 and 1975); the DES for unpublished data; Heinemann Educational Books Ltd, London, for a diagram from Wallace (1969); ISIS for unpublished data; Longman Group Ltd, Harlow, and authors for data from Davie, Butler and Goldstein (1972); Penguin Books Ltd, Harmondsworth, and author for a diagram from Barnes (1976); Andrew Pollard for diagrams from his chapter in Barton and Meighan; John Wiley and Sons, London, for a diagram from Gannaway's chapter in Stubbs and Delamont (1976).

# 2

# Sociological Perspectives
on School and Schooling

What this book tells is what every teacher knows, that the
world of school is a social world. . . . It is a unique world. It is
the purpose of this book to explore it . . . I believe that all
teachers, great and small, have need of insight into the social
realities of school life; that they perish, as teachers, without it.

*Willard Waller (1932)*

## 2.1 A topic for all

Nearly everyone in our society goes to school. This long and
intimate exposure to institutions of learning, together with parents'
subsequent concern for their children's education and the political
and economic importance of education, appear to ensure that we all
have well-developed ideas about education. We tend to hold these
opinions with far greater confidence than those we hold about other
common institutional experiences, for example, of the family, the
community, the workplace, medicine, the law and so on. Indeed, it
is clear that there are more self-appointed experts in the field of
education than in almost any other. Yet very rarely are teachers and
others working in education recognized by the public as authorities
on the subject of schools and education. In conversation, their
expertise and professional opinion is much more frequently
challenged than that of others, including motor mechanics,
plumbers and doctors. In the framing and implementation of
educational legislation the education profession is likely to be given
a back seat.

In the education of teachers and the academic study of education we see a similar diversity of expertise and competition for authority. In teacher education there is a tension, however artificial, between 'method' (essentially concerned with the practical – how to teach a subject, an age or type of child) and 'theory' (those aspects of certain disciplines which are seen as necessary for teachers to experience). The tension between the two is clearly false, but well established and rarely overcome other than by the individual student or teacher. The diversity goes much further. Within 'theory', the typical teacher education course includes recognizable elements of at least the psychology, sociology, history and philosophy of education, to mention only the best established areas.

This book takes a very particular set of views of classrooms, schools and education – those gained from the sociology of education. This chapter outlines the particular characteristics of such an approach, while the chapters which follow demonstrate the approach in action. This book is written in the belief that any understanding of teaching and learning which neglects the social factors involved will be partial and misleading.

## 2.2 What is the sociology of education?

Subjects or disciplines can never be identified or distinguished by reference only to their content. As we have seen, schools and education feature in a very large number of disciplines. The only factor which allows one to identify a discipline and to set it apart from any other is the approach it adopts towards its subject matter. This then is our first consideration.

The sociology of education is best seen as a particular approach to the explanation of educational phenomena – an approach distinguished by the fact that it is *sociological*. Sociology is by definition concerned with the social. One way of appreciating this is to think in terms of levels of abstraction. A human being can be viewed at a variety of such levels – as a chemical, physical or biological entity, as a discrete individual in the psychological or theological sense or, from the sociological viewpoint, as a social being – a part of a social situation or system. Hence sociology is not particularly concerned with individuals but with *people*. People are essentially social beings: in very many senses they do not exist other than in a social setting, nor can they be seen as other than participants in, or products of, social experience. Sociologists do not ignore the non-social aspects of human beings but in referring to these they use knowledge from other disciplines. What is peculiar about the sociology of education is that ultimately it approaches education at a level of abstraction which is essentially concerned with the social institutions of education, from peer groups through classes and schools to the system of education, with institutional compositions, structures, procedures, ideologies and functioning (workings and outcomes), and with inter-relationships between education and other institutions.

The most basic assumption of the sociological approach to school and education is that these are social institutions, involving social beings and social processes and behaviour. At one level this is an obvious statement, to which most people would subscribe. At another it is easy to see that the approaches of other disciplines are asocial, in that they concentrate, for example, on the individual rather than the social.

Hence, being *sociological* is the first basic characteristic of the approach. There are three more – theoretical, empirical and objective. Together they can be seen as a set of reasonable criteria of recognition for the discipline.

*Theoretical.* The word is used here in a general sense to suggest that the sociology of education goes beyond pure description. It is concerned with explanations of educational phenomena which are couched in terms other than the characteristics of the phenomena being explored. One simple example, abundantly illustrated in this book, is the way in which factors from the social structure are seen as important in explaining what goes on in classrooms and schools.

*Empirical.* Sociology of education, in all its forms, depends on observation of one type or another. The variety is considerable – from information from existing sources, through data collected from questionnaires, tests and interviews (sometimes treated statistically), to various forms of direct and indirect observation and experimentation through change or comparison. The importance of empirical investigation is that such knowledge can be checked by further observation, either of the same type (replication) or using other methods. In this way the knowledge gained is both developmental and accumulative.

*Objective.* Sociology of education is more than merely a single individual's reflection upon, or reaction to, a social situation or knowledge. Of course, it has to be appreciated that facts never speak for themselves, presentation implies interpretation, and consequently objectivity is only relative. However, an expectation of the discipline must be some degree of objectivity. This is attained either by sociologists viewing phenomena from a variety of perspectives (see 2.3), a proper use of their data, or by their being explicit about the perspectives, values and evidence they use. In any case a measure of objectivity, or at least opportunity for appraisal, is afforded by subscription to the two other tenets – theory and empiricism.

In so defining the sociology of education, a clear statement is being made that the discipline is directly and substantially part of sociology *per se.* There are two main implications. On the one hand, the sociology of education is affected by the interests, content and direction of sociology itself and, on the other, it makes considerable contributions to it. This relationship is intimate and has no predominant direction, as Gouldner (1956) has argued: 'Any metaphor which conceives of applied social science as the offspring, and of the basic discipline as the parent is misleading. It obscures the point that the applied sciences often contribute as much to pure science as they receive from it.' The subject matter of the sociology of education and the fact that the discipline is mainly practised in teacher education also indicate that it has contributions to make at a more pragmatic level. This is not to imply that the discipline is or necessarily will be about providing specific prescriptions or answers to practical teaching, classroom or school problems. Indeed none of the other contributory disciplines to education addresses itself to such direct problems. What the sociology of education does provide is both a unique picture and a questioning analysis of education. This is precisely the value of the discipline. Its role is educative rather than prescriptive or directly utilitarian, in that it enables disciplined thinking about education in a separate and different way. Its prime contribution is its singular insistence on viewing schools and education as pre-eminently social. Such a view is in contrast to, and corrective of, both common everyday inclinations of the public, professionals and policy makers and of other disciplines in education, particularly some forms of psychology of education.

The influence of the sociology of education can be recognized in educational-policy documents. Compare the following examples:

> Intellectual development during childhood appears to progress as if it were governed by a single central factor, usually known as 'general intelligence', which may be broadly described as innate all-round intellectual ability . . . We were informed that, with few exceptions, it is possible at a very early age to predict with some degree of accuracy the ultimate level of a child's intellectual powers . . . (*Secondary Education* 1938).

> The numbers who are capable of benefiting from higher education are a function not only of heredity but also of a host of other influences varying with standards of educational provision, family incomes and attitudes and the education received by previous generations (*Higher Education* 1963).

In the first quotation the singular contribution is that of psychology. The pupil is seen as an individual with a given innate potential. In the second quotation (some twenty-five years on) there is a clear if not predominant sociological consideration. The pupil is seen as a person whose potential is related to social factors.

## 2.3 Sociological perspectives

Like most other disciplines, the sociology of education contains a number of approaches, variously called theories, models, or, as we shall refer to them, perspectives. The value of an appreciation of the perspectives in use can be easily illustrated. First, by a somewhat extreme analogy. Suppose we were to go for a walk on the Yorkshire moors with four people. While we are enjoying the physical experience, we observe the behaviour and (since it's a story) peer into the minds of our companions. One, a geologist, stares into the distance, fascinated by an outcrop of unusual rock. Another, an archaeologist, looks at mid-distance to the site of a neolithic long barrow. The third, a botanist, is looking at the ground, having just avoided crippling a rare flora. The last – this one an ornithologist – stands transfixed, eyes heavenward, homing in on a flock of migrating birds. The walkers are all human, all are sharing the same time and space, but viewing different aspects of the same reality because of their separate perspectives. Even if they were to pool their perspectives we would not have a total view, we should need others. Fortunately it is extremely unlikely, but, if they were so encapsulated in their separate perspectives, it is possible that they could overlook what many would assume to be the most important feature of the landscape – an isolated pub! The perspectives that sociologists bring to bear on the school and education are not quite as bizarre as those in our analogy.

Secondly, we can appreciate the role that the perspectives play in the process of research and the establishment of knowledge. They provide, through their assumptions, a framework or structure within which a person recognizes problems to be solved and frames questions (hypotheses) to be answered. In turn it shapes the observations made, the methods used to collect information or make observations and a framework within which findings are presented and generalized statements made. These components and processes are illustrated in Table 2.1, which suggests two further points: all stages are interrelated – perspective affects observation and in turn observation affects perspective – and that the process has no obvious starting point. A common fallacy is that all science begins with theory, but a moment's consideration shows that observation or experience must precede, and be intimately related to, any theory.

The exact number of perspectives in the sociology of education is open to debate and, according to Bernstein (1974), depends upon who is counting. Initially, it is useful to view them in two groups,

**Table 2.1**
The components and process of sociology

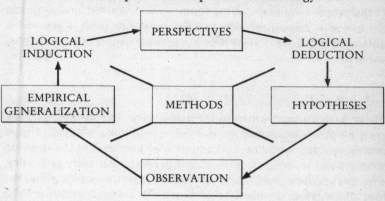

Based on page ix, Wallace 1969.

defined by the emphasis placed on either side of the basic dilemma about the nature of social reality. This dilemma, which is not new, can be simply illustrated by two questions – to what extent are *people* made by society? and to what extent is *society* made by people? Put that boldly the dilemma appears silly, since people and society are clearly products of each other – without people there would be no society, without society no people. The perspectives which favour emphasizing the first part of the dilemma we shall refer to as *structuralist*. A variety of alternative terms are to be found in the literature; each draws attention to particular aspects of the approach (as will be seen below): systems, macro, normative and holistic. They are concerned to explain how social behaviour is shaped by institutional and societal factors. They emphasize how similarities in the behaviour of, for example, teachers and pupils are the result of social/cultural pressures along a spectrum from legislation and school rules to mild ridicule and humour. We are all aware, at least on reflection, how our behaviour and, to an extent, our thinking are constrained by the social situations of which we are part. In the same way we recognize that teachers have similarities and that they are as they are because of what they have to do, where and how they have to do it, and that this relies on the expectations of the people around them, the training they received, and so on. At the extreme, these perspectives may appear to paint a somewhat unflattering picture of people as puppets on strings being pulled by society.

## 2.3a STRUCTURALIST PERSPECTIVES

These have a long history as the mainstay of the discipline. They emanate from what sociologists for a long time viewed as their central problem – the explanation of social order. That is, why do societies and social systems exist and persist? – or, more pointedly, what makes them tick? There are two main types, one based on the idea of *consensus* (general agreement), the other on *conflict*. The most common form of the first is structural functionalism, which has unique importance in the sociology of education; the best-known example of the second is one form of Marxist sociology. A useful introduction to these forms is to consider their theoretical defences.

### i *Consensus*

Social life would be impossible if there were no norms (recognized standards or patterns) in social situations, together with some commitment to these norms on the part of the people involved. This commitment, it is argued, comes from the fact that underlying the norms are shared values and beliefs about them (consensus). All apparent divisions in society – for example, differences in power – are countered by these values. Hence power is viewed as legitimate authority. In a similar fashion the social systems that make up society are in basic accord with each other. Society is viewed as being rather like a body: all parts are related to each other, change or movement in one affects the others, and parts cannot be autonomous from, or in conflict with, others. Functionalism has further implications. To appreciate these it is necessary to realize that the ideas were developed from problems faced by anthropologists

28

attempting to understand societies which had no written history. A basic assumption that developed was that there is no such thing as a redundant social activity. If the participants in rain dances don't believe they dance to cause rain, then the dance must be fulfilling some other function for society and the dancers or else it would not happen. As Cohen (1968) has pointed out, the development of this is Parsons's (1949) claim that one of the major tasks of sociology is to analyze society as a system of functionally interrelated variables. Parsons (1951) treats personality needs and social needs as variables of the social system. Hence analysis of professional rules (for example those of doctors) displays that they have functions for: *the profession* – they regulate entry, maintain rights and obligations; *society* – they provide and control a service; *practitioners and clients* – they regulate and structure their relationships allowing each to anticipate the other's behaviour and facilitate the exchange of the intimate without risk and involvement.

## ii *Conflict*

Society exists because it serves human beings' interests; however, such interests are not the same for all groups in society. Groups vary in their access to scarce resources in society – wealth, power, prestige, knowledge, etc. – and these differences are the basis of the conflict between interests and groups. Consensus exists only within a group with shared interests. General values in society are the values of the group which has control and hence the ability to impose (by coercion or inducement) their group values on the rest. Conflicts may not always be apparent – they become institutionalized or remain latent – but this situation cannot remain for long because group interests seek expression and autonomy. Marx saw the major axis in society as the relationship of groups to the means of production. The chief area of conflict was in social-class terms and between those who owned and those who did not own these means. Dahrendorf (1959) suggested that the axis was authority (power to impose one's will on others) and that the arena for viewing conflict should not be society as a whole but any area that was subject to the same authority (e.g., industrial enterprise, school); accordingly, there are many different conflicts within society and not one as suggested by Marx. Van Den Berghe (1963) proposed that the theory be developed to include conflicts over all types of scarce goods in society.

### iii *Consensus and conflict*

These are two views which may appear to be incompatible and opposed. They are far from mutually exclusive, however, since consensus and conflict are obviously both characteristic of social life. Thus it is not a question of accepting one and rejecting the other. Some commentators, for example Dahrendorf, have suggested they vary in their utility depending on the nature of the social situation one is observing. Most agree that the two forms not only contain elements of reality but also of each other. Van Den Burghe has identified how they overlap or converge.

*Both present a holistic view*, seeing society as a system of inter-related parts, and may be criticized for overstressing this factor while under-estimating the relative autonomy of some parts of society (including education).

*Consensus and conflict have dual roles*. As Coser (1956) has pointed out, conflict can be a stabilizing and integrative force within the groups involved. At the same time, consensus about such norms as individual *laissez-faire* or competition is hardly likely to contribute to social solidarity.

*Both share an evolutionary model of social change*. Conflict sees a dialectical process towards progress, while consensus sees society moving towards greater structural complexity.

These two forms are then partial and complementary. Their main objective is to examine the ways in which features of the social structure affect (or are related to) observed behaviour in social situations. In pursuing this approach they are often criticized for failing to give sufficient consideration to the subjective under-standing and active involvement of the social beings who constitute society.

Perspectives favouring the second part of the dilemma about the nature of social reality we shall refer to as *interpretative*. Again, a variety of terms are used to indicate aspects of this approach: action, micro, interactionist and atomistic. These perspectives emphasize the role of people in constructing or negotiating their own meanings of social reality. Hence we recognize among teachers that each has a certain uniqueness. Teacher X is not exactly the same as teacher Y – and for such mercies we are often very grateful! The more intimate our knowledge or experience of people or situations, the more likely we are to be aware of such differences and variety. At the extreme, these perspectives may be seen to be suggesting that people are all discrete individuals and each social situation is unique and unrelated.

## 2.3b INTERPRETATIVE PERSPECTIVES

These emphasize the importance of the processes which lie between social structure and behaviour. The central character in these processes is the person (not an individual, as in psychology or theology) who is active in the construction of social reality. There are three main forms which are not too easily distinguished from each other.

### i *Interactionism*

This perspective has had a major impact on the sociology of education. It has its roots in the basic ideas of a classical social philosopher, G. H. Mead, which have been neatly presented by Blumer (1965). Mead's central concept was that of the *self*: that a person has the ability to be an object to him/herself – can see, communicate with and even act towards him/herself. In a social situation a person is capable of deciding what his/her needs are and how these can be satisfied, review the possible ways of achieving them, decide on the most appropriate action, undertake it and change course if their predictions prove incorrect. It may be helpful for readers to relate these ideas to such situations as a meeting of two people of the opposite sex, or a headteacher interviewing a pupil about an incident. The picture of social action or situations that emerges is active, involving interpretation and definition by the social actors, rather than pure response to external factors. Established social behaviour – the type we all rely on – is seen as an ongoing dynamic process, maintained only through common definitions and reactions. Most importantly, it suggests the whole and full range of possible human associations – co-operation, conflict, domination, exploitation, compromise without duress, and so on.

The implications for the sociological enterprise and research are considerable. It suggests that the 'objective' or outside view of a social situation has limited utility. It is only by gaining knowledge of the actor's perceptions and reactions to situations that an understanding of the action involved is to be achieved. Similarly, one should not assume that when two or more people occupy the same relationship with another – say, pupils to a teacher – they share similar views or necessarily engage in the same behaviour. Only by concentrating on the *subjective* meaning of the actor can one avoid a situation in which an investigator holds a different view or understanding of social reality from that held by the subjects studied. This is not to claim that structural factors are to be dismissed, but that a clear change of emphasis is called for: rather than suggesting, for example, that the bureaucratic organization of a tax office *determines* the behaviour of tax officers, the assertion is that it *affects* tax officers' definitions and interpretations.

## ii *Phenomenology*

This is derived from the philosophy of Husserl who suggested that we should be concerned only with phenomena – that (literally) which can be directly understood by our senses, or how things appear to our consciousness. What remains behind the phenomena cannot be determined. Hence phenomenologists are concerned, after Schutz, with how reality is contructed through social process and how the individuals involved acquire ways of thinking. The major concern, then, is to explore the 'commonsense', 'everyday' world of how people understand each other and share similar perceptions of the world. Each person, it is claimed, has a unique stock of knowledge and therefore to some degree views the world differently. Interaction takes place on the assumption that we can take for granted other people's knowledge or views, and ignore some of the differences between them and us.

Generally speaking, and particularly with people we know, such 'commonsense' assumptions work. With less familiar people and situations we must improvise, and this leads to some modifications in our 'typifications' (classifications or categories). Few distinctions are drawn between everyday life and the activities of social scientists, who construct typifications for scientific rather than 'practical' purposes. As Mennell (1974) suggests, 'to speak of multiple realities conveys an impression of the relativity and even subjectivity of truth, that all perspectives on reality are equally valid.' Thus the abiding impression, or task, of phenomenology is to question and explore the commonsense assumptions pervading everyday life.

### iii *Ethnomethodology*

This considers the way people understand each other – communication and interaction – as being problematic. It claims that actions and statements have an infinite ambiguity, suggesting that generalizations brought from one situation to another are most difficult, if not impossible. Douglas (1971) distinguishes *situational* ethnomethodologists, who are concerned with the negotiation of social order; a basic research method here is to disrupt everyday situations in order to expose the underlying assumptions. Garfinkel (1967) asked students to act as 'lodgers' in their own homes (with predictably disruptive effects!). Douglas's other group are *linguistic* ethnomethodologists who concentrate on language exchanges. All conversations contain more than their words convey – think about your 'family talk' and how understandable it would be to an outsider. In conversations we all assume 'knowledge' on the part of others. Most sociologists believe that the participants could explain a conversation to outsiders, though some ethnomethodologists might not accept such as acceptable evidence of their meaning and intentions.

These three perspectives emphasize respectively the importance of the processes, meanings and practical accomplishments of social life and reality. In pursuing this approach they are often criticized for failing to give sufficient consideration to structural pre-conditions (being ahistorical) and constraints, and for presenting an over-active picture of the typical social actor.

## 2.4 Bridging perspectives

It should be appreciated that so far we have indulged in the somewhat dangerous art of characterization (it's only dangerous to the extent that you believe it – so be warned). Our description of the two major perspectives in sociology, while making for clarity, is over-simplified in suggesting a separateness which neither should nor really does exist. The separable emphases are to an extent a reaction to the complexity and scope of the phenomena to be analyzed, together with the ideology implicit in the approaches and that of sociologists and the institutionalization of knowledge (see 2.5). Hence, while sociologists may identify with, or work within, a particular perspective, as in the case of the dilemma over the nature of social reality, they cannot deny others. Interpretative sociologists cannot ignore (or do so at their peril) the fact that social behaviour takes place in social contexts which have structures and histories, any more than structuralists can deny the importance of subjective meanings and how people's actions affect social reality.

It would also be incorrect to believe that sociologists are unable to work within both major perspectives. Indeed, two major classical writers (the main criteria for classical are being both dead and remembered), Marx (1818–83) and Weber (1864–1920), quite clearly recognized the essential duality of the nature of society. Marx wrote, 'Men make their own history, but they do not make it just as they please; they do not make it under circumstances chosen by themselves, but under circumstances directly encountered, given and transmitted from the past.' (From *The Eighteenth Brumaire of Louis Bonaparte*, quoted in Feuer 1969.)

Weber echoed and greatly developed this idea. He was intent on developing ways of explaining the nature of society which encompassed both its constraining influence on people *and* its construction and maintenance by people. He was sceptical of approaches which started from either extreme – social structure or individual – and suggested what amounts to starting in the middle by studying what he referred to as the 'specific acts of men'. Two 'schools' of sociology – Marxist and Weberian – have arisen and become the pervasive influence in contemporary British sociology of education. Both provide an analytical framework which is capable of encompassing the constraining aspects of society, the subjective understandings of its members and their activities in shaping and changing social reality. For some, the political connotations of Marxist sociology, particularly assumptions concerning the evolution towards socialism and communism, may be a distraction or grounds for rejection. Such reactions would ignore the fact that all social theories contain ideology (see 2.5) and, as we have seen (2.3), all imply views of the future as well as of the present. At our present state of knowledge it is appropriate to adopt a utilitarian approach to perspectives, taking from each what they have to offer rather than rejecting any on other grounds.

## 2.5 Perspectives on perspectives

Academic disciplines do not develop in isolation, identifying their own problems, producing new ideas, approaches and theories, presenting findings, and so on. They have a complex relationship with the social setting in which they operate. This is at once a simple and complicated point to make. If society, or its government, becomes interested in the effectiveness of education in relation to producing certain types of workers, then this interest, and probably the money made available, will encourage those disciplines involved to develop work and research in this area. Of course it works the other way round too: disciplines, because of their intrinsic interests, may reveal problems or research findings which capture the imagination or interest of society; or the interests of both society and disciplines may coincide. A good example from the sociology of education is the interest in the relationship between children's social class and their performance in education. As I have suggested elsewhere (Reid 1977a/81), a number of interrelated factors can be identified with this interest and the direction it took in the late 1950s and early 1960s. In its simplest form it can be seen as follows. On one side there was the continuing interest of the public, politicians and educationists in equality and equal opportunity in education, and in particular in the results of the 1944 Education Act. On the other, there were sociologists whose type of sociology (structural functionalism) gave them an interest in large-scale research and in seeking explanations for educational achievements outside the classroom, in the social structure. The coincidence of these two interests gave rise to a number of large-scale studies of social-class achievement in education (see also 7.2, 7.7).

An understanding of the sociology of education and the contents of this book requires some appreciation of the discipline's development and academic, social and ideological settings. While the discipline is obviously related to sociology *per se*, it is fundamentally an enterprise within teacher education. Though some 'academic' degree courses and 'A' level GCE syllabuses contain options or elements of it, the discipline is predominately taught and researched by those engaged in the pre- and in-service education of teachers. So the producers and consumers are, by definition, involved in teaching and the discipline is shaped by teacher education.

This relationship is well illustrated in the short history of the sociology of education in Britain. Despite the nineteenth-century writings of Spencer – one of the few, and oft-forgotten, British classical sociologists – those of Mannheim (published posthumously in 1962) and, indeed, Ottaway's text, *Education and Society* (1953), it was not till the early 1960s that the discipline 'took off'. The extension and expansion of teacher education was dramatic. In 1962 college courses were extended from two to three years, and after 1966 to three or four-year degree courses, as they all are now. The number of entrants rose from 16,785 in 1962 to 39,574 in 1966, peaking at 42,133 in 1972. Over the same period the number of graduates in training increased by two-thirds (*Statistics in Education 1970* and *1975*, Vol. 4). With the extention of college courses came a move to make education more academically respectable, by attempting to identify with the disciplines of which it is composed. Courses in education became courses in the history, philosophy, psychology and sociology of education. Elements of these had existed before. I well remember the vice-principal of the college I attended as a student displaying in his lectures such a fascination with the effect on children's school performance of growing up in the slums of Scunthorpe that we presented him with a single railway ticket to go there! In those days it was all called education, however, and appeared to owe little to the contributory disciplines and a great deal to the direct aim of producing people who would be adequate classroom performers. Such was the strength of the discipline in the 1960s and early 1970s that its literature and research was more than sustained through the period of very rapid decline in teacher education numbers that followed. During the period when it was best established, sociology became the only social science to be widely taught as a main academic subject in teacher education, being offered by six colleges in 1960 and 46 in 1968 (Reid and Wormald 1974; Reid 1975).

In terms of its perspectives, the discipline's development can be seen to have passed through three phases (Reid 1978b). The early courses were almost exclusively structural functionalist in perspective, reflecting the important role played by the London School of Economics' brand of sociology which held sway in Britain until the late 1960s (Banks 1976; Bernstein 1974; Shipman 1974). This phase was characterized by fairly direct links with the sociology of Durkheim and little discussion about perspectives and theory, almost entirely on account of the lack of alternative models. A second phase is conveniently, if not accurately, marked by the 1970 conference of the British Sociological Association at which a series of papers (Brown 1973) was presented from interpretative perspectives. This gave rise to what is erroneously referred to as the 'new sociology of education'. This phase was characterized by attention being directed to previously neglected aspects of schooling, for example, the curriculum and classroom interaction (see 4.5 and 5), and to a great deal of debate and conflict over what were then seen as conflicting perspectives. A third and overlapping phase was that in which a synthesis between structuralist and interpretative perspectives was and is sought and taught. Its beginnings were marked by the Open University's course E202 (1977) and work such as that of Sharp and Green (1975) and Reynolds (1976).

To this very brief outline of the development of British sociology of education we need to add some consideration of two further, related factors. First, to how the efforts of sociologists of education have been received into the ideology (body of ideas forming the basis for political, economic or social system) of society and educational institutions. Second, to the demands made upon the discipline by users of the sociology of education. These two aspects are intimately related and shed some light on the development and use of the current perspectives in the sociology of education. Our concern with these aspects will be limited to the main users of the sociology of education – teachers and teacher-education institutions. Somewhat similar points about sociology and society in general are available elsewhere (see, for example, Wright Mills 1959; Gouldner 1973).

Sociological theories, like most statements about man or society, can be seen to contain or reflect an ideology. A theory that sees the parts of society (institutions or systems) as related to each other, and conflicts between them as being underlaid with agreement or acceptance of certain values, can be characterized as conservative. Suggesting that society is coherent or in balance (equilibrium) may be seen to carry the assumption that it is as it should be.

Without stretching one's imagination too far, it can be seen that the above characterization of structural functionalism suggests a possible reason for its acceptance and past monopoly in the sociology of education: it fitted in with the teaching profession's ideology. Teachers and teacher-education institutions have been found to be basically conservative (see, for example, McLeish 1970). The view of social reality presented by this type of sociology accorded reasonably well with teachers' perceptions of their teaching and their relationships with children and society. Moreover, and without being too cynical, its message was as appealing as that of the psychologists about intelligence: basically, that educational achievement was to some extent due to factors outside the classroom and teachers' control – in this case, the family and community as opposed to innate ability. Both these ideas to some extent protect the teachers from total responsibility for the end product of their teaching. In a difficult task like teaching such protection can be welcome.

At the same time, there were aspects of teachers' professional beliefs

38

which conflicted with this approach – for example, the stoutly defended idea of the uniqueness of each teacher, class and child. Hence there was a tendency to reject bold suggestions from sociologists of education that teachers were performing roles for society at large, such as occupational placing and cultural reproduction, and that it was possible to talk meaningfully in a generalized way about what *teachers* did in classrooms, rather than viewing them as helping children to realize their individual capabilities and goals. In this case interpretative perspectives, emphasizing the uniqueness of social situations and individuals, were welcomed and assimilated by a profession where such understanding was traditional and perhaps necessary. These perspectives can also be seen as conservative. Their concentration on the immediate social situation and actors can detract attention from the underlying structural factors affecting the practice of education.

In some contrast, conflict and Marxist approaches tend to appear radical or revolutionary, in presenting change and conflict as endemic. Consensus/conservative and conflict/radical perspectives taken to their logical conclusions lead to opposing outcomes. A consensus view of society can lead to the conclusion that significant educational change lies well outside the educational system itself. Since education is shaped and controlled by the economic and social structure, that is, then, where change must happen – a radical conclusion indeed. Conversely, conflict perspectives which view change as inevitable can give rise to a 'sit back and wait for it to happen', conservative stance.

As there is no indication of the superiority (in any real sense) of any of these perspectives, it seems probable that choice between them is affected by how well each fits into one's or an institution's ideology, beliefs and understanding of social reality. Also important is the purpose for which this knowledge is required. As we have seen, the sociology of education is strongly related to teacher education courses, which have two clear objectives: to prepare people for the professional role of teaching, and to continue their education. There are clear indications that the first is the overriding one, so that the content of such courses is both evaluated by teachers and taught in terms of its relevance and utility to professional goals. This criticism was made public and shifted, between the mid 1960s and early 1970s, from questioning whether sociology and sociology of education had any value for teacher education to what type of sociology was most useful (Reid and Wormald 1974). McNamara used Jackson's (1968) 'summation of teacher-talk' – that it was characterized by uncomplicated views of causality, an intuitive rather than a rational approach to events, opinionated stances regarding teaching practices, and a narrowness in applying abstract terms to work situations – to suggest that the sociology of education taught was inappropriate to teachers and students, 'Not particularly because he does not want to but because the pressures of work and the practical demands of the situation in which he finds himself make it particularly difficult to stand back and look objectively at what he is doing' (McNamara 1972). He went on to claim that sociologists had, for too long, been interested only in developing and verifying general theories about social situations. The answer lay, he suggested, in grounded theory, which would 'develop a sociology of education . . . based upon observation and research in school situations . . . concerned with deriving explanations of the behaviour of individuals in schools from data collected in schools rather than applying theoretical perspectives from elsewhere'. Gorbutt (1972) argued that only by adopting the interpretative rather than the structuralist paradigm would the sociology of education produce a self-critical, researching teacher, a result he saw as necessary for revitalizing schools and colleges. This emphasis towards what could be termed as utilitarian sociology (designed to be of use to schoolteachers) I noted was true of main courses in sociology and social science in colleges of education. 'Of the 103 syllabuses in the Guide to Social Science Courses (McCready 1972) . . . only 38 are specifically referred to as sociology. The majority are directed towards more direct classroom skills or curricula, or to the extension of the role of the teacher' (Reid 1975).

Similarly, Burgess (1977) reported that professional ideology dominated the sociology of education on PGCE and certificate courses. More recently, the tendency for the discipline to be subsumed into professional studies, noted by Alexander and Wormald (1979), has been heightened by increasing government involvement in approving and seeking 'relevance' in teacher education courses

(*Command 8836* 1983 and *DES Circular* 3/84 1984). There has also been a marked change in the balance in such education away from the BEd degree towards the short (36-week) PGCE. There are, then, real pressures for a return to the 1950s model of thematic education courses in which contributory disciplines are disguised and used in a utilitarian fashion. (Reid 1986b).

Thus the ideological and utilitarian settings of the sociology of education must be seen as helping to shape the development of the discipline. It would appear that the interests and demands of teacher education provide an apparently more fertile bed for interpretative than structuralist perspectives. There is, however, a tension in that sociology itself and the nature of the phenomena dealt with exert definite pressure towards what we have called the bridging perspectives.

## 2.6 This book's perspective

As will be evident from our discussion above, the sociology of education has to be viewed as a single discipline within which there are discernible perspectives that are obviously complementary and supplementary to one another. Any other view is to ignore the nature of what is being studied and the approach of the discipline. While distinctive contributions are made by particular perspectives, they remain contributions to the whole. Hence, this book does not take part in what became an extensive debate within the discipline during the 1970s over whether one or other perspective is superior, more useful, contains more of the truth, and so on. Neither does it examine to any extent the way in which perspectives may operate in the development of the discipline: by challenging, or posing questions for, one another (see, however, 9.2a).

At the same time, as has been stressed (2.3), there is a need for an awareness of the perspectives because of their underlying assumptions and the way in which they frame approach, research and presentation of findings. Also required is an appreciation of the social context of the discipline. Together these amount to what might be called a sociology of the sociology of education. This should deter readers from assumptions, sometimes accorded to disciplines, about a free-standing, unrelated, single-minded, objective body of knowledge. Since in much of the literature the perspectives are neither very clearly defined nor agreed upon, it is not possible to specify that used in each contribution – even were this to be desirable. However, some indication is given in the presentation by reference to where and how data was collected/ observations made/findings interpreted. This allows interested readers to refer to and from this and other sections of the book.

This book has an essentially pragmatic aim: to inform those who work, are preparing to work, or who are interested in schooling and education of the useful and necessary knowledge that the sociology of education can supply. To this end, it draws from that body knowledge in a fairly utilitarian manner, paying no particular allegiance to any perspective. The topics covered are those which appear relevant to those who work in the educational system, guided to an extent by existing syllabuses in teacher education. Similarly, as we have seen, the perspectives have different histories and stages of development and/or have concentrated on particular topics or addressed differing questions. As a consequence they have, at the time of writing, differing contributions to make to the concerns of this book. As this book is written primarily for British readers it is also biased, though not exclusively, towards British sociology of education. Finally, as its main aim is to provide an understanding of educational phemonena of value to those involved in their practice, there is an emphasis on empirical studies.

# 3

# The Sociology of Schools and Schooling

## 3.1 Scale and complexity

While we all share some first-hand experience of schools, many are not aware of the scale and complexity of schooling in our society – an appreciation of which is an essential part of the context of our concerns.

In 1983/4 there were 36,505 schools in the United Kingdom containing some 9.7 million children and over half a million teachers, together with a further 4.7 million people engaged in non-compulsory education (including part-time) outside the schools. The cost of this immense enterprise was some £15,824 million, or 5.2 per cent of the Gross National Product of our society (*Education Statistics for the United Kingdom 1985*). This last figure does not include expenditure in the private system of education. While such figures provide an indication of the scale of education in our society, they do not illustrate its complexity. In order to grasp that, we must appreciate that the 8.28 million children in the 25,000 maintained schools in England and Wales in 1983 were taught in nearly a third of a million separate classes (*Statistical Bulletin 6/84*). To which it is necessary to add a consideration of the wide range of type of school, private and LEA, nursery, primary and secondary, and the variation in their size, organization, curriculum and teaching methods. Such simple facts suggest that the description let alone the explanation of schools and classrooms as social institutions, or the typification of teachers and pupils, is a formidable task.

A further aspect is that we do not have one system of schooling in Britain, let alone the UK, but several separate ones. As with health, there is a private system of independent and 'public' schools (see

6.3). This sector is growing and assisted with public finance made available, directly and indirectly, by central government. The major sector, despite being commonly referred to as such, is *not* a state system. There are fundamental differences between the Scottish, and English and Welsh, systems, involving different types and lengths of schooling and qualifications. A third system in Northern Ireland is distinctive in not having changed towards comprehensive secondary schooling (maintaining a grammar/secondary modern system) and with Roman Catholic and Protestant church schools operating in some isolation from each other. While overall control of education in the UK is by central government, four separate ministries are involved: the DES for England; the Welsh Office Education Department; the Scottish Education Department, and the Department of Education in Northern Ireland. Local administration is by LEAs in England and Wales (104) and Scotland (12) and Education and Library Boards (5) in Northern Ireland. Such diversity gives rise to considerable variation in provision and service (see 7.2b and 7.10). It also poses severe problems for the proper discussion of schooling, since few studies (including governmental) cover more than one part of our society. The neglect of Northern Irish education is very considerable (although see Darby 1973 and 1977 and Sutherland 1973). Consequently, this book uses material mainly based on Britain rather than the UK, and care is taken to locate the data presented.

A further dimension is that some schools have voluntary (mainly religious) foundations and those within the LEA sector have joint control and finance. While the distinctiveness of 'church schools' may have declined (at least outside Northern Ireland), they have played a significant role in the development of schooling in the UK and constitute a further aspect of our educational diversity (see 6.2).

## 3.2 Paradox and limitations

The sociological study of schools provides a good example of the major paradox of sociology. Through our experience we have both intimate knowledge of, and a set of values and beliefs about, school.

These frequently contradict or question statements about schools in general and about specific schools and classrooms. These contradictions are similar to those involved in studying any social institution of which we have been part – for example, the family. But one can go further and state that at one level we know what goes on in schools and classrooms, while at the same time maintaining that we shall never know. These levels of abstraction range from the very high – schools are places in which knowledge and skills are passed from teachers to pupils – to the very low – knowledge and experience of a particular classroom and teacher over a year. The first gives little insight into any particular school; the second little into an understanding of schooling in general, and may or may not provide any insight into other classrooms. In the latter case it could well be that another person who shared the experience might have gathered different information. Neither form of knowledge on its own is very useful to a proper understanding of schooling, nor, as was argued in 2.3, can really be called sociology. Obviously what is needed is a combination or something in between, allowing us to relate both to the general and the specific.

These problems are, of course, true of many other phenomena. In the case of the human body, medical scientists know how bodies in general function, but such knowledge can be found lacking in relation to specific bodies, the abnormal or sick. Working in the other direction, that is from knowledge of a specific body, also has its dangers. Clearly, to understand bodies, schools or any phenomena, both types of knowledge are needed, especially as it is difficult to see that they don't both contribute to each other. Still within the medical analogy, a great deal of knowledge about the functioning of the normal body has come from the study of the sick and the dead.

At the outset, then, we should recognize that the sociological treatments being reviewed are limited in a number of ways. Our knowledge of schools is limited by being:

- *partial*: either    (a) limited to only some aspects of the social reality of schools

         or    (b) limited to only some (few) examples of schools

         or    (c) both (a) and (b);

- *dated*: schools change constantly: both through social and educational change and because people in them are replaced;

- *problematic*: it is difficult to relate the specific to the general, and the general to the specific.

## 3.3 Unique places

Schools, as you may have noticed, are pretty odd places – there is nothing else quite like them. They are, as sociologists would have it, unique social institutions ('aspects of social life in which distinctive values and interests, centring upon large and important social concerns, are associated with distinctive patterns of social interaction', Weeks 1972). Before exploring the ways sociologists have viewed and researched schools, we can pick out a number of commonly accepted but unique characteristics of schools. The most important of these is that we all have to go to school; the law insists upon it. Indeed, in Western society, schools are the only social institution, of any real importance, of which we must all be part. We can assume that virtually the whole population experiences school – certainly a much larger proportion than is involved in other institutions including the family, marriage, religion, politics, and so on. Basically schools are a significant part of people's lives, apart from anything else, because of the large amount of time spent in them. At present the minimum number of years at school is eleven (from approximately five to sixteen years of age). This could amount to something like 15,400 hours at school, or the equivalent of 10,266 football matches, 7,500 feature films or around 32,000 episodes of 'East Enders'!

School is an important feature of life, not only for the children in them but also for adults. It is to be hoped that those who count schooldays as the happiest of their lives are balanced by those who do not – otherwise it's a sad reflection on the rest of society and adult life. Although not easy to trace directly, our experiences at school, to varying degrees, remain of some consequence throughout our lives, and affect our views, attitudes and behaviour over a range of facets of adult life. It is certainly possible to see relationships between what people do, or do not do, at school, and income, style of life, occupation and social class in adulthood (see 8). The same experiences appear to be related to the educational performance of our children (see 7). It is in these terms that schools perform their very significant social role. Together with the family and other institutions, they produce a social adult in the full sense – that is, a person who takes, or makes, their place in society. This implies that schools are about more than just learning in the cognitive sense of mastering subjects on the timetable, and are about learning in the social sense. Indeed, as we shall see, it is possible to argue that they are *more* concerned with social than cognitive learning (4.2).

There are other unique features of school, some of which require brief identification here. Schools bring a small number of adults (teachers) and a much larger number of unrelated children (pupils) into an association. It would be difficult to see this association as purely voluntary. Children do not necessarily choose to go to school – either generally or regularly – neither do they choose the particular school or teachers. Likewise teachers have little real freedom of choice about the children they teach, or about where, what and how they teach (though in the latter cases their freedom is much greater than that of the children). This feature of schools, as we shall see, raises interesting questions about social order in schools. What makes schools exist and endure, or what stops the children taking them over, or schools being almost deserted (see 3.4)?

Schools can be seen, at one and the same time, to have quite specific and diffuse aims. In the first place they are instrumental, concerned with getting children to read, write, learn and pass exams. At the same time it is difficult to draw boundaries around schools and their activities since they attempt to influence pupils on a broad and deep front. They try, with varying degrees of success, to affect children's attitudes and beliefs, the way they dress and behave, not only in school but also outside. It is interesting to speculate how much of a school's energy and time is spent on these non-instrumental aims, enforcing standards of dress and appearance, checking swearing, chewing and smoking, developing or demanding courtesy and attitudes of respect, and so on. It should also be noted that parents and society have high expectations of schools in terms of the non-academic characteristics of their products. Indeed, the law holds schools wholly responsible for pupils from arrival to departure. Schools are increasingly held responsible for, or seen as the agent to combat, a growing variety of social ills.

All this is in stark contrast to institutions concerned with adults. Imagine a factory attempting to maintain a similar regime with its workers. Even colleges and universities don't try very hard. It needs bearing in mind too that schools set out to achieve their specific and diffuse aims with children who have widely different levels of ability and willingness to fulfil them. In some cases, and for a variety of reasons, schools are attempting the near impossible. This should not only be seen with regard to the children they have to work with. Teachers, as we are all too aware, also vary in their ability and willingness to teach, or help children to learn, in these areas. Schools, their facilities and equipment, together with the educational systems in which they function, are often inadequate. Nor is competency and adequacy merely a question of having it or not – not all good scholars are paragons of virtue and no school or system works in all directions and with all its pupils. If we put these considerations into a dynamic situation, with the demands made upon schools and the aims they set themselves changing over time, then we can begin to appreciate the complexity of the institution we are viewing.

A further unique feature of schools arises from the values and beliefs they exhibit. These are different, rather than in opposition to, those of the general public, or at least significant parts of it. Here we consider only two aspects, the academic and social. Schools appear to believe that education is good in itself or for its own sake, whereas many people see it rather as a means to an end, say, getting a particular type of job. Within education schools appear to give less regard to subjects which may have high intrinsic value (enjoyment) for pupils – like PE, games and domestic science – and those most directly related to adult occupational roles – wood and metal work, typing and commerce. At the same time they give high regard to subjects, whose enjoyment and initial, or subsequent, utility pass many pupils by. This concern with education itself leads to a valuation of pupils within school on what is a narrow part of a person – academic ability. With this rewarding of academic ability goes what is often referred to as an élitist view of education. In schools the more gifted are treated differently and enjoy higher status than the less able. They are often taught different subjects differently by different teachers. Outside educational institutions, in the real world, a wider range of aspects of ability and personality are rewarded. In contrast to the family, for example, schools (particularly secondary ones) emphasize and demand a narrow and instrumental part of the person and pay less attention to the rich diversity of talents that make up a person. Such educational values may be held to be middle-class, the values of which permeate and characterize the regime, rules, atmosphere, language and expectations of classrooms and schools (although see discussion in 4.2). In many ways schools are middle-class institutions. This implies that the extent to which the social world of school is congruent or incongruent with children's other experience is dependent upon the social class of the children. This is discussed further in 4–7.

So far we have identified schools as institutions which are universal, compulsory, and have specific and diffuse aims which are effective in the short and long term, and display values and beliefs different to those of significant parts of society. We have also recognized the scale and complexity of schooling in our society. It will be clear that sociologists adopt a number of approaches to the study of schools. These arise both from the nature of the phenomena involved (schools) and the body of the discipline (sociology). We now turn our attention to some of the results of these approaches.

## 3.4 Order and purpose; consensus and conflict

The explanation of social order has been a basic concern of sociologists throughout the discipline's history. Order and/or discipline in schools is a fundamental issue for teachers, pupils and society (see also 5.2, 5.3) and this, together with a consideration of what schools are for, is the appropriate topic for us to tackle initially. Most early attempts at a sociology of schools adopted a social systems approach within structuralist perspectives. 'The term social system may refer to small or large-scale phenomena. Thus "a" social system exists when two or more people are involved in social interactions; their behaviour is shaped by similar conceptions of the social norms and roles appropriate to that situation' (Weeks 1972). As we saw in 2, two main versions of structuralism have evolved, one based on consensus, the other on conflict; the former has been most influential in the sociology of education. Talcott Parsons has provided much of the best known consensus-structuralist sociology, and in 1959 published an essay which identified the functions of schools for society and described the processes involved. He claims, and it is easy to agree with him, that schools are involved in four simultaneous functions (purposes they fulfil).

(i) Emancipation of the child from the family
(ii) Internalization (learning) of social values and norms, at a higher level than is available in the family
(iii) Differentiation of pupils (see also 6) in terms of (a) their actual achievement and (b) the differential valuation of achievements (some are more valued/rewarded than others, see also 4.5 i)
(iv) The selection and allocation of pupils into the adult role system, including the occupational structure.

It is the third function (differentiation) which he views as the most important, seeing school as an agency which differentiates pupils broadly along a single scale of achievement, the content of which is relative excellence in meeting the expectations imposed by teachers as agents of adult society. It is on this process that we

50

concentrate. Parsons recognizes that achievement differentiation will inevitably be a source of strain, because it gives higher rewards and privileges to one group and denies these to others. This strain is relieved by what he calls integrative mechanisms. The most fundamental of these is the sharing of a common value by family and school: that of equality of opportunity. This value recognizes that it is fair to give differential rewards for differential achievement providing there has been fair access to opportunities. Hence it assumes an initial equality and that differing subsequent achievement and rewards are just, enabling those involved, who presumably might otherwise object, to accept differentiation in school. Parsons sees this as particularly important in respect to 'losers' in the school competition. Certainly one has to agree with him that it is useful for school and society that 'losers' should blame themselves rather than teachers, school, educational system or society for their failure. It is also true that most failures at school do not blame the educational system, at least openly. However, it is a rather bold step from that to assume that it is because they share a common value of equality of opportunity. Nor is it clear what evidence there is that such a value exists, or whether it is widely shared by all the groups involved. Presumably both points might be answered by the fact that very few parents and pupils are in open revolt against schools for differentiating them from others. There are, however, a number of logical reasons, other than a shared value, why this could be so, ignorance and perceived lack of power being the obvious ones. It seems difficult to believe that parents can accept the idea of initial equality other than through ignorance. Widely reported evidence has drawn attention to a variety of inequalities in educational provision, process and achievement (see 7, 8 and *passim*). Further, evidence suggests that many parents have but a sketchy idea of what goes on in schools. Despite recent efforts – such as the publication of school policy documents and examination results, broadening the recruitment of school governors, the development of PTAs – schools and the educational system remain largely a closed shop. Several studies (for example Pallister and Wilson 1970, Ghodsian et al 1983) have shown that knowledge of and attitudes towards education vary along social class lines – the middle classes being best informed and most favourable (see also 7.9c). It is worth noting that parents with the most knowledge of what goes on in schools are in fact those most likely to object – to teachers, via PTAs and local politics, and by removing their children from the LEA system and placing them in the private sector. These sorts of considerations suggest that alternative views to those of Parsons need to be taken into account. For example, that 'such autonomy as . . .[school system] possesses is derived from their custody of the mysteries and records, rather than from any considerable measure of popular deference to their authority' (Friedenburg 1063).

Parsons does not rest his case on the fact that a common value is the sole integrative mechanism counteracting the strains imposed by differentiation. However, the evidence and operation of his further three factors is similarly far from clear cut, as is illustrated below and extensively elsewhere in this book.

● *Family differentiation cuts across achievement differentiation and the family supports the child in directions other than achievement.* We can accept the latter part of the statement with little comment. The first part, though, is a surprising claim, given the well established evidence of the relationship between family status (particularly social class) and children's educational achievement (see 7.2). Indeed, Parsons produces such evidence himself while simultaneously claiming, 'the evidence also is that the selective process is genuinely assortive'. What he is claiming is that those for whom the relationship does not hold true, for example, the minority of children from disadvantaged backgrounds who succeed in education, are of considerable importance to the system. In other words that minorities justify the majority pattern (this is further discussed at 6.1 and 8.9).

● *Teachers like/respect pupils on grounds other than achievement status.* While this has some truth – everybody loves a clown – direct and indirect evidence suggests that teachers have a preference for able pupils (see 5.3).

● *Peer-group friendships cross-cut achievement status.* Again, Parsons is resting his case on the fact that there are exceptions. In Britain, with its emphasis on ability grouping in schools, achievement has been consistently shown to be an important factor in friendship choice (see 6.46).

Further, it needs to be recognized that Parsons appears to over-emphasize that schools are about teachers and families, and to forget the children. The essential element of schools is the direct face-to-face relationship of pupils and teachers. Finally it can be recognized that in writing about 'functions' and 'integrative mechanisms', Parsons has depersonalized the school and its social system. This criticism has been well sustained by Levitas (1974).

> . . . the function definition . . . [calls] the practice serving certain purposes a function. And in doing so the vital interests inherent in these purposes, the identities of their creators and executors and the social class intentions behind them are effectively hidden. When a sociologist talks about goals, anyone may ask 'Whose goals?'

Once one accepts the idea that schools (or any social system) are inhabited by distinct groups which have their own goals, then it is obvious that these goals may not coincide and there is therefore the potential for conflict. Certainly this was how Waller (1932) perceived schools.

> The teacher-pupil relationship is a form of institutionalised dominance and subordination. Teacher and pupil confront each other in the school with an original conflict of desires, and however much that conflict may be reduced in amount, or how-ever much it may be hidden, it still remains. The teacher repres-ents the adult group, ever the enemy of the spontaneous life of groups of children. The teacher represents the formal curriculum, and his interest is in imposing that curriculum upon the children in the form of tasks; pupils are much more interested in life in their own world than in the dessicated bits of adult life which teachers have to offer. The teacher represents the estab-

lished social order in the school, and his interest is in maintaining that order, whereas pupils have only a negative interest in that feudal superstructure. Teacher and pupil confront each other with attitudes from which the underlying hostility can never be altogether removed. Pupils are the material in which teachers are supposed to produce results. Pupils are human beings striving to realise themselves in their own spontaneous manner, striving to produce their own results in their own way. Each of these hostile parties stands in the way of the other; in so far as the aims of either are realised it is at the sacrifice of the aims of the other.

However much teachers and their like may wish to believe that education is about filling empty jars or feeding the hungry, the reality is somewhat different. Anyone with classroom experience in secondary schools could hardly fail to be impressed by the centrality of discipline. While the problems of order are apparent and often recognized in such schools, it is also true that children in the reception classes of infant schools pose problems of control – as many a student teacher could witness. Indeed, even Sunday school teachers, working with very small groups (mostly between four and seven children), reported discipline problems as one of their major concerns in teaching (Reid 1977b).

The basis of a conflict-model approach to schools can be established by identifying the points of conflict. These lie with:

(i) *the instrumental goal emphasis of schools* being imposed on pupils who vary in their ability and/or willingness to accept it
(ii) *the partial exclusion of affective goals and interests*
(iii) *the normative value emphasis*, with concentration on what can be seen as middle-class norms
(iv) *conflict between young* (pupils) *and old* (teachers), or between the formal (school) and informal (pupil) cultures in schools
(v) *conflict inherent in the teaching process*: since teaching is about attempting to change pupils by introducing new ideas and knowledge, it involves conflict and subordination (Greer 1968).

These premises are fleshed out and discussed in 4 and 5. From them it can be predicted that conflict will be greatest where: pupils are of low ability, and in school situations where instrumental demands are heavy; pupils come from widely different social class and/or ethnic backgrounds from their teachers; the age group differences are accentuated – by their closeness. What these conditions identify are the older, less able/achieving pupils in formal downtown city secondary schools, which is of course precisely where the greatest overt conflict is to be found. Conflict is a fairly strong word, and it is necessary to describe it by reference to its manifestations. Given the differences in power between teachers and pupils, the most common overt reactions to conflict should be seen as forms of passive resistance. This involves playing up the teacher and playing down the class. Such activities use up a good deal of time in most classrooms. Pupils develop the 'old lag syndrome' – well known in places like prisons and the armed forces – a form of mechanized semi-conformity. They laugh or hate teachers out of real existence and most effectively neutralize teachers' control by indulging in activities that are just outside the regime and so just avoid punishment, while causing the maximum disturbance. Teachers, on the other hand, withdraw mentally, and sometimes physically (I once worked next to a teacher who did little else in the classroom other than read novels – to himself). They use sarcasm and verbal haranguing, avoid direct conflict by permitting marginally unacceptable behaviours, allow themselves to be sidetracked from the lesson, and so on. You have probably done and seen it all yourself (see also 4 and 5).

In the same way, approaches to the sociology of schooling from interpretative perspectives share a view that the process involves, to a varying degree, an essential conflict. We can in fact say that conflict and coercion must be features of schools, since they are never really voluntary or democratic. In arriving at this conclusion we are in good company, including not only sociologists but also philosophers of education. Much of what goes on in schools is best viewed as institutionalized conflict. The relative lack of overt conflict or violence appears to be due either to the very strong normative pressures in schools or to the fact that the balance of power there is very much in the teachers' favour. Conflict as a reality of school life is ignored at their peril by both sociologists and teachers. Shipman (1968) recounts the difficulties of student teachers in tough schools when headteachers refuse to see conflict and discipline as a school or group problem, viewing them only as problems of individual teachers.

## 3.5 Shifting analysis

The sociology of the school can be seen to have had three developmental stages. The first, a social systems approach using structuralist perspectives, which we have just discussed. The second develops from the first using the mobilizing concept of schools' culture(s) and involves both structuralist and interactionist perspectives (see 4). The third is a more intimate view of schools as social worlds, seen through the eyes of the participants with interactionist perspectives (see 5). In following this order of presentation we are not so much tracing the development of the discipline as moving from macro to micro views. However, as was pointed out in 2, this is not to imply a separateness or appropriateness to the order. As the text below stresses they are all complementary and need to be considered as one.

Space precludes full and separate treatment of two related approaches: the socio-historical and the organizational. The importance of the first lies with the fact that schools and the educational system cannot be properly understood only in terms of the present. They are clearly shaped by and through the past, as is all social reality. While this fact is recognized throughout this book, interested readers will find useful and full treatments in the following: Shipman (1971) provides a consensus (structural-functionalist) account, Vaughan and Archer (1971) a Weberian conflict and Bowles and Gintis (1976) a Marxist one. A general structuralist view is that of Musgrave (1968 and 1970), while Lawson and Silver (1973) provide a most readable historians' account. For a short review of these see Reid (1978a, Chapter 5). The second approach, while having a distinct emphasis on aspects and operation of schools as organizations, covers much the same ground as the one here. For example, Banks (1976) does not distinguish between social system and organizational approaches, referring only to the first. For useful and full reviews of organizational analysis of schools, read Davies (1973 and 1981), or King (1983).

While we quite extensively view aspects of socialization and family background in respect of their relationship to schooling and education (see 7), space again precludes a full treatment of the family and of child-rearing practice. Young and Willmott (1975) provide a useful study of the family, while a valuable longitudinal study of child-rearing which displays social class and sex differences is that of Newson and Newson (1963, 1968, 1976, 1977). For accounts of the different socialization of girls see Sharpe (1976) and Belotti (1975). The diversity of family and child-rearing among ethnic minorities in Britain is illustrated in Khan (1979). An intimate view of six different ethnic minority children's families, homes and their entry into first school is provided by Jackson (1979). Aspects of the cultural diversity and 'home' cultures of ethnic minorities in Britain is illustrated in Watson (1977).

# 4

# The Culture of Schools

## 4.1 The cultural approach

We have recognized schools as relatively isolated social institutions with some explicit objectives. A major sociological approach to their study is via school culture. Potentially, given the definition of culture (all that is not innate, i.e., not universal and unlearned), such an approach includes nearly everything that goes on in schools, and could encompass all approaches. The underlying assumption is that schools have characteristic patterns of behaviour, values, beliefs and physical environments which are to some degree different from those of other institutions in society. Further assumptions are that, while we are aware of variations from school to school, there is sufficient similarity for meaningful characterizations to be made and that these assist in the explanation of the processes of schooling and their outcome.

Such an approach has considerable currency and history in the sociology of education. For example, Waller (1965) identified, 'a separate culture . . . within the school. This is a culture which is in part the creation of children . . . and in part devised by teachers in order to canalise the activities of children. . . . The whole complex set of ceremonies centring around the school may be considered a part of the culture indigenous to the school.'

Considerable use has been made of these two aspects, often referred to as the formal and informal, or pupil, cultures (or sub-cultures). They have often been contrasted; for example, the formal probably accords high regard to academic achievement while the informal may accord it to 'being one of *the* boys/girls'. As we shall see the relationship between, or similarity of, the two varies from school to school. There are, though, inherent dangers in viewing the two separately. In essence they are simply different perspectives on the same social reality of the main parties involved in school. Views implying that teachers uphold the formal aspect and that pupil culture is a response to it are simplistic. They fail to recognize that teachers have an informal culture and that while teachers and pupils have different levels of power and autonomy, it is through their interaction that the culture of school becomes reality. Hence the number of cultures in school is larger than two and depends on the level of abstation at which analysis is undertaken. Finally, as should be obvious, much school culture comes from outside the school, is legally defined, socially shaped and/or involves taken-for-granted cultural assumptions from a range of sources. Bearing these caveats in mind we can now view some of the characteristics of school culture, starting with macro considerations.

## 4.2 Social and educational aspects

The culture of schools, like that of any social system, can be seen to serve three broad functions: *instrumental* – from it people select techniques of doing things, the means to reach objectives; *regulative* – the actions of persons and the use of instruments are subject to rules and regulations, the dos and don'ts of living, specifying what should/should not be done; and *directive* – from it individuals derive ultimate and immediate values, their interpretation of life and goals for which they strive (after Dahlke 1958).

As would be expected, the formal culture of schools is concerned with motivating and facilitating the achievement of pupils. Within schools that achievement can be defined as the 'relative excellence in living up to the expectations imposed by the teacher(s)' (Parsons 1959). As such it is fairly obvious it involves both cognitive and social aspects, which can only be theoretically separated. The inter-relatedness of the cognitive or academic with the social is a major theme of this book. It is pointedly illustrated by Rist's observations (1970) of a classroom in a black American kindergarten (a rough British equivalent would be the reception class in an infant school). The school did not stream by ability. The teacher, who was herself black, very quickly grouped the children into three groups, which were seated at separate tables and given names to differentiate them. This allocation was made mainly on the basis of the teacher's observations and judgements of their behaviour (remember this was their first experience of school). Rist was able to show that the resulting groups were distinguishable by the following criteria – family income, family size and level of parental education. Observations revealed that the groups received differential treatment and experience. The lowest group received more control-orientated teacher behaviour, had less interaction with the teacher, and received more ridicule from the other pupils in the class, than did the other two groups. The initial groups were maintained, the only movement between them being the demotion of two children from the top group because of their inability to be as tidy as the teacher expected top group children to be. When the class reached the end of kindergarten their IQ was tested and revealed very slightly higher scores for the top group but overlaps between all the groups.

The question now is the extent to which such initial decisions and treatments – based on social criteria – help to predetermine the school careers of children. Subsequent teachers will be affected by school records and will support initial grouping and labelling, while the children will respond with, or be socialized into, appropriate behaviours and achievements. Keddie (1971), in a study of a British secondary school, has displayed how teachers' 'knowledge' of the ability or stream of the classes they teach – based on previous teachers' assessments – affects which parts of the curriculum they teach, how they teach them and the way in which they respond to pupils' questions. The best illustration is that the question 'Why are we learning this?' was regarded as serious enough to require an answer if from a high-stream child, but as 'Why do we have to learn anything?' if from a low-stream child (see also 5.4).

The question of the mixture of the social and educational in schools can be taken further. We might, for example, reason that, since schools are consciously produced and maintained institutions (they don't happen by chance!), underlying their culture would be firm and clear educational principles. Or, to put it more forcefully, that it would be appropriate to attempt to explain what goes on in schools in terms of their contribution to learning and achievement. Of course, this is a somewhat mechanistic view of a human institution. Most schools are far from being factories since their 'products' are people, not objects, and the processing involved has few similarities to that of production lines for a standard commodity like beer bottles. In other words, schools have to be effective – catering for the social needs of their members – as well as being instrumental – promoting the learning of certain types of knowledge. There is also the question of the relationship of schools to society and other social institutions.

Our present concerns have been admirably discussed by Young and Beardsley (1968), who argue that what goes on in classrooms is better understood in terms of social systems theory rather than teaching or learning theory. The content of a lesson, which can be seen as an information exchange, is quite secondary to the importance of a lesson in structuring behaviour and socializing children to function in a social system. In other words, its purpose is more to socialize than to educate; social as opposed to cognitive learning is at a premium. For example, a basic requirement of living in modern society is an ability to accept a common definition of social situations and to change readily from one situation to another. Young and Beardsley suggest that this is taught in schools via the timetable, as children have to move mentally and/or physically from subject to subject. When the bell rings, it breaks up what could be a useful learning situation in the hope of producing another one; alternatively, useless learning situations have to be maintained until the bell. As they comment, 'socialisation imperatives clearly outweigh the educational'. But it goes further: teachers' concern with making children indulge only in 'game-directed' behaviour acts in much the same way. Misbehaviour, however vital it may be to the individual, has to be checked. Examples of this would be reading a history book during a mathematics lesson (even where the latter was a waste of time), or the following piece of typical classroom conversation:

*Teacher*: You are not paying attention.
*Pupil*: Yes I am.
*Teacher*: Well, what's the answer?
*Pupil*: 362.
*Teacher*: You don't know how lucky you were to get it right. Now, stop looking out of the window and pay attention.

In much the same way, experience of classrooms teaches children that many of their personal needs – affective, psychological and even physiological – are irrelevant to that situation and should be ignored. The overriding general rule is that behaviour should be rule-directed, hence the preoccupation with rules in school and class. If these are learnt properly, the child will be able to function well in most social systems in the outside world. Moreover, if schools do their job, social systems can confidently be constructed in the knowledge that there are suitable people to person them.

It has occurred to many writers that the formal culture of the school is rather similar to middle-class culture. For example,

> The orientation of the . . . school is predominantly that of the middle class. There is a strong emphasis upon the character traits of punctuality, honesty and responsibility. . . . While both competitiveness and cooperation are valued to varying degrees, there is always stress upon mastering and achievement. These middle class values are expected to be binding upon both children and adults (Havinghurst and Neugarten 1967).

The usual explanation is that teachers are by origin, and/or by virtue of their occupation, middle class (see 4.8), and that they impose their values on school and pupils. Another explanation, along Marxist lines, is that since the middle class is the most powerful (as opposed to the largest) in society, it attempts to impose its values on the whole of society, and the most potent means for this are schools and the legal and occupational systems. Quite different explanations have also been put forward, for example:

A current interpretation of the public school is that it merely reflects and upholds middle-class values. The norms apparently support this idea, but continuity of school and middle-class norms is incidental. Many of the norms and values emphases occur not because of middle-class influence but because the school is a group . . . [the norms and values] are necessary conditions if any group is to persist. (Dahlke 1958).

This idea – that the values and norms of the formal culture of the school arise from schools' institutional needs, and that without them schools could not operate – has a certain appeal. Banks (1968) commented on findings that teachers thought lower-class children unrewarding to teach because they had low motivation, were difficult to control and had habits which annoyed them. 'However, while some of these attitudes appear to reflect middle-class values, others are just as likely to be a reflection of teachers' occupational needs. It is, for example, much easier to teach children who are highly motivated to learn, and who respond to the teachers' efforts.'

From one perspective the elements of school culture can be seen as middle-class, from another as being requisites of teaching (as we know it). However, it is necessary to go further and question where the ideas of teaching came from, and why and how they are maintained, often in the face of a spectacular lack of success. The important factor to grasp is that, regardless of how it is caused, the formal culture of schools embodies strong elements of what can loosely be termed middle-class culture. The reality is that children from differing social-class or ethnic group (normative) backgrounds are differently equipped to respond to it. Given the intimacy of the social and the academic in schools, the ability to fit into these aspects of the formal culture is clearly a factor in achievement.

Before viewing school culture in action we further our understanding by exploring three of its important ingredients. These rehearse and develop our considerations so far, and are also of interest in themselves.

## 4.3 Buildings, space and territory

Despite, or because, of their obviousness the physical aspects of schools are often neglected in educational discussion. Our concern here is to recognize that buildings and their use are cultural products, embodying ideas and 'messages' which affect social activities taking place there. This is not to suggest that they provide a clear, unambiguous structure (sic) – they are open to interpretation and inventiveness – but they set some of the parameters for teaching and learning.

The existence of specialist school buildings supports the false but commonly accepted idea that school learning is divorced from other forms of learning which happen spontaneously and continuously elsewhere. Physically, schools help to set aside schooling from everyday life and perhaps, again erroneously, suggest that schools are exclusively about academic learning. School territory is marked by boundaries within which different rules apply. Schools are places where the general public, often including parents (other than at specific times, or by appointment) are kept out, and teachers and pupils kept in – though out of school hours the latter's attendance may constitute a trespass. Some challenge to this isolation has come from the community school movement, in which the school becomes the plant for a whole range of activities and persons (see, for example, Fletcher and Thompson 1980). Nearly all schools contain classrooms, which are based on assumptions about the size of learning groups and the space required for learning activities. Specialist rooms reflect assumptions about the importance and role of particular subjects and their needs. Wanzel (1970) pointed out this implies that education becomes defined as that which can be 'fitted into' the school, rather than the other way round. The timetable offers similar constraints (see 4.4).

Separate classrooms also imply or impose a level of privacy to the act of teaching; an autonomy for the teacher in the classroom, which is jealously guarded (see 4.8). In many schools, especially primary ones, classrooms become the sovereign territory of particular teachers who display proprietorial attitudes to room and class. The layout of the classroom demonstrates the educational assumptions in the use of school space. The traditional, typical, secondary school classroom, with teacher's desk in the front at right angles to the door, near the 'technology' of blackboard and wastepaper basket, indicates who is in control of learning, communication and interaction, and the received nature of knowledge. Informality, spontaneity and sharing may well be inhibited by such a layout. Primary school classrooms show greater variation. However, while Evans' (1974a) study of 145 infant classrooms did not find any example of the rectangular grid pattern, only six lacked a teacher's desk or table, mostly in the traditional place. As she remarked, 'elements of tradition and continuity are stronger in English infant schools than is sometimes assumed.'

The most clearly marked and stoutly defended spaces in the typical school are the headteacher's office and the staffroom (although sometimes these are matched by the caretaker's and secretary's territory!) These serve to indicate the status/authority differences between adult and child and between teachers. Headteachers inhabit the only or best office, reflecting their status and authority over pupils and staff. Access to the room is limited and its layout typically involves the use of desk or furniture to denote the barrier between the public and private space, which is usually difficult to cross. Evans (1974b) suggests that this typical layout relates to the way heads wish to present themselves and to manage relationships. The use of staffrooms is discussed below (4.8). Pupils are not normally allowed any territorial rights, and often lead a nomadic existence in school. While they do have more claim to the playground and toilets, these remain open to the legitimate invasion of teachers. The same is true of recent developments in LEA secondary schools of sixth and sometimes fifth form common rooms.

Hardy (1977) has drawn attention to how the design and equipment of schools predisposes teachers to an authoritarian and custodial role. Fragile fittings and furniture and the need to protect them induce what might be seen as petty teacher concern with aspects of pupil behaviour – rocking a seat, leaning against walls, and so on. Similarly, the poor design and construction of many schools in comparison with other public buildings often calls for heightened discipline in respect to factors such as safety, noise and interference. Insufficient toilets, lack or unsuitability of accommodation for meals, assemblies and wet break times all produce potential trouble spots and anticipatory action by teachers.

Educational ideas and practice change much more rapidly than school buildings. Indeed, schools have a durability unknown to other buildings. In the industrial north many mills built for nineteenth-century methods of production stand empty or are used for storage, partly because of their unsuitability for modern processes. Schools of similar age remain in use, despite educational changes at least as great as the industrial ones. Dale (1977) has appropriately commented that until recently there was a fairly high level of agreement about what and how to teach and hence about school design. Currently, there is less agreement which, together with inherited buildings, lowers the level of congruence between school buildings and what goes on in them. At the same time, buildings do not determine practice; as Joiner (1971) suggests, regardless of the architect, people can impose quite a lot of themselves on their surroundings. Consequently, it is not particularly difficult to observe open plan schools which are ingeniously partitioned or traditional schools in which classroom boundaries are removed and activities spread across, and into, other available spaces.

## 4.4 Timetables

Modern society is very time-conscious and almost every social activity is related to time. Nowhere is this quite so apparent as in school. The most vital piece of equipment for secondary school teachers and pupils is their timetable. In one sense it is simply the central organizational device, facilitating the distribution of personnel and resources across the school. The finished product, however, contains a number of educational assumptions and values, together with practical considerations relating to the available rooms, number and type of people. At some stage educational ideology meets social reality!

Secondary school timetables are detailed and explicit; infant and primary ones are typically less so, although teachers work for balance in activity and subject – often on an individual pupil or group rather than a class basis. The assumption often prevails that intellectually demanding mathematics and English should be done first thing in the day, while the children are fresh. For years I thought mental arithmetic naturally followed assembly! The subjects included reflect values about the curriculum (see 4.5). Interestingly enough, the only subject which legally has to appear – religious education – does not always make it. There is clearly a core of subjects whose non-appearance would cause consternation and others which are open to choice.

There are also more fundamental assumptions. One is that teaching and learning fit into given times and space. This rather precludes spontaneity for the activities and, since periods in school vary from 35 to 90 minutes, suggests there is little agreement about desirable or optimal length of lessons. The time slot clearly constrains what can be undertaken and favours the use of the lecture and second rather than first-hand experience. The message is that knowledge comes in chunks, with labels, delivered by a variety of teachers, in different rooms, with no clear link or inter-relationship. The importance attached to subjects can be deduced by their regularity of appearance and the length of time allotted to them. Hence mathematics and English often appear daily and constitute a major block of time. Timetables also imply that some subjects are related to age, sex, ability and aptitude. Sometimes this is done overtly, through streaming or banding the timetable and pupils (see 6.4), at others it is done through 'choice'. In reality, this choice often amounts to segregation, since the timetable simultaneously presents second languages, separate sciences and other subjects together with integrated studies and practical subjects. Resulting 'choice', even without the typical guidance, results in the more able opting for the former, the less able for the latter. Much the same happens between the sexes where subjects like craft and design and home economics are timetabled together.

The timetable has implications for teachers. First, in secondary schools they are typically required to face a large number of classes in sequence, which requires the facility to switch into and out of social situations and limits particular knowledge of each class and the pupils in it. Second, their identity is shaped by their timetable role – who and what they teach. Generally speaking, single subject, academic and examination teaching is held in highest regard and is often achieved only through time. As a new teacher I was given a very mixed subject timetable with the lowest streams and taught them in drab surroundings – an old hut with a coke stove and a changing-room behind the stage. Next year, I was promised, it would be different!

The timetable, then, is capable of being used as a teacher control mechanism, conferring reward and status, or offering constraint. Most teachers, like nearly all pupils and parents, are not directly involved in timetabling decisions.

## 4.5 The curriculum

Literally, the word means 'a course of study' and refers to what is taught and studied in educational institutions. Until comparatively recently the curriculum was commonly viewed as a neutral stock of knowledge and skill, identified on a timetable or syllabus, which was passed on to pupils and students. It is fairly obvious, however, that, like all things human, knowledge is socially constructed. What passes as knowledge in education and how it is taught are socially defined, and vary between and within societies and across time. Similarly, a good deal of what is taught and learned does not appear on any syllabus, and may well happen unintentionally and pass officially unrecognized. As we shall see, along with facts children are taught, often implicitly, a whole series of views, attitudes and patterns of behaviour. It is this aspect of the curriculum that has led some sociologists, following Jackson (1968), to elaborate the term 'hidden' curriculum. The only real value of this term is to draw attention to those parts which are not official or explicit. The term 'hidden' is unfortunate to the extent that it implies that one can separate two aspects of the curriculum. In fact, the explicit and implicit aspects are intertwined much in the same way as Parsons' distinction between cognitive and social learning (see 4.2). Any clear-cut dichotomy is false. Further, the term raises questions as to what is being hidden and who does the hiding and from whom? It is intellectually and socially insulting to imply that teachers are unaware that they are involved in more than teaching an official syllabus in an objective, factual way; or that they and their female, black or working-class pupils and students fail to appreciate the sexist, racist and class assumptions inherent in the subjects they study. Consequently, our consideration of the curriculum will lean towards a definition along the lines of 'all that is taught and learned in school'. As such it should be appreciated that other parts of 4 and of this book are relevant to its discussion. Here, the concern is to illustrate some of the important characteristics of schools' curricula and to identify some of their consequences and implications.

### i *Stratified curriculum*

The idea that subjects on the curriculum are stratified into a hierarchy and that access to them is related to social stratification in society is clearly indicated in Durkheim's statement, 'there are as many different kinds of education as there are different milieux [locations] in a given society' (1911). Current British interest in the sociology of the curriculum may be conveniently marked by the work of Young (1971). He usefully identified the criteria for the stratification of school knowledge as: *literacy* (written as opposed to oral); *individualism* (not group work or cooperation) – both of which are related to how work is assessed; *abstractness and compartmentalization* of knowledge (independently of the learner); and *unrelatedness* (to daily life and experience). Hence, high-status academic subjects are 'abstract, highly literate, individualistic and unrelated to non-school knowledge'. It is not difficult to see the appropriateness of this model to subjects on the secondary school curriculum. Think about the status differences between mathematics and science on the one hand and 'lifeskills' or child care on the other. A study of the acceptability of A level GCE subjects for university admission revealed a declining order of: mathematics and pure science; humanities and language; social science, RE, music, art and housecraft – sometimes counted as an O level! (Reid, W. 1972). Young also points out that curriculum change involving shifts away from the criteria of high status towards integrated study, group and oral work in areas of topical relevance are typically developed only for those who have 'failed' academically. The low status of such courses confines pupils' status and removes from them access to high-status knowledge.

One consequence of the stratified curriculum is that pupils and teachers are themselves stratified by their involvement with particular parts of the curriculum. Identity and status are derived from the subject and level of study. The same status assumptions affect the distribution of resources – materials and personnel – between subject areas.

A number of issues are raised by this analysis. For example, who stratifies knowledge and supports the criteria, and for what purpose? Young dismisses the idea that the differentiation takes place because knowledge is best made available in this manner. In other words, it would be difficult to justify in pedagogical terms, as is the case with much of what goes on in schools (see 4.2). He sees the process as 'the conscious or unconscious choices which accord with the values and beliefs of dominant groups at a particular time'. The control of the curriculum and education is a complex issue, discussed further at 9.1. Allied to control is another question: who gains access to high status knowledge and what are the effects of differential access? The short answer is the most able, successful pupils. High-status subjects are followed predominately by middle-class and male pupils, while success in these subjects typically leads to high-status occupations characteristically pursued by males. In bold terms, the stratified curriculum assists the reproduction of the existing social differences in society. The curriculum can be seen to have cultural and class bias which favours the dominant groups in society. Consequently, any radical change in the stratification of knowledge or curriculum might well redistribute educational success and failure and, consequently, affect occupational and life chances and style (7 and 8).

## ii *Biased curriculum*

Since school knowledge is socially constructed, it can be expected to embody social values reflecting the basic dimensions of power and inequality in society. These can be quite easily seen across the whole curriculum, so the specific illustrations used below should not be taken as an indication of bias, or its lack, in any particular subject(s). Here we are concentrating on content bias; presentation, methods, and context also contain less easily identified and more variable bias. The forms of bias presented below are not exhaustive and are typifications – exceptions do exist and, in some areas, may be growing in number.

Social stratification bias in the curriculum is pretty obvious. History and literature provide many examples of social class bias. While history reveals much about monarchs, aristocrats and the captains of agriculture and industry, little insight is provided into the lives of the masses. Working people when featured are often depicted as being problems to rulers: rioting, striking, resisting the industrial revolution, being wretched and poor and in need of relief and education. In literature, from reading schemes through story books to texts, much the same is true. Middle- and upper-class settings and characters dominate, albeit with occasional rough diamonds who, like working-class scenarios, are often treated in a paternalistic and moralising way.

Sex pervades classrooms, albeit socially neutered and justified. Surveys of reading books used in British primary schools showed boys possessing a wider range of toys and taking the initiative more often in mixed sex settings in comparison with girls who typically display passive behaviour. Female adult roles were limited to familial ones, whereas males have many additional occupational roles. Only two unisex jobs were featured, teachers and shop assistants (McDonald and Thomson 1975; Lobban 1976). Much the same is true of the majority of other subjects. Millstein (1972) has neatly pointed out that history is, indeed, *his* not *her* story. Women rarely feature in history and are typically portrayed in subordinate and traditional, familial roles. The exceptions, such as Joan of Arc and Queen Elizabeth I, are notable for being just that. Apart from sexual stereotyping, it is possible to instance sex bias in timetabling, curriculum expectations, resourcing and tests and examinations (Byrne 1975, 1978 and Deem 1978).

Despite the reality of our multi-cultural society, the curriculum typically represents only the majority culture. The number of black faces in most textbooks remains lower than their proportion in the population. Examples of unfortunate and inaccurate stereotypes remain in much literature used in schools (Broderick 1973). History and geography which deals with India and Africa tells the white person's (man's) story and presents an unflattering and inaccurate picture of black society before white arrival. In an analysis of fourteen primary school textbook accounts of South Africa, Nash (1972) found only two which indicated history beginning before the whites arrived, only four which gave an account of slavery and only two which discussed apartheid, while ten used derogatory terms in discussing Africans. He drew very similar conclusions about the treatment of the history of India.

Among other bias in school knowledge is that away from the everyday, which was mentioned in discussing the stratification of the curriculum. There are two main forms of bias here. The first, which is a variant of class bias, is towards 'high culture' (or upper-class culture). The effect of this is to exclude other forms of knowledge and experience from proper consideration in schools. For example, Vulliamy (1978) has highlighted the culture clash in music. School music is typically 'highbrow', notation-based, viewed as being free from commercial concern, pure, highly technical and respectable. It is typically but falsely seen as being in contrast to popular and jazz music – which often plays a very significant part in pupils' lives. Hence the curriculum creates the irony of pupil disinterest in school music and schools' failure to capitalize on the learning potential of a major preoccupation of the young. Rather similar observations can be made about not only art, literature, media, sport and drama but most of the curriculum. The timetabling convenience of turning knowledge into subjects is a further indication of how school knowledge is made abstract and it is interesting to speculate upon how much effort some teachers put into breaking down that abstraction to return to the meaningful!

The second bias is towards the academic, which here means more than simply being amenable to classroom learning, embodying a number of value assumptions about knowledge. These amount to status differences between types of knowledge and subjects; the most respectable is the abstract and theoretical. These values are well illustrated in the attempts made by some subjects to gain academic respectability, of which there are numerous examples: housecraft to domestic science to home economics; wood and metal work to craft and design or craft design and technology; social studies to social science. Movements in the opposite direction towards greater practicality and relevance have typically been reserved for those deemed to be unsuitable for the 'real thing'. An interesting current example is the response to micro-computers in education. As I have remarked elsewhere (Reid and Rushton 1985), the response has been classically academic: 'some syllabus and teaching appears premised on the assumption that everyone needs to be an expert, capable of an understanding and appreciation that includes the ability to write programmes and full knowledge of the technical and developmental aspects of computers.' In fact, computer developments already underway will make redundant such knowledge and skills; the majority of the population are likely to require only user-skills akin to those for a car or video machine.

It is apparent, then, that bias is a characteristic of the curriculum, including the way in which it is taught. The question arises – does it matter? Many educators believe that interest in, and identification with, the curriculum is a vital ingredient in learning. So bias may be seen to predispose some towards successful effort and others towards alienation and failure. Recently, this argument has been most strongly put forward by those concerned to improve the performance of females and ethnic minorities. Apart from educational achievement, they see the curriculum as important in the development of the self-concept, which has importance within, and well beyond, learning at school – supporting and perpetuating the existing differences and inequalities between social groups. The same arguments apply to social class and the socially deprived (Midwinter 1972).

Obviously, such a line of argument is attractive; if curriculum change in the direction of relevance would enhance performance and produce greater equality, it would be welcomed. However, a number of issues are raised. Given the received nature of our understanding of what goes on in school it is difficult for many to visualize what such a curriculum would contain and how, and on what, such a balance might be struck. Probably the most difficult to imagine would be a truly multi-cultural curriculum, since it begs the questions of which, and how many, cultures are to be included (see 7.4). There are some quite well-developed ideas in the field of urban education, including those of Midwinter (see also Rayner and Harden 1973 and Rayner and Harris 1977). However, there remains the inherent danger in specific curricula for social groups, that of stratification. Separate tracks usually lead to different destinations. As history informs us, different schools, curricula and examinations, designed to cater for the interests of identified groups, have tended to add to differentiation in education rather than to diminish it (see also 6).

Tailoring the curriculum to fit the assumed needs, or interests, of pupils may only be effective in terms of easing the passage through school for pupils and teachers if society and the occupational market regards the products as ill-clothed and continues to reward the traditionally dressed. It is these considerations that have led some radical commentators to argue that what is needed is not the reform of schools but the deschooling of society. Illich (1971) not only saw schooling as an artefact, but also as unnecessary and corrupting – 'depriving education of reality and work of creativity'. If real progress is to be made it seems likely that the curriculum will have to be changed for all children, rather than for specific groups, for only in that way will discrimination be avoided. In other words, a truly common curriculum be instituted. Such a dramatic change seems unlikely in Britain. What is apparent is that curriculum innovation and change, together with its evaluation, has to date been so limited as to preclude an answer to the vital question – will it work? We do not know, for a fact, whether a less racist, sexist, classist, more relevant curriculum would lead to the enhancement of educational opportunity for those presently disadvantaged, and greater equality in attainment. However, that is to take too narrow a view of schooling. Curriculum reform also has social and moral objectives. If racism, sexism and classism are to be decreased, a vigorous and early start must be made in school.


## iii *Contrived curriculum*

From our discussion so far it is clear that teaching and learning in schools are not a spontaneous phenomenon, but constrained and somewhat artificial. The curriculum cannot be viewed simply as a vehicle which assists pupils' factual learning, designed and executed for that purpose. Like education itself, the curriculum performs important functions for society. There is a surprisingly high level of agreement among a wide range of sociologists that the major function of education is economic and cultural reproduction (Apple 1980). Hence Bourdieu's (1971) view that schools 'reproduce in transfigured and therefore unrecognisable form, the structure of prevalent socio-economic relationships – which are consequently perceived as natural.' Bourdieu (1973) also suggests that educational processes exist to maintain illusions concerning participation, open competition, equality and democracy. Bowles and Gintis (1976) stress the similarities between the social relations in schooling and those in capitalist production. Althusser (1971) draws attention to the role of ideology (social beliefs that guide action and serve particular social interests). He sees the educational system as the most effective ideological device in a technological society and that which creates the precondition for the expansion of capitalist social relationships. These Marxist views are clearly similar to that of Bernstein (1975) when he writes, 'How a society selects, classifies, distributes, transmits and evaluates the educational knowledge it considers to be public reflects both the distribution of power and the principles of social control', and 'the form and content of educational transmission embody class ideologies'.

It is relatively straightforward to recognize such relationships between schooling and society, as is the identification of the considerable list of parties involved in the production and execution of the curriculum. Much more difficult to describe, let alone demonstrate, are the mechanisms involved – not only because of their complexity but also because they vary from situation to situation. In effect, this question is the same: Who controls education and for what purpose? These issues are taken up in 9.1.

## iv Contradictory curriculum

It would be quite wrong to form a view of the curriculum as a monolithic structure imposed upon pupils and teachers – it only feels like that sometimes! In secondary schools, for example, there are common complaints of the constraints of the external examination syllabus from pupils and particularly from teachers. Cornbleth (1984) has drawn attention to the contradiction both within the curriculum and between it and other aspects of social life. Classrooms and subjects vary – from 'think-for-yourself' to 'use-the-textbook'; cultural diversity is praised but pupils are rewarded for conforming to the teacher's idea of a good student; schooling is about equal opportunity but clearly involves inequality of treatment. School plays out the contradiction between the individual and society – celebrating the former but providing little, if any, opportunity for involvement in decision-making in respect of behaviour and dress rules, the curriculum or assessment. The curriculum and its teaching involve compliance with authority, whereas TV and cultural heroes and heroines typically display the opposite. Schooling often stands in contrast to family, peers, the media and other institutions and values. Some people would argue that the successful in schools are those who experience the least incompatibility between the curriculum and other aspects of their social situations.

Such a view would, however, neglect the fact that the contradictions are mediated by teachers and pupils, who play an active, though not an independent, role in respect of the curriculum. It is not a simple question of their accepting or rejecting, since most adopt a form of accommodation (or 'playing school') which varies from cynicism and not taking it all too seriously, through detached involvement, to attempts at redefinition and subversion. There is, then, a sense in which what is taught and learnt in schools is negotiated in the classroom between teacher and pupil. Teachers often valiantly strive to interest their classes, or convince them of the value of what they want to teach. Pupils often seek to divert teachers towards their own interests and values, using a variety of means, see 4.7 and 5.6 to 5.9.

In similar fashion, Willis (1976/7) and Apple (1980) question the extent to which schools simply and passively reflect the dominant values of society. They argue that schools have some relative autonomy and are therefore one of the sites of ideological struggle. This issue is taken up in 9.1b.

## 4.6 School culture in action

The major objective of school culture is to produce successful (achieving), well-behaved pupils. Common-sense tells us that schools and teachers spend most of their time attempting to get pupils to behave in fairly closely-prescribed ways (the ideal-pupil role) in order to achieve. At the same time, all schools to some degree or another fail in this aim – whether over all or for individuals. It is of sociological as well as professional interest to attempt to explain why this happens. Merton (1957) suggested that social systems exert definite pressures on certain people to be nonconforming rather than conforming; in other words, that social systems designed to produce saints also produce sinners, and that the explanation for this lies not with the nature of human beings, or original sin, but with the social system. Merton identified two theoretically separate elements in culture: *goals* (purposes and interests) – these apply to all members and are those things held up by the culture as worth striving for; and *means* – the ways in which goals should be achieved in a socially accepted manner. Social systems, via their culture, provide both goals and means, but, even if the *goals* were accepted by all, groups of people would have different access to the *means* of achieving them. A good example is the goal of wealth or ownership which is very widely spread among the population. At the same time the opportunity (access to the means) to achieve this goal in a socially acceptable way varies greatly – from the wealthy businessman's clever child, say, to the unskilled, unemployed person. People who are variously situated in a social structure can adapt to it in a number of ways.

We concentrate on pupils' adaptation to school culture. It has to be borne in mind, however, that the extent to which teachers vary in support of the goals and insistence on means affects pupils' response; indeed it shapes the presentation of school culture. The extent to which goals are generally accepted clearly varies, although research into this has been limited. It could be argued that, judging by pupil behaviour, they are more commonly accepted in infant schools than in secondary ones, possibly because the goals in infant schools are more realistic – can be achieved by the majority – than those in secondary schools. More relevant, however, is the fact that access to the means is differently distributed. The most important ingredient here is ability, both in the academic and the social sense. Almost as important is that aspects of the formal culture of schools actually provide structural barriers to access to the means for individuals. The most obvious example is ability grouping (see 6.4) where staff, facilities and the curriculum are differently distributed, so that low-ability pupils may be effectively denied the means to achieve O level GCE, even if that were their goal. At a more subtle level, teachers may categorize and group pupils, thus building barriers to some pupils' achievement and helping to determine their educational outcomes (see 6.5).

In effect, then, we are saying two related things. First, that the formal culture, in operating, as it does, to produce well-behaved achieving pupils, at the same time produces delinquents and disruptive non-achieving pupils. This is probably partly explained by the culture's emphasis on rather narrow instrumental and normative standards; a broader-based culture *might* be more successful over all. (This is the essence of the arguments of the de- and free-schoolers, especially in respect of those children who don't achieve in traditional schools.) Second, that in order to achieve in school pupils must accept and be a part of the school's formal culture. Some evidence exists to show that some children have problems in relating to, and becoming part of, the formal culture. Jackson and Marsden's (1962/66) now almost classic study revealed that successful adults from working-class backgrounds retained vivid memories of clashes of culture between their family and community and that of their schools. Success at school either called for rejection of the first or for the adoption of a Jekyll-and-Hyde existence. Those unwilling or unable to do either, dropped out of or failed at school.

Merton's ideas, modified by Haray (1966) have been used to analyze, in general terms, the working of secondary schools. For an account of 'public' schools see Wakeford (1969). We shall use some of the contributions of Woods (1977, 1979) whose account is based on LEA schools and added the adaptations of colonization and intransigence to Merton's five (all are shown in Table 4.1), together with a depth of understanding. We consider the adaptations in the order of the table, which should be consulted to identify their relationship to goals and means. *Conformity* (ideal pupil) can be seen to vary according to the depth of acceptance; from the 'creep/teachers' pet' who courts favour without concern for peer-standing to those whose conformity is based on trust or because they see it leads to better ends (mainly jobs). *Innovation* could be disruptive, but would include, for example, the able (even very able) achieving pupil who, say, refuses to do homework or work in the prescribed manner, because it is seen as inappropriate or there are better means. It is possible that in a strictly enforced culture such a pupil might be stopped or discouraged from achievement. More common, as Woods has pointed out, is a milder form, *colonization*, where there is indifference/ambivalence towards goals and means. This adaptation involves playing the system to maximize comfort – taking short cuts, avoiding punishment, playing off teachers and situations against one another. *Ritualism* is common and schools depend on those who, while not striving after the goals, nevertheless play the game, abiding by the rules. *Retreatism*: school is meaningless and boring since there is no identification with it; 'in society but not of it', as Merton put it. Passing time is the central problem and this can be achieved passively or actively. Indeed, it is difficult to distinguish between retreatism and ritualism since passive resistance can flow from both. Woods used *intransigence* to refer to active and disruptive rejection of means based on hatred. This serious and immediate problem for schools claims much of its resources, though as Wakeford observed it is often short-lived and fades into colonization or rebellion. *Rebellion* varies in nature depending on whether the substitutes conflict with, or can be accommodated in, the school. The examples given by Woods, like acting out parts of shop-floor culture (see also Willis 1977) and devising a 'pop scene' curriculum, are less of a threat than intransigence and akin to retreatism. On the other hand, rebellion may amount to outright delinquency.

Behaviour related to these adaptations obviously varies in degree, extent and context – nor is it always clearly related to one. An extreme but not uncommon example is complete withdrawal –

## Table 4.1

Types of individual adaptations to the culture of school

| Adaptation | Goals | Means |
|------------|-------|-------|
| Conformity | + | + |
| Innovation | + | − |
| Colonization | ≠ | ≠ |
| Ritualism | − | + |
| Retreatism | − | − |
| Intransigence | ≠ | − |
| Rebellion | ± | ± |

Key: + = acceptance; − = rejection; ≠ = indifference/ambivalence; ± = rejection and substitution.
(Devised from Merton 1957 and Woods 1977 and 1979)

truancy – which can arise from both retreatism and rebellion. It is important to appreciate that adaptations are not total responses by individuals to everything in school. They vary considerably over time and school career and in regard to specific aspects, like particular teachers and parts of the curriculum. The response received or invoked by teachers varies, while conformist pupils in, say, mathematics, can become rebellious in games or craft lessons (and vice versa). Bearing these strictures in mind, readers are capable of applying their knowledge of school and its members (including staff) to the schema in order to illustrate it more fully. For example, innovative teachers may be very successful (popular) with their classes, but are they so with other teachers, the head, parents and so on? See how well the adaptations work in respect of pupils and teachers you know or have known, and their behaviour. As you will appreciate, the analysis so far has been at a fairly high level of abstraction. Later sections deal with classroom behaviour and interaction in more detail, but now we turn to the question of whether, or to what extent, there are informal cultures of the school.

## 4.7 Pupil cultures

The basic question addressed here is whether life and school provide a number of cultures rather than a single one. As is characteristic of the discipline, there has been more research into the existence and nature of pupils' culture(s) than those of teachers, and that is where we begin. Much of this interest centred initially on the existence of pro- and anti-school cultures and their role in explaining success and failure, and, alternatively, the extent to which they were produced by the then prevalent form of ability grouping, namely streaming. Apart from Waller (1965), the antecedents of this work appear to be Parsons' (1942) conceptualization of youth culture and Coleman's (1961, 1965a) large-scale study which found American high school pupil culture to be anti-intellectual and the existence of strong social pressures on youth to conform to it. Parsons' ideas merit our reflection. His structural-functionalist analysis attempted to view facets of society in terms of the functions they performed (purposes they fulfilled), both for the social system and for the individuals in them. Writing about 'youth culture' in society at large, he claimed that its function for the social system was to hive off a potentially dangerous threat to the social structure into relatively harmless pursuits. In other words, while the young were busy making the 'pop' scene, they were unlikely to be actively criticizing the political structure. In much the same way the mere labelling of behaviour and ideas as 'adolescent' renders them harmless or insulates them from serious consideration by adults. For the individual, Parsons saw youth culture as helping to emancipate the child from the family by providing an intermediate culture between that of the family and adult independence. Following Parsons' thinking, one can see that, if there was a culture(s) in schools which was different from the formal, then it could function in similar fashion. In secondary schools in particular, pupils who could pose problems for the school might not do so if interested and involved in such cultures. At the same time, an alternative culture might particularly attract under-achievers, the disinterested and disenchanted, and allow them to become emancipated from the formal culture.

An early British study, Sugarman (1967) was based on 540 fourth-year boys in two secondary modern, a grammar and a comprehensive boys' school in London. Sugarman argued that schools are successful to the extent to which they can get children to play the *pupil role*, as defined by teachers, which has two characteristics:

- *deferred gratification* – the restriction of present pleasure in favour of the less agreeable but better in the long run (for example, doing homework and not messing about in class, in order to achieve)
- *subordination to all teachers* – accepting and carrying out what teachers say because they are teachers.

He proposed that there is also a *teenage role* roughly opposite to the *pupil role*. Not surprisingly, high commitment to teenage role was related to low commitment to pupil role and to poor conduct rating by teachers. The question arises as to the direction of these relationships – does commitment to teenage role produce poor conduct, or the other way round? Sugarman demonstrated that both are related to what he called the 'intellectual quality' of the home (crudely measured by pupil's reports). His data suggested two distinct patterns – conformity across the home, commitment and school behaviour; and deviancy. He claimed that the teenage role does not have equal appeal to all, but does so strongly to two groups: pupils from poor, non-supportive homes, for whom the teenage role reinforces differences between their backgrounds and schools; and pupils who are beginning, through lack of success, to be alienated from school, who turn to the teenage role for support. He concluded that youth culture is the culture of the non-mobile working class, the downwardly-mobile middle class, and of individuals seeking mobility or goals along non-school lines.

Murdock and Phelps (1972) identified two distinct types of youth culture, which they claim that Sugarman had confused by treating them together. The first, *street culture*, involves mucking about in streets, playing football, going to cafés, and having a central value of solidarity of the group. They argued that this is basically working-class. The second is *pop media culture*, where the central value is immediate gratification and expression of emotional and physical capabilities. It is individual and open to all, but characteristically middle-class. Their study was based on a working-class secondary modern and a middle-class grammar school. They found pupils to be involved both in school and youth culture, though those with relatively low commitment to school were the most involved in the alternative cultures (the secondary modern almost exclusively with *street* and the grammar with *pop media* culture).

*The Culture of Schools*

The relationship between high ability and commitment to the school formal culture and low ability in opposition is supported by two studies in boys' schools – Hargreaves (1967) in a secondary modern and Lacey (1970) in a grammar school. Both these schools were streamed by ability, which was seen as a factor in the polarization of the two contrasting pupil cultures. The higher the stream, the more pro-school the pupils' subculture. Social class was also a factor – hardly surprising given its relationship with achievement and streaming (7.2, 6.4). Willis (1977) takes this latter factor further and sees the polarization arising from working-class (shop floor/factory) culture brought by the 'lads' he studied into school, which they used to anticipate the future. The lads were low achievers and anti-school. He argues that shop floor and anti-school cultures share the same determinates – the need to create meaning from what can be seen as harsh conditions and external direction, and the need for strategies to cope with boredom, blocked opportunities and alienation. Common characteristics of both are masculine chauvinism, attempts to gain control, a developed opposition to authority, and solidarity based on language and humour. The subculture thereby provides a continuity for the worlds of school and work (in both directions) – sustaining them in school and leading to the 'choice' of 'shop floor' work. In contrast, the subculture of conformist pupils (affectionately labelled by the lads as 'ear-holes') appears grounded in a different social class location and is generally supportive of school and teachers (see further discussion, 9.1b). A study in a multi-racial, working-class London comprehensive school showed that lower stream and black pupils were immersed in peer groups which were both racially and academically exclusive (Troyna 1978). Ball (1981) identified pro- and anti-school cultures in his study of a banded comprehensive school. He points out that teenage culture provides an alternative to that of school culture for lower ability pupils, whereas the more able combine both. He suggests a refinement of pro-school culture into supportive and manipulative, and anti-school culture into passive and rejecting. He also notes that not all pupils can be simply fitted into these categories, and they may move between them.

Further research based in a variety of schools and on pupils of different sex, age, class and ethnic group serves to bear out such reservations and refinements. Here, we have space to review only a few of these studies. Furlong (1976) studied a small group of mainly West Indian female pupils in a secondary modern school and discovered no consistent culture, suggesting that 'interaction set' better describes the fluid groupings and variable responses to situations and time observed. Meyenn (1980) argues that middle-school, female pupils' peer groups do not fall into the pro- or anti-school schema. For example, the less able had strategies to make school tolerable, but these did not include causing trouble and they claimed to be happy at school. Unlike those in Sugarman's study, the most pro-school were equally involved in the teenage culture. Pollard (1979) reports that for most of the time in the primary school under study, there was a negotiated consensus and therefore no pro-/anti-school groups or real polarization. In a comprehensive school Fuller (1980) identified a small aspiring subculture positively based on being black and female. The girls' rejection of what they saw as a double subordination (sex and colour) led them to work hard towards qualifications while maintaining the appearance of not doing so – by indulging in forms of marginal confrontation and having friends from among non-academic black girls rather than aspiring whites. Delamont (1976) in a private, middle-class, flexibly organized girls' school found no polarizing subcultures or friendship groupings. Similarly boys 'public' boarding schools were found to display pupil culture more or less agreeing with formal school culture (Lambert 1968). Davies (1984) concluded from a study of 'problem' girls in a mixed comprehensive school that the term 'pupil subculture' had limited application because it had been developed in respect to boys. The girls in her study were indifferent to school rather than challenging, while their individualism and private interests limited the effect of the subculture. Hence the girls lacked the social solidarity of Willis's 'lads', being perhaps true deviants in lacking integrative group support and using the group to celebrate differences rather than similarities. Lambart (1976) similarly supports the idea that female peer groupings are more elaborate and complex than male, and they have also been seen as typically smaller and more intimate (Murdock and Phelps 1973).

Our review leads to a number of overall considerations. Early research was carried out with male pupils in streamed secondary schools, subsequent work involving females and other types of school drew attention to the socially specific nature and variation of pupil cultures. Research again illustrates differences in the level of abstraction applied. Pupil cultures may be viewed simply as pro- and anti-school, or as a series of more detailed corporate adaptations – note the similarity of Ball's cultures and the adaptations outlined in 4.6. Allied to this are differences in relation to the research techniques employed. Interpretative research with its protracted study of small groups of pupils is, by definition, going to produce finer tuning than macro approaches. However, it is also true that particular pupil cultures must not be viewed in isolation. They must be studied in relation to, and interaction with, all cultures in both the school and the society and communities in which they exist.

Overall we can conclude that pupils in school, like people in any social system, have their own ways of viewing, reacting and coping – a corporate survival kit! These cultures display variation based on: status within school (mainly a product of ability and conduct); forms of social stratification (social class, sex, age, and ethnic group), both within and without school; and the organizational base of the school. These cultures are dynamic and, while not all pervasive, do affect behaviour of members and non-members. They are clearly an important aspect of school life which needs to be recognized and understood by those wishing to affect what happens in school and classroom. These aspects are taken up in greater detail in 5.

## 4.8 Teacher cultures

Perhaps because teachers are educated, work in such a variety of types of educational institution, and come from such a large, diverse workforce (3.1), their culture has yet to be explored at other than a relatively high level of abstraction. There are four main elements to the work culture of teachers – their social background, their professional and other education, the nature and status of their employment, and their response to working in school. Here we take a brief view of the first three factors before looking at some general aspects of their culture as presented in schools.

While there is no up-to-date, large-scale data on teachers' social background, it is clear that the majority come from the middle and upper working classes. Analysis of the class origins of student teachers in 1961/2 revealed the following percentages (for definition of RG's classes see 10.2): I:7 per cent, II:33 per cent; III(nm): 14 per cent; III(m): 29 per cent; IV:9 per cent; V:2 per cent; unknown 6 per cent (*Higher Education* 1963). These percentages were not dissimilar to those for postgraduate students, of whom 46 per cent were working class; a larger proportion of women than men were middle class. Floud and Scott (1961) found a higher percentage of working-class teachers in primary and secondary modern schools than in grammar schools, and we can suspect the proportion of teachers with middle-class backgrounds to be much higher again in 'public' schools (6.3). Further variation has been observed in smaller-scale studies. I found that just over half of a sample of Bradford teachers (many of whom were non-graduates) were from working-class backgrounds and were the first in three generations of their families to have a middle-class occupation (Reid 1980). By definition, teachers are drawn from among those who have been successful in education and can be expected to have some commitment to, and interest in, education. *Higher Education* showed that 80 per cent of student teachers had attended grammar or independent schools. The contrast between the social and educational backgrounds and interests of teachers and many of those they teach can be seen to pose problems in terms of cultural clashes – which in turn can call for fairly dramatic adjustments on the part of some teachers. This clearly varies according to the type of school and pupil involved. Finally, in this respect it should be noted that there are extremely few ethnic minority teachers in British schools – a situation likely to continue for some time since the proportion of ethnic minority students entering PGCE courses in 1983 was considerably lower than their representation in the population (Searle and Stibbs 1986).

Something of the nature and complexity of becoming and being a teacher is revealed by Lacey's (1977) study of a PGCE course. In this he uses the concept of social strategy – the intentions and acts of an individual in a social setting. On entry to the course, students already have an internalized view of the world gained from life – Lacey sees degree subject as of particular importance, but the concept can easily be widened – which forms 'the basis for but also limits the number of strategies open to an individual in a given situation'. He identifies three types of sub-strategy: *compliance*, in which the prevailing definitions (of course and/or school) are accepted but the person maintains his own view: *internalized adjustment*, where they are fully accepted; and *redefinition*, in which ideas and methods which challenge the prevailing view are held and used. This schema is useful in that it corrects some over-deterministic views of teacher education, schools and teachers' roles. There is, however, evidence to show that compliance, in which the ideals of teachers and teacher education give way to an extent to more traditional ones of the typical school, is common (see below and 5.4).

Hargreaves (1980) has drawn attention to the relative neglect of the occupational culture of teachers and identifies three major concerns on which it is centred: status, competence and social relationships. The principle factor of status is dissatisfaction with the standing of teaching in society. Teaching is a long way from the status of traditional professions (medicine, law, etc.), but shares some aspects of a profession, together with the sustained desire to be recognized as one. Hargreaves sees a rift between teachers who see pay as the crucial factor and those for whom respect is more important. Professional status is clearly related to expertise and competence, not always or fully recognized by the public despite an improvement in teacher education and the realization of all-graduate entry to teaching. There remain important divisions between teachers who take the PGCE and BEd. routes to the classroom and those who teach children in primary, or subjects in secondary, schools. Such divisions are further reflected in the internal status hierarchy within teaching itself and that accorded to teachers by pupils, employers, parents and public. Despite changes in curriculum and school organization, subject specialism and level of teaching remain important distinctions.

Teaching is a very diffuse occupation with broad and relatively unspecific goals in academic, social and moral, and vocational spheres. It is also an activity in which there is only limited feedback about success and failure. Hence teachers appear to rely on extremely short- and long-term indications: the lesson just taught is *felt* to be good or bad; great pleasure of association is felt about the pupil returning to school having achieved success in higher education or career.

Hargreaves states, 'Like sexual activity, teaching is seen as an intimate act which is most effectively and properly conducted when shrouded in privacy', and relates this to teachers' concern for autonomy from not only the conflicting demands of teaching and relationships with pupils, parents, LEA officials and governers, etc., but also from each other. In other words teachers (like many others) have a fear or dislike of being judged and criticized, having what Hargreaves called a 'cult of individualism' which leads both to security and insecurity. Earlier (1972) he supplied a useful description of the characteristic norms and values of secondary school teachers:

- *autonomy* – mainly concerned with the privacy of the classroom, providing teachers with the freedom to do what they believe to be right in their own room
- *loyalty* – to each other, avoiding criticism of other teachers in front of pupils, the headteachers, and to some extent other teachers, and backing each other up
- *mediocrity* – much like the behaviour of students, avoiding giving indications to one's peers that one works particularly hard or that one is over-keen
- *cynicism* – often humorous, but amounting to the derision of belief in the possible success of innovations or the achievement of objectives
- *anti-intellectualism* – a pragmatic, on-the-job (chalk-face) attitude, unencumbered by consideration of abstract theory
- *categorization* – the characterization or labelling of classes and/or pupils (see 6.5).

As suggested above, there appear to be considerable variations according to type of school. In contrast, for example, King (1977) reports that there was little evidence of mediocrity or cynicism in the infant school staffrooms he observed. Children were the main topic of conversation and teachers were secure about their ideology; consequently, there was little talk about educational issues other than techniques. Among the many differences which may account for this contrast is the important fact that infant teaching is undifferentiated: subject identities do not exist in such schools, whereas in secondary schools they are the basis of organization and of staff groupings (Lacey 1977, Grace 1978, Ball and Lacey 1980). However, staff groupings show considerable variation in terms of the criteria on which they are formed. In one school at which I worked, the two major groupings – which cut across all others – were those who played basketball and those who played bridge!

Such variations do not detract from the importance of staffroom culture in affecting members' understanding of, and behaviour in, school. This is pointedly revealed to the newcomer who is likely to be given a rapid rundown on the corporate views of the classes, pupils, rules, system, and hierarchy in the school. Subsequent experience will be reinforced, challenged or modified by staffroom discussion. In an occupation as complex and involving demands as conflicting and heavy as teaching, the attraction of staffroom culture as an aid to making sense of it all is likely to be high. Woods (1979) has drawn attention to the role of staffroom laughter in neutralizing the alienation that teachers experience from the institutionalization of schools and the conflict and discrepancy between appearance and reality. And, we might add, between what teachers as professionals want to do and what they can, or do, achieve. Whincup (1983), from his twelve years' participant observation of the male staff of a comprehensive school, shows how their humour and antics were corporately used to 'combat' the status division and to control aspects of members' behaviour which were socially or professionally irritating. He draws a direct analogy with Willis's (1977) 'lads' who attempted to counter the school's formal culture with their own informal one, which gave negative meaning to that of the school's. In staffrooms, humorous disrespect for the hierarchy and unacceptable peer behaviour appear to function in the same way.

Although not researched to the same extent or in the same manner, teacher culture appears then to parallel the functions of pupil culture. Both provide members with socially based coping strategies and a grouping to deal with the demands of teaching and learning in the context of members' abilities and motivation and within the vagaries of the structure of schooling and education. As we have seen, while the two cultures are intimately related to school, they draw on, and are related to, features of the social structure well beyond its boundaries.

## 4.9 Do schools make a difference?

Having reviewed a number of individual aspects of school culture, we turn now to consider differences between schools' overall culture. Like all social institutions, schools have reputations (not always accurate ones) and appear to vary in their ethos or climate. Whether schools differ in their success, how success is defined, and what ingredients are involved have entertained the users and providers of educational systems as well as sociologists of education for some time. The general weight of opinion, until recently, has been that the affect on children of school is slight in comparison with that of their home background. Such views were informed by mammoth American studies (Coleman et al 1966 and Jencks et al 1972) which argued that school performance was largely independent of schooling and that significant increases in resources were unlikely to affect it. Similarly, in Britain, the influential *Children and their Primary Schools* (1967) expressed the view that home influences were of greater importance than schools. The general view was perhaps characterized by the title of a paper by Bernstein (1970), 'Education cannot compensate for society'. However, the situation is neither quite so simple nor so comforting for those in control of resources in schools, since recent British research has challenged these assumptions. It is at least suggestive that differences in the effectiveness of schools are related to differences in their climate and culture.

The most directly relevant study to our discussion is that of Reynolds and Sullivan (1979). Their six-year research in eight almost exclusively working-class secondary modern schools in a

Welsh LEA revealed differences in the 'ideology, conscientiousness and beliefs' of the participants. Five of the schools were seen as *incorporative*: pupils were encouraged to take active part in lessons and in control within the school; interpersonal relationships between teachers and pupils were good (a low rate of corporal punishment, a 'truce' about some school rules, e.g. smoking and chewing, rewards for being good); and parents were involved. The other three schools were *coercive*: they made little attempt to involve pupils and parents (who were viewed as the enemy); there was a high level of institutional control, lack of truce, and high rates of corporal punishment. The latter schools produced twice as many delinquents as the former, and poorer attendance and academic performance (Reynolds 1976) from pupils whose ability and parental social class was similar (Reynolds et al 1976). These differences were not accounted for by differing record-keeping or examination entry policies. The cause of the differences was seen as lying with teacher perceptions about the pupil intake. For example, in one *coercive* school 70 per cent of pupils were seen as being socially deprived and there was a tendency to under-estimate ability and to emphasize the need for firm control and character training. In comparison, in one *incorporative* school only 10 per cent of the pupils were so viewed. These different perceptions, it is argued, are passed on to new pupils and teachers and thus affect their behaviour. In short, it is argued that the more successful schools succeed because social control in them is conflict-avoiding and pleasant.

The research in this field to receive the most attention was that of Rutter et al (1979). Twelve comprehensive schools in inner London were found, as might be expected, to vary markedly in terms of their pupils' attendance, behaviour, delinquency rate and academic attainment in public examinations. At the extremes, for example, in one school the average 16+ examinations score of the lowest band of ability (as measured across ILEA) was equal to that of the highest ability band in another. The factors involved in producing such different outcomes were seen as intake measures (pupil) and process measures (school). The first were operationalized as verbal reasoning (VRQ) scores, parental occupation and behaviour ratings by primary school teachers. Process measures, which were collected by the researchers, numbered 46 and included: academic emphasis; teacher action in lessons; rewards and punishments; rewards and praise; pupil conditions; responsibilities and participations; stability of teaching and friendship groups; staff organization; skills of teachers. An 'overall school process effect' combining the variety of these factors was statistically analyzed to show that it was more powerful than intake measures in predicting the schools' outcomes. Rutter et al, while maintaining that for a causal explanation controlled experimental studies would be needed, concluded that the ethos or climate of a school affects outcomes and characterized good schools as 'schools which set good standards, where teachers provide good models of behaviour, where they (the pupils) are praised and given responsibility, where the general conditions are good and where the lessons are well conducted'.

This research received a good deal of telling criticism. We concentrate on that not directly aimed at the statistics used (for which, apart from sources quoted below, see Preece 1979). Heath and Clifford (1980) point out that the percentage of the variance in examination performance explained by verbal reasoning test scores is 27, by school factors 6.5, leaving 66.5 per cent unexplained (if verbal reasoning is held constant the effect of school remains the same). Hence, the results are open to a wide interpretation. A researcher such as Jencks could conclude that verbal reasoning and school factors explain very little – the evidence clearly suggests much within as well as between school variation. On the other hand, one like Eysenck, a proponent of IQ, could claim that verbal reasoning is much more important than school factors. Gray (1981a) argues that Rutter et al used a model which supposed that differences between school outputs, which cannot be explained by simple input measures, *must* be explained by school factors. This, of course, assumes that other factors, particularly home background (which is more than amply illustrated in this book as a vital factor in achievement, see 7) are adequately catered for. In fact, as we have seen above, only one measure of home background, parental occupation, was used which itself was crude (see 10.2 and discussion at 7.2a), compared with 46 measures for schools. As Heath and Clifford remark, further background factors such as educational level of parents and parental interest might well have diminished the apparent effect of school. Gray points out that in his work he found stronger correlations than those of Rutter et al between proxy home background variables, such as free meals, and examination results (1981b). He calls for more open-ended research and concludes that it would be wiser at this time to say 'we don't know very much about whether schools make a difference'. It could be that *both* outcomes and functioning of schools are a consequence of input variables.

A later study used more detailed measures of pupils' background (sex, father's occupation, number of siblings and mother's education), together with pupil's measured ability (VRQ) and related these to the outcomes of 15 Scottish secondary schools (Williams and Cuttance 1985). Again, considerable variation was found: average pupils left the 'best' schools with five or more O level SCEs, but left the 'worst' with only one or two passes. Schools were successful or otherwise across the curriculum. Unlike Rutter et al there were a few schools which were particularly effective with low- but not with high-ability pupils and vice versa. Over all there was a relationship between school effectiveness and average VRQ, which would appear to confirm that pupils perform better (perhaps particularly the less able) in schools with high overall levels of ability. The collective properties of a school's pupils may affect performance in a number of ways – through peer influence, disciplinary climate, established school expectations, the curriculum adopted and the type of teachers and pupils attracted to the school.

The implications of such findings, if further substantiated, would be considerable and far-reaching. If the products of schools with similar intakes and resources vary according to their social climate or culture then the possibility of significant advance in equality of educational opportunity would be held out by the spread of good or best practice. Certainty in this direction will, however, have to await further research, better balanced between home and school factors, using larger samples of schools together with more detailed analysis and intimate views of schools' objectives, organization, resourcing and cultural climates (see also 7.10).

# 5

# Pupils, Teachers and Classrooms

## 5.1 A view from inside

The views of school and schooling in 4 were mainly expressed at a relatively high level of abstraction and concerned with macro aspects. Here we take a closer, more detailed, micro view more directly through the eyes of the participants of the ways in which they construct, interpret and negotiate the meaning of the social world they inhabit. While this emphasis is clear, it is in no way a separate approach; as argued in 2, it is part of an overall, composite understanding. Work in this field arises not only from shifts in sociology towards interpretative perspectives, but also from other fields of interest (see Delamont and Hamilton 1974). Important contributions have been made by the allied disciplines of social psychology, social anthropology and socio-linguistics. Apart from being relatively under-researched, classrooms had until the mid 1970s been investigated mainly through 'interactional analysis', which involves recording teacher and pupil behaviour in prescribed categories. Critics argued that these categories assume a particular style of teaching – the traditional chalk and talk – and over-emphasize the teacher's importance. This leads to ignoring important aspects of social interaction in classrooms and current trends towards different types of teaching. Further stimulus is identified as coming from the perceived failure of teacher education and lack of teacher interest in educational research, both seen to be due to the apparent distance of educational knowledge and research from the 'chalk face'.

Since the mid 1970s, interpretative classroom research has blossomed into a major field of interest, so that the range of available material approaches something of the social and physical complexity of life in the classroom itself. Consequently, some considerations have had to be made in the selection and presentation of material. First, it has been chosen to relate to the material and areas dealt elsewhere in the book. Hence, it concentrates on contributions to our knowledge of what goes on in schools rather than on the justification and utility of the approach and its research techniques. It is concerned only with the major social actors' (teachers and pupils) views of each other and their interaction in their immediate environment of the classroom. Second, wherever possible British studies have been used. While this is true for this book in general, it is crucial in relation to approaches particularly concerned with, and sensitive to, the meanings of social situations. While the research reviewed uses a variety of techniques, its major characteristic is the very full if not complete recording of events, interviews, and so on. Often this is achieved by using tape recordings, subsequently transcribed and analyzed. The reason for these, it is argued, is that they allow readers to reinterpret the material differently to the author. Actually, however, this is rarely the case, in that the researcher always has more 'evidence' available than can be presented in written form. Here we lack the space to follow this convention of quotation. For the full flavour of this interpretative research, readers will need to consult the references given.

Not using predetermined categories for observation does not solve the problem of what to select to observe, but shifts some selection from before to after the research act, and allows the researcher greater interaction with the data. But this form of research is far from straightforward; note taking is severely limited by speed of writing and interferes with observation; mechanical recording is likely to affect social interaction in classrooms, pose technical problems, or result in vast quantities of material, and thus pose problems of sortage and use. Indeed, it may be impossible fully to capture the sheer complexity of the classroom. Walker and Adelman (1976) have argued that, particularly in informal classrooms, the mere recording of speech is not enough. Visual recording (film and video tape) is required in order to make sense of pauses, hesitations and fragments of speech together with non-verbal cues – facial expressions and gestures, for example. Even this is not the whole answer. Anyone who has attended a football match and then watched it on television appreciates the limitations of filming social reality.

As suggested above, our entry into the social world of the classroom begins with examining the participants' views of each other and moves on to their relationship and interaction. Teachers are for pupils a vital aspect of school; in some senses they are synonymous with school. They are the front line, representing, or being, the school in the classroom. Hence the ways in which pupils see and react to teachers, and the bases on which they do so, are of prime importance in understanding what goes on in classrooms and schools. A similar case can be made for teachers in respect to pupils. This is not to overlook the importance of each for themselves (6.6). Since pupils are the majority – they outnumber teachers by around twenty to one in schools and often by greater numbers in classes – we start with their views.

## 5.2 Pupils' views of teachers

Pupils' views of teachers appear remarkably uniform and stable, varying little according to the age of pupil, type of school or research technique used to investigate them. Unremarkably, pupils expect teachers to do their job properly and humanely. An early study (Taylor 1962) analyzed children's essays and identified four categories of teacher behaviour – teaching, discipline, personal qualities and organization. From these were developed scales which were given to 980 pupils in a number of primary and secondary schools. Over all, good teachers were seen as those who were firm and kept order, had good knowledge, and were able to explain, and to be helpful and encouraging. Nash (1974) asked twelve-year-olds to describe the differences in behaviour between a teacher they 'got on with' and one they 'didn't get on with'. In analyzing the interview transcripts he found six common constructs (ways in which pupils discriminated between the two teachers): (i) keeps/unable to keep order (the strongest construct, used by almost all children); (ii) teaches you/doesn't teach you; (iii) explains/doesn't explain; (iv) interesting/boring; (v) fair/unfair; (vi) friendly/unfriendly (this one was seen as a bit of a bonus – teachers were not really expected to be friendly!). These are then the members' (pupils') rules; the more in accord the teacher is with each of the first of the above alternatives the more acceptable they will be to the pupils and consequently the more 'acceptable' will be pupils' classroom behaviour.

It is important to appreciate that the research reported here is more than a catalogue of pupils' likes and dislikes about teachers. What is being explored is the basis of the rules or expectations which pupils hold for teachers, similar in process and effect to those held by teachers of pupils (5.3). For example, Ball (1980) observed that comprehensive school pupils, including those who were most pro-school, were quick to take advantage of teachers who failed to take action, got angry, lost self-control or displayed signs of confusion.

Similar findings are presented by Furlong (1976, 1977) from observation of a low-ability class of mainly black secondary school girls. Their acceptance of teachers and behaviour in their classrooms related to whether the teacher was strict or soft (in control and discipline) and effective or ineffective (in getting the girls to learn or not). Woods' (1979) study in a small secondary school revealed teachers evaluated on four criteria: (i) *teaching techniques* – those liked were helpful and explained, provided variety and allowed more freedom; (ii) *disposition* (not personality, but their presentation of state of mind or mood) – a preference for those who were more cheerful, humorous, friendly and understanding; (iii) *control* – firmness was appreciated, but excessive severity was viewed as being as bad as excessive softness; (iv) *fairness* – most disliked were those who had 'pets' or who were always picking on people.

While differences between the sexes of pupils in respect to views of teachers have yet to be fully explored, it is interesting to note Davies' (1984) highlighting of girls' distaste for contradiction. They disliked teachers who were rude, inconsistent, smoked or chewed, and they expected teachers to be very moral. They took advantage of soft ones and rejected those who did not make them work, who encouraged poor work or failed to provide pupils with marketable skills. They were quick to recognize and take advantage of teachers who appeared to have status problems – who showed off or 'showed up' pupils, called them names or displayed arrogance. Stanworth (1983) interviewed sixth-formers to explore whether sex affected pupils' attitudes to teachers. She found that pupils of both sexes thought male teachers were more effective disciplinarians (even where this was not borne out in their current classroom experience) and more successful in academic and teaching terms than female teachers. However, both male and female pupils felt more at ease, attentive and able to participate when being taught by members of their own sex. All pupils thought male teachers were more friendly towards male than female pupils, the latter being kept at a distance.

Even less well researched are ethnic group differences. Stone (1981) provides a rare example of West Indian pupils' views of teachers as hostile, authoritarian and arbitrary in their use of power. This view may well be related to differing levels of achievement (see 7.4). West Indian youths who had not achieved CSE were found by Ratcliffe (1981) not only to resent teachers' authority but also to be dissatisfied with their teachers' interest in them.

Interesting further detail is provided by Thompson's research (1975) which entailed first- and fourth-year secondary school pupils rating teachers and adults in general. Teachers were more favourably rated on what can be seen as role characteristics – wisdom, success and hardness – and less well on the more human qualities of kindness, fairness and warmth. Older pupils made lower ratings of teachers than the younger, not in respect to human but to role characteristics. As would be expected, pupils identified by teachers as deviant had less favourable overall attitudes to teachers than those seen as well-adjusted. Human characteristics, which featured prominently in Blishen's (1973) analysis of 'bad' teachers from children's essays, identifying remoteness, lack of sympathy, attachment to trivial rules, and failure to admit to ignorance and uncertainty.

It is important to appreciate two aspects of pupils' major and prime concern with teachers' ability to maintain order and control in the classroom and over them. First, it is shared by all, the good

## Table 5.1
### Pupils' evaluation schema for teachers

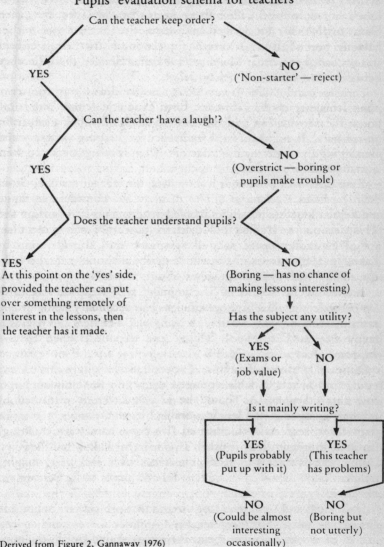

(Derived from Figure 2, Gannaway 1976)

and the bad. While such concern may be simply seen as in the self-interest of the well-behaved, it is less obvious that the badly behaved not only expect teachers to keep them in order, but often blame teachers for not doing it and, implicitly, for their own misbehaviour. Second, it is not simply a question of strictness, a certain style is called for, what Meighan (1981) has labelled the difference between 'nice strict' and 'nasty strict'.

The research of Gannaway (1976) neatly draws our considerations together in diagrammatic form (Table 5.1) and, more importantly, provides an analysis of the process of pupils' evaluation of teachers. It highlights the centrality of keeping order, while identifying and ordering other factors. What is being suggested then is that pupils are 'sizing up' teachers and, having measured them, relating their own behaviour to how well the teacher matches up to their yardstick. Delamont (1976) displays the considerable range and depth of factors possibly involved in 'sizing up'. The girls in the private school she studied took teachers' posture, gestures and their use of classroom space as well as speech into consideration in making judgements about a teacher's personality and mental condition. They had their own views about acceptable fashion with respect to teachers' clothes. The younger staff were seen as more sympathetic, the older as more efficient and better at keeping order. Being married was associated with being placid in class and having a happy life out of school! Heads and deputies, when in the classroom, had an aura of authority stemming from their status.

Quite apart from their status, of course, teachers have careers and reputations in school which precede them into the classroom and their pupils' evaluation. These become characterized in the school folklore, encapsulated in nicknames and legend. Among the more graphic and respectable nicknames I've come across are: Bulldog, the Cow, Pregnant Pussy (a man), Thumper, Mr Dillon and the Fairy Queen. Pupils' views of student teachers have also been sought. Meighan (1977) showed secondary school pupils to be perceptive, reflective, sympathetic and constructively critical in their comments. Cortis and Grayson (1978) found that primary school pupils particularly noticed student teachers' abilities in recognizing the quality of work, organizing, answering questions and explaining.

Pupils also reflected on the extent to which lessons contained new material, were enjoyable, exciting, difficult or understood.

The studies we have looked at clearly show that pupils' reactions to and evaluation of teachers are in no way blanket responses to a generalized concept of the teacher. Rather they are the result of considering a large number of factors related to particular teachers, pupils' past experience and the context in which it takes place. Such variation and range should not, however, distract from the overall picture. A reading of the studies shows that some pupils see teachers along a line from positive to neutral (love to tolerance), and others from negative to neutral (hatred to tolerance). The exact ingredients involved in the production of such a range of evaluations, together with the possible strategies to affect them, calls for more extensive and deeper research into the participants, their school careers and the contexts in which they meet.

In general terms, however, the fundamental pupil requirement of teachers is that they should do their job properly – which at heart involves keeping order and teaching something, if possible in a humane way and with fairness and humour.

## 5.3 Teachers' views of pupils

Teachers' views of pupils have been researched in a variety of ways. Early work used the concept of the ideal client that other professionals were thought to hold of the people they work with or for. Becker (1952) identified the ideal pupil as one who displayed ability in learning, conformity to classroom rules, and avoidance of offending the teacher's moral codes. The unsurprising implications were that teachers have a preference for pupils who ease the job of teaching and that they measure pupils against that ideal. Becker identified social class as a major variable in teacher typification of pupils, middle-class pupils fitting, working-class not fitting, the ideal. Many British researchers have emphasized the relationship between the ideal pupil concept and institutional categories. For example, Keddie (1971) and Ball (1981), among others, related pupil typification to ability bands in secondary school. The top academic band provides a shared model stereotype, on which teachers base their evaluation of pupils. As Ball puts it, they are 'constraints which the teacher brings into the classroom and with which the pupil has to deal'. There are also clear indications of this type of thinking in respect of views on pupils by sex, see below.

A second type of research seeks to identify pupil characteristics which form the basis of teacher typification. The work of Nash (1973) and Taylor (1976) provides interesting comparisons, since they both employed a technique in which teachers identified and ranked the constructs they used in evaluating their pupils with different results (similar research to that of Nash with pupils, see 5.2). With eight teachers in one 'progressive' junior school, Nash identified three common core constructs: hardworking/lazy; mature/immature; well behaved/poorly behaved. He concluded that the constructs relate to work habits, maturity and behaviour, which are, according to him, aspects of the child's personality. Pupils were judged on personal attributes associated with good progress in school. Taylor, using 48 teachers in 18 more traditional schools teaching nine-year-old children, found that academic ability was more important than personality. He also found that male teachers valued academic ability more than female teachers; the latter tended to treat other characteristics with equal importance, being especially aware of pupils they 'got along with' and those who were helpful. This could reflect differences in the patterns of authority in male and female teachers' classrooms. The contrast in findings between the two studies may be due to differences between 'progressive' and traditional schooling and attendant perceptions of pupil and teacher roles.

A third approach, labelled by Hargreaves (1977) a 'dynamic interactionist model', involved observing and investigating teachers in action. A substantial study in this vein sought to discover how pupils in secondary schools became labelled as deviants (Hargreaves et al 1975) and in so doing illuminates some aspects of classroom interaction. Deviancy was seen as involving three elements: (1) an act by party (person) one; (2) the interpretation of (1) by a second party as rule-breaking, the labelling of the first party as deviant, and then according him suitable treatment; (3) the reaction of the first party to (2). Their study was limited to (2) above, hence their first concern was to identify rules in school. They found three main types: *institutional* rules which were applied universally, such as punctuality, no litter, etc; *situational* rules which were applied in specific places, e.g., assembly, the classroom; and *personal* rules which were particular to individual teachers. They chose to concentrate upon situational rules and found that neither teachers nor pupils had any coherent concept of a set of rules. This, of course, does not mean that either party was unaware of the rules, but rather that they could not identify them in that manner. The researchers were able to identify the themes of the rules, which were related to talk, movement, time, teacher/pupil and pupil/pupil relationships. The importance and recognition of the rules appeared vitally related to the context in which they occurred. This was illustrated by the way in which the same words could either be an instruction or what they called an 'imputation of deviancy'; for example, 'Pay attention' is an instruction when the pupils are working well but the teacher wants to give further instructions, but is an imputation of deviancy when the teacher is talking and the pupils are not listening. According to the researchers, the importance of the context was also revealed by the fact that the teachers could not always explain why they had said certain things in class and sought to explain them by tracing the context. The importance of the context to rules had not been expected by the researchers. In exploring rule contexts they found that lessons are typically composed of phases (or contexts) in which rules and their application change: entry – settling down – lesson proper – clearing up – exit. Teachers use 'switch signals' to define the change from one phase to another, whereupon all members move from one set to another. This suggests that members have a common-sense understanding of the classroom, a point further illustrated by the fact that teachers only rarely state which rule is being broken, expecting the rule breaker to know. Hence 'Reid!' in context would, as it often did, mean 'Pay attention!' The researchers' next concern was to find out how teachers interpret their pupils' behaviour as being deviant in the sense of breaking rules. They distinguish between *conviction rules* – where the teacher actually witnesses rule breaking or has direct evidence for it, for example, in relation to 'paying attention' when the pupil cannot answer a question – and *suspicion rules* which operate when there is ambiguity; for example, if there is talking or movement during a test it could amount to cheating but may not. The teacher is likely to adopt various strategies to find out: direct questioning, physical searching or the later inspection of the two scripts. Teachers, as we may expect, have a vast knowledge of deviancy in classrooms and the ways in which it is disguised, as indeed pupils have of presenting plausible cover-ups! However, the research also reveals, as we might expect, that teachers also use their knowledge of the particular pupil involved in deciding whether behaviour is deviant. In investigating how teachers build up this knowledge of pupils, interviews were held to find out the constructs which teachers applied in their description of pupils (see also above). These were identified as appearance, conformity to discipline, conformity to the academic role, likability and peer-group relations. One of the major contributions of the study is the illustration that, while the teachers made initial identifications of pupils, not only were these qualified through more contact but a process of verification took place over time, resulting either in the initial reaction being substantiated or in a retyping. Over time, too, the teachers' greater knowledge of pupils led to more extensive (wider-range) typing of pupils which consequently became much more individualized. For example, motives were associated with deviancy of particular pupils. Some pupils appear, even at the early stage, to 'stand out' from the others. Three main factors were identified here. (1) *Sibling phenomena* – pupils with older siblings in the school are likely to be recognized early and their behaviour seen in the light of the latter's performance, both for good and bad. (2) *Staff discussion* – this can bring individuals to a teacher's attention before meeting them in class, or confirm or modify their initial impressions. (3) *Particular problems* – for example, information received by the school about a medical condition. Note that, although it does not occur in this particular study, record cards and reports, where they exist and are used, could operate in this way. Finally, some 'spectacular' classroom happening or accident may make a pupil 'stand out'. Pupils who emerge from the teacher's process of typing as established deviants are seen as indulging in a diversity of types of deviancy, and as being persistent at it, incurable and not likable.

Having presented a very considerable amount of evidence on typing, the authors conclude:

> Although deviant pupils may be classified together under the diffuse label of 'troublemaker' there is nevertheless a uniqueness about every typing when pupils are considered as individuals. Deviant pupils emerge as distinct individuals, each with his own methods of deviating on particular occasions and for particular motives. . . . There is a certainty and confidence to the teacher's knowledge of these pupils which, based on multitudinous events few of which are remembered . . . has been built over time into a coherent and resistant characterization.

Their final concern was with how the teachers treated deviant acts. On detecting such an act the teacher has to decide (1) whether to intervene, and (2) how to intervene. These decisions were explored by asking teachers to explain their behaviour in scenes of 'deviancy' observed by the researchers. The considerations relating to intervention were: would intervention be more disruptive than ignoring the act? how serious was the deviancy? who did it (what type of deviant)? what is the emotional state of the deviant? what is the likely outcome of the intervention (success or failure)? In choosing the type of action, teachers aim for the most effective (it'll work) and efficient (quickly and well) and this again is chosen in relation to the type of pupil committing the deviancy. Really stable deviants are subject to higher levels of threshold (will be acted upon less frequently) than other members because teachers do not expect anything from them – intervention is unlikely to be successful and will possibly cause more problems by giving rise to confrontation.

A somewhat similar study, this time in three infant schools, is that by King (1978). He notes that typifying and assessing pupils are inseparable processes flowing from teachers' ideologies of development and individuality. Three main characteristics of teacher typification are identified. (1) Teachers mainly relied on their own experience, rarely consulting other teachers' reports. (2) Teachers used three aspects of pupil behaviour: obedience to classroom rules, relationships with other children, learning progress. (3) Typifications were not absolute but varied over time.

Some research has focused on sex as a factor. Teacher preference for the sex of pupils displays an interesting contrast between primary and secondary schools. In the former, females are preferred (Ingleby and Cooper 1974). In infant schools, male pupils are seen as untidier, more impatient, lazier, rougher, noisier, more immature and lacking concentration in comparison with females (Hartley 1978). Douglas (1964) reported that primary school teachers saw boys as working less hard, being less able to concentrate and less willing to submit to discipline than girls. This might be thought to reflect the fact that most British primary school teachers are themselves female and exhibit chauvinism. However, Davies (1984) has examined evidence across Europe, where the sex ratio of teachers varies considerably, and concludes that 'the picture remains amazingly similar'. She also points out that the situation is not simply due to sexual prejudice, in that it involves both what teachers believe pupils of each sex expect from teachers, and the differing behaviours presented by them (see 6.5aii). There has been less research in secondary schools and there is some variation in the findings. Douglas et al (1968) found that teachers rated girls more favourably than boys at the ages of 13 and 15 years. A later study found that teachers of both sexes, given the choice, would prefer to teach male pupils who were seen as more enthusiastic, quicker to grasp the concepts and better 'on the oral side' (Davies and Meighan 1975). Female pupils were seen to present less behaviour problems, as in primary schools, but teachers had suspicions about female submissiveness and maturity. Male pupil discipline problems were interpreted as 'boys will be boys'; female ones as devious, insolent and insidious. Stanworth (1983) found male sixth-form teachers more attuned to sex differences of pupils than female staff. However, teachers of both sexes were more responsive to male pupils, to whom they were more attached. This greater involvement with male pupils was true even where females were academically more successful. Pupils reported as difficult by teachers of both sexes were, without exception, female.

As in the case of pupils' views, those of teachers in respect of ethnic groups have received little attention and been limited to West Indian, Asian, and Other (see 7.4). Brittan (1976) found a high degree of agreement among the 510 teachers questioned about West Indian pupils – that they were of low ability and created discipline problems – but that the stereotyping was contradictory, embracing both 'lazy/passive/withdrawn' and 'boisterous/aggressive/disruptive'! Carrington (1981), reviewing literature in the field, writes, 'teachers, it would seem, tend to regard West Indian pupils as a problematic group – disruptive, aggressive, unable to concentrate, poorly motivated and with low academic achievements'. In contrast, teachers have been found to hold positive stereotypes of Asian pupils. A majority of headteachers surveyed commented favourably on Indian and Pakistani pupils' manners, keenness to learn and industry (Townsend and Brittan 1972), while Asian pupils have been viewed similarly and seen as not having the behaviour problems associated with West Indians (Stewart 1978). Such differences in teachers' views may be related to the differences in the educational achievements of the ethnic minorities involved (see 7.4) and to differences in pupil role performance, as well as aspects of teacher prejudice (see 6.5a and b).

Teachers make public or formal their typification of pupils in writing reports, either for parents or school. King (1978) observed that the words and expressions used were similar to those employed in controlling infant pupils in classrooms. In one school, 'A' pupils were typically described as well behaved, quiet, sensible and mature; 'C' were badly behaved, noisy, silly and immature. Woods (1979) analyzed secondary school reports and argued that while they appear to be written to absolute standards (implied by grades), the marking was relative, in accordance with the stream of the pupil. Two considerations were paramount: the gaining of skills and social adjustment, which, while involving an 'ideal pupil' concept, varied according to the aims of school and teacher. Report categories were based on pupils' performance according to teachers' instructional and disciplinary expectations. Hence the desirable categories used of the children were: concentration, quiet, industrious, willing, cooperative, responsible, mature, courteous, cheerful and obedient.

This pattern was disturbed only by outstanding pupil excellence, nuisance or other particular teacher/pupil relationships.

Our review suggests that while teachers' views have been more extensively researched than pupils', knowledge remains fragmentary. Both display considerable variation according to the context and type of research involved. Teachers' major consider ations are clearly ability and behaviour, though a range of other factors are involved (see also 6.5 on categorization). As Hargreaves et al (1975) have shown, there is a depth and subtlety to the process of teachers' typifications. Before turning to classroom interaction we consider further the contexts and effects of teachers' views of pupils.

## 5.4 Views in context

It is important that teachers and pupils are not viewed in isolation; in relation only to each other, or only in classrooms. They, their views and their actions relate outwards to the school as a whole, the community and to society beyond. Our consideration is limited to two aspects. The first indicates how persuasive the cultural climate of school is in affecting teachers' views and practice. Keddie (1971) reveals differences between what teachers as educationists think and how teachers as teachers operate. She found that the humanities staff in a comprehensive school disagreed with the rest of the staff about teaching methods but agreed with them about evaluating pupils. As educationists, these teachers rejected the ideas of intelligence primarily determined by heredity, of streaming, and of a curriculum differentiated according to the ability of pupils, and thought of social class and ability as being separate. Such beliefs underlay the introduction to a new CSE Mode 3 syllabus they introduced for all pupils – inquiry-based, and in which the pupils worked at their own pace using work cards. The objective of the course was to help pupils become more autonomous and rational beings, by developing modes of work and thought. However, while the course embodied a concept of the ideal pupil, this concept was identical to that which already existed in the academically able child. The school was banded, pupils being broadly grouped by ability into bands A, B and C (see 6.4). Those in the A band were seen in ideal-pupil terms, those in C were not. Hence, as the A band worked more quickly than C and the course ran in a structured way from one topic to another, it could be seen to be more compatible with the A band than the C. Similarly the individualistic and competitive nature of pupil work (via work cards) favoured those who, through academic achievement, enjoyed and were good at this type of work. While the course appealed to A-band pupils in that they saw the manner of working as being valuable in terms of their future academic pursuits, pupils in C band were more concerned with the immediacy of the course's content.

In operating the course the teachers appeared to adopt (or fall back on?) the school's general ways of categorizing and evaluating pupils, which as educationists they denied. This is illustrated by the following quotations from teachers:

... it's O level material ... but some of the human elements may be C material

I didn't know any more than was on the work card ... this was all right with Cs but it wouldn't be with As

The Cs who fail can't meet [the head of department's] criteria [of autonomous work] ... Many have working-class parents ...

According to Keddie, teachers translated what they 'knew' about pupils in social, moral and psychological terms into what they knew about them as intellects. Similarly she argues, by implication, that teachers fail to appreciate that the pupils in different bands approach knowledge in different ways. The A-band pupils accepted the teachers' definition of the subject and its framework, and asked 'relevant' questions, whereas the C-band pupils used more immediate contexts for their approach. For example, they wanted to know why the mother of an isolated (feral) boy had treated him so, to which a teacher responded with, 'Well, we are not too interested in that but in the actual influence on the development of the child.' The differences were viewed by the teachers in terms of lack of ability – that is, the C band could not deal with concepts and subjects and required more concrete examples. It seems that hierarchical categories of ability and particularly knowledge persist even in unstreamed classes because teachers differentiate between pupils on what they see as high or low ability.

Sharp and Green (1975) provide a more detailed, intimate picture of the relationship between teachers' thought and practice. In their study of three teachers and their classrooms in a progressive, working-class infant school, they attempt to illuminate the extent to which classroom practice is the result of, on the one hand, teachers' ideology and, on the other, the material and social constraints imposed by the classroom, school, its catchment area and society. The researchers identify the school's progressive ethos through an interview with the headmaster. They report that he combined a child- centred perspective on education with a social-pathological view of the community from which the pupils come. The major objective of the school was to provide a socializing ('civilizing' was his word), supportive context in which the children can develop. While he recognized an obligation to teach pupils to read and write, this was not the prime aim, which was to cater for the developmental needs of the whole child. Underlying this, the researchers report, was a pessimism about the effectiveness of the school in counteracting the effects of the home environment. The ambiguities are due, they argue, to a clash between the ideology of child-centred education and the conflicting pressures brought to bear on the headteacher.

Observation and interview showed the three class teachers to hold individual views – from accord to mild disagreement with the school's ethos – and variations in practice accordingly. The researchers argue that these differences should have given rise to differing classroom stratification and differentiation. In fact, they found the stratification to be very similar in each of the classrooms and little different to that of 'traditional' classrooms. This arises, they argue, because the common features of the material and social environment impinge on practice and cannot be 'merely intended away in consciousness'. The common features are seen as 'what to do in the classroom' (problems of management and control), the need to live up to (with) colleagues, superiors and parents, and the constraints of the classroom and of pupil numbers. The classrooms were stratified along a line from 'odd' (problematic) through 'normal' to 'successful'. This situation is a paradox in that while the three classrooms were 'child-centred', the children in them had reified identities which gave rise to differentiation. Those seen by teachers as being closest to their common-sense understanding of 'normal' or 'successful' received the most attention and were viewed most as individuals. Put the other way round, the style adopted by the child in coping with the classroom situation is important in the way pupils and teachers construct his/her identity. At the same time some classroom differences were revealed. One was relatively more dominated by teacher and rules than the others and there was more reified typing of pupils. Hence, a higher proportion of pupils acquired low-status and deviant identities and there was less mobility within a narrower range of identities.

Sharp and Green trace classroom practice to society and its 'need' to reproduce the economic and social system for the next generation. What they imply is that teachers, wittingly or not, are concerned with creating society in miniature in the classroom. 'The processes we have observed in the classroom . . . can be seen as the initial stages of the institutionalization of social selection for the stratification system.' Like Keddie they see a difference between ideology and practice but their explanation, unlike hers, transcends the school: 'the educational ideology of child-centred progressivism fails to comprehend the realities of a given situation of a stratified society whose facilities, prestige and rewards are unequally distributed'. While such reasoning has its attractions, particularly perhaps from a sociological standpoint, its demonstration is a long way off. Its value lies in indicating that there could be limits to the understanding of micro social realities gained only through the eyes of their actors. As they write, 'there may well be social situations where, for whatever reason, the individual may find it very difficult to give a meaning to his situation or his actions at all, or where he is completely constrained to do things irrespective of how he defines the situation'.

111

The Sociology of School and Education

## 5.5 Teacher-talk

As you will have noticed and heard, teachers talk a lot. Research shows they spend 60 to 70 per cent of lesson time doing it and speak three to four times as much as all their pupils together. Wragg (1973) observed student teachers in secondary schools using 73 to 81 per cent of their time talking, while pupils' share of classroom talk ranged from 32 to 23 per cent. Galton et al (1980) found that primary school teachers devoted about 60 per cent of classroom time to talk, three quarters of it in making statements and the rest in questioning. Informal classrooms follow this general rule, though not all the pupils hear all the teacher says (Walker and Adelman 1975; Edwards and Furlong 1978). Teachers not only monopolize classroom talk, they also control it in ways that from others in school would be regarded as most rude and unacceptable. They typically ask questions to which they already have answers and check up on and interrogate pupils almost constantly. They consistently state and impose on pupils their definitions of order, discipline, knowledge, ability and so on. Of course, as this is teaching as we know it, it is both familiar and acceptable.

As Stubbs (1976) has pointed out, a good deal of what teachers say is *metacommunication*, that is, communication about communication. Using material from his observations in a Scottish secondary school, he illustrates that metacommunication involves: (1) attracting or showing attention: 'Now, don't start, just listen'; (2) controlling the amount of speech: 'Anything else you can say about it?'; (3) checking or confirming understanding; (4) summarizing; (5) defining; (6) editing: 'Now that's a good point'; (7) correcting; and (8) specifying the topic: 'Now, we were talking about structures.' Stubbs argues that what teachers actually say – the style of language – is unimportant in comparison with what they are doing. The teacher is about 'staying in touch' with his pupils and directing their discussion and language. This is very one-sided since only very rarely do pupils use such words as 'That's an interesting question' or 'What do you mean by . . .?' to their teachers. Again, Stubbs is pointing up the part played by language in supporting the teacher's role, his/her values and the maintenance of social order in the

112

classroom: 'By the very way in which a teacher talks to his pupils, he inevitably communicates to them his definition of the situation and the form of teacher/pupil relationship which he considers appropriate.'

Other researchers have attempted to outline the structure of classroom communication rather than analyzing its content. Sinclair and Coulthard (1974) say that the typical exchange structure of classroom communication is:

teacher asks question ⟶ pupil responds ⟶ teacher evaluates
    (initiation)        (response)        (feedback)

Notice that the sequence begins and ends with the teacher. In contrast, the much rarer initiations of pupils may receive a response but are unlikely to give feedback to the teacher. Again, these authors stress the role of language in the social structure of the classroom, illustrating the complexity of these exchanges well in the following example. A class have listened to a tape of someone speaking in a very 'posh' accent which is followed by laughter on the part of one pupil. The teacher asks 'What are you laughing at?' The pupil wrongly assumes that this is a disciplinary statement, when in fact it is a genuine question aimed at exploring the child's reaction and attitudes to the tape. A misunderstanding of a language form – as command instead of question – had taken place. Some classroom talk can only be understood within its context. Walker and Adelman (1976) point that out. Teacher: 'Is that all you've done?' Pupils: 'Strawberries, strawberries', followed by laughter, can only be appreciated if one knows that the teacher in question had a favourite expression about pupils' work: 'Like strawberries – good as far as it goes, but doesn't last nearly long enough.' In other words, shared meanings have shared history.

The centrality of teacher-talk, and the consequent subordination of pupils and pupil-talk, reveals quite a bit about classrooms – about power, roles and expectations in them. Most important though, teacher-talk is a vital ingredient in learning. Most commentators see classroom dialogue, heavily teacher-biased, as the major part of the educational process for most pupils. Obviously then in an ideal setting teacher-talk should be about facilitating learning. Unfortunately, and perhaps predictably, it can also be a distraction or hindrance. Barnes (1976) has differentiated teachers' use of specialist, subject language (some of which teachers are aware of and carefully present), and what he calls 'language of the school' (which is only heard in school). We shall concentrate on the first, which most teachers see as 'natural': all subjects have their vocabulary of particular words or specific uses of words. Perhaps to be a sociologist one has to sound like one!

As Barnes points out, while such language may not be necessary to explain certain ideas it is convention to use it. At the same time, for some pupils it is both unfamiliar and confusing, while teachers may find it difficult or be unwilling to accept pupils' contributions other than in what they see as the appropriate language style. In some cases teachers' recognition of pupils' learning is related to their ability in using teacher-language as well as, or even rather than, their knowledge. The two are often not easily separable, though it appears easy to instance examples where teachers fail to recognize valid ideas from pupils. Asked how to remove a chlorophyll stain from a piece of material, a pupil suggested putting shoe polish on it and then washing it. He had the idea of using a solvent, but not the language which allowed the teacher to understand him. The problem may be even deeper; Mercer (1981) points out that pupils had the ability to use words like 'evaporation' and 'liquid' in class but not an understanding of the concepts (for example, liquid was thought of as thick and sticky). Careful probing of primary school children has revealed that they do not have the basic sexual knowledge that designers of sex education programmes believe they have (Kimberley 1986). Edwards and Furlong (1978) have analyzed how teachers work to persuade pupils to adopt 'the teacher's system of meanings, which either confines or extends or even replaces his own'. This is achieved through questioning and the management of answers which shape pupils' responses and knowledge into the teacher's framework until they are 'right'. Barnes (1976) has distinguished three types of teacher questions in respect to lesson content: factual (what?s); reasoning (how?s); and open. The teachers he observed used mostly factual, some reasoning and few open questions.

The language used by teachers clearly implies that school knowledge is different from everyday knowledge, that it is received from the teacher, and that learning it involves listening and reproduction rather than questioning. In many ways it mirrors the written language of textbooks, which poses for some pupils the problem which Rosen (1972) has graphically described: 'the gap between their own language and the textbook is so great that the textbook is mere noise. . . . The textbook is alien both in its conventions and its strategies. The subject never comes through: it is another way of life. Though this is not a matter of language alone, language plays a big part.'

Readers may wonder whether our account so far relates only to traditional chalk and talk lessons, and the extent which more open, 'progressive' classrooms differ from it. The answer appears to be only a matter of degree: most accounts suggest that freedom and spontaneity are more apparent than real. Atkinson and Delamont (1977) have disclosed how guided discovery science lessons amount to carefully staged 'mock-ups' which recapitulate known facts rather than real discovery. Edwards and Furlong (1978) concluded that a resource-based humanities programme they studied was a change in teaching technology rather than a move away from the transmission model of knowledge (note the similarity with Keddie's work, 5.4). Barnes (1976) has commented that the most commonly used 'self-directed' learning aid, the worksheet, rarely does more than get pupils to rehearse textbook or teacher knowledge. Perhaps the end line is provided by Kozal (1968) who visited 'free schools' which prided themselves in their progressiveness and the range of choice offered to pupils. He concluded that teachers and adults in them dictated opinion and preferences in important ways, offering a similar range of choice (albeit different to an extent from that of an ordinary school). While most of the research reported has been conducted in secondary schools, King's (1978) observations from infants' classrooms fit in well:

Teachers defined the reality of everyday life in their classrooms. Within this they created other orders of reality, the story worlds of reading, the writing worlds of news and story, and the world of number and mathematics. Children learnt to share their teachers' definitions of the nature of these provinces of meaning by reproducing them in their reading aloud, in their writing and in doing sums or problems. They also learnt which of these worlds they inhabited at a given time.

The evidence of a generalized pattern of structure and use of teacher-talk is convincing and firmly rooted in the socially defined, accepted and regulated activity of teaching as we know it. However, the picture is not total, though differences are of relative variation rather than absolute difference. The work of Barnes (1976) alerts us to the relationship between teachers' ideologies of learning and teaching and their use of language, organization of classroom language and evaluation of pupils' work. Working from the responses of secondary school teachers to questions concerning written work, Barnes hypothesizes two polar types of teacher.

(1) *Transmission teachers*, who believe that knowledge exists primarily as a public discipline; value pupils' performance to the extent that it conforms to the discipline's criteria; see the teacher's role as evaluating performance according to those criteria; and view pupils' access to knowledge as difficult, since qualification is through tests of performance.

(2) *Interpretation teachers*, who believe that knowledge exists in pupils' ability to organize thought and action; value pupils' performance in terms of their commitment to organize thought and action; see the teacher's role as setting up a dialogue in which pupils reshape their knowledge through interaction; and view pupils as already possessing relevant knowledge and the means to shape it.

Barnes suggests that the two types produce differing classroom communication systems as illustrated in Table 5.2. Hence, Type 1 teachers will tend to use a communication system in which transmission and assessment play a major part, compelling pupils to adopt presentation-type performance and encourage boundaried knowledge which is not brought into relationship with pupils' purposes and interests. Type 2 teachers will tend to use communication systems which emphasize the reply aspect, making possible the negotiation of teacher and pupil knowledge – involving collaborative and exploratory communication in which knowledge is related to pupils' purposes and interests. Useful as the model is, it clearly involves extreme typifications – most teachers would lie somewhere in between and probably shift according to the subject they were teaching – and it does not take into account the disposition of pupils, which is likely to be critical to classroom outcomes.

**Table 5.2**
Teacher type* and classroom communication system

| Teacher type* | Teacher's role | Pupil's role | Kind of learning encouraged |
|---|---|---|---|
| 1 | **Transmission** assessment predominates | **Presentation** final draft | **Boundaried** school knowledge |
| 2 | **Negotiation** reply predominates | **Collaboration** exploratory | **Related to everyday** action knowledge |

* See text for definition
(Based on table p. 146, Barnes 1976)

## 5.6 Initial encounters

On my first day teaching in the East End of London a senior teacher gave me the sound traditional advice that generations of recruits have received. The pupils would be fine initially, then they would 'try it on' and finally settle down. So I was to be as strict as possible and impose myself on the classes – I could always ease up later but, I was assured, I would have no second chance if I let them get away with anything early on. These honeymoon, coming out and settling down phases, well known and anticipated by teachers and pupils, have been explored by researchers. Most commentators assume a level of conflict between teachers and pupils and, hence, assess initial encounters in terms of the parties testing each others' strengths and weaknesses. Beynon (1984), for example, observed how first-year male pupils in a comprehensive school were set on 'sussing out' (their term), by a series of well orchestrated check and challenges, their teacher's tolerance, coercive power and essential knowledge. This allowed them to locate the teacher on a number of dimensions (and also allowed strict teachers to prove and establish themselves). Ball (1980), however, suggests that pupils may be after several things ranging from understanding to confrontation: a competent understanding of how the teacher defines a situation (what the teacher wants); negotiating a mutually acceptable and congruent definition; or challenging, in whole or part, the competence and authority of the teacher. In essence, pupils want to know where they are in relation to the teacher, so that they can anticipate the future – this may well reflect their appreciation of teachers who are strict and fair (see 5.2). Similarly, teachers are about establishing a (their) regime for the same purpose. The basic picture is one of the two 'sides' negotiating meaning and establishing order. While teachers may be assumed to hold the greater power they can only sustain it with the agreement (coerced or voluntary) of the class, within which there are likely to be differently disposed groups of pupils (see below). While initial encounters may be critical classroom events, they are not complete or final: the relationships are dynamic. Hence the best approach is to look at pupils' and teachers' interests and the coping strategies they use for dealing with the classroom.

## 5.7 Coping strategies

Whatever the dispositions of classroom participants, they have to live within classroom social reality and cope with it. In facing this common problem, which is in part defined by themselves, teachers and pupils adopt a range of strategies. This approach is particularly useful since it provides a bridge between the structural constraints on classrooms, interaction within them, and members' interests, thus incorporating macro and micro concerns. Teachers' coping strategies have received most attention and are our first consideration.

Hargreaves (A, 1978) sees teachers' coping strategies as the products of both constructive and creative activity, and adaptation to institutional and societal constraints. He identifies three major constraints: the fundamentally contradictory goals of the educational system (egalitarianism and personal development as against preparation for the occupational/social order, involving selection); material considerations (school buildings, class sizes, educational resources); and proliferation and change of educational ideologies (through public debate and political action). Such constraints are institutionally mediated within schools, where they are expressed differently according to the age and social class composition of pupils. Whether strategies persist or not is in part related to the response of pupils and they are validated through teachers' experience. Strategies are based on a set of taken-for-granted assumptions about schooling, children and learning.

Woods (1977, 1979) provides a similar but more descriptive view. He identifies conflict or tension between teachers' own commitment to teaching, the institutional momentum of schools and the social pressures (including the clientèle) applied to schools by outside agencies. While recognizing that these pressures vary, mainly in terms of type of school and level of teacher commitment, he argues that teachers are after the accommodation of these pressures through the use of a series of strategies. He argues that for a highly committed teacher in very difficult circumstances there is a survival problem involving 'physical, mental and nervous safety and well being, continuation of professional life, way of life, status and self esteem'. In more typical settings we can perhaps best see the following strategies in terms of coping rather than survival terms. As readers will see, the strategies are not as clearly separate as Woods' presentation implies.

- *socialization*: attempts to fashion pupils, via school rules and routine, towards the ideal pupil role; likely to succeed mainly with those already disposed towards school culture, but can itself cause alienation
- *domination*: what we would recognize as discipline, from physical to verbal strictness, assault and aggression; epitomized according to Woods by PE teachers and, aimed at achieving conformity

119

- *negotiation*: based on exchange principles – 'now you play ball with me and I'll . . .' – over school work, rules and pleasure; includes appeals, apologies, cajoling, flattery, bribes and so on; designed to sustain order and get some work done
- *fraternization*: 'if you can't beat 'em' join 'em, by becoming less adult and joining the pupils; good relationships induce more obligation. Several forms: culture identification (more readily available to young teachers) – display of interest/ knowledge in pupils world/mass media, etc.; entertainment – use of humour, film, fieldwork projects and so on; indulgence – tolerating certain behaviours or individuals to get pupils' interest and cooperation; flirting – use of sex as a form of control and humour
- *absence or removal*: ranging from physical to mental absence from classroom, – including not volunteering, keeping out of the way, wasting time between and during lessons and using group and individual pupil projects
- *ritual and routine*: well exampled by assembly routines, but also evident in the individual classroom. Dictating of notes and work cards can be seen as examples; pupils believe that they are spared from work and thus their cooperation is secured. According to Woods, teachers become addicted to routine
- *occupational therapy*: certain activities provide relief and opportunities to occupy the mind while cutting out from the overall scene, – drawing maps and pictures, practical activities, setting up and taking down apparatus or displays, etc
- *morale boosting*: teachers' group solidarity is high (even if staffrooms usually have a number of groups) and this is sustained by rhetoric and humour which supports the belief that teachers' accommodation is forced on them by outside factors – the pupils, the examination system, etc

Woods concludes that these strategies do not necessarily facilitate teaching (and presumably learning) and that they often take its place, becoming ends in themselves. Contemporary schooling, he argues, increasingly forces teachers 'to think of survival first and education second'. He sees the strategies as explaining why there has been so little real change in schooling despite the efforts of theorists – because many ideas (for example, open-plan schools and integrated teaching) threaten to destroy the basis on which the strategies are constructed, while providing no clear alternative. He further claims that pressures on teachers, rather than a conspiracy on the part of capitalist society, explains why 'education is removed from the essential being of the learner and objectified as an alien commodity which can be consumed or rejected . . . schools make alienation preparatory to life' (Holly 1973). In similiar fashion Burgess (1983) identified three teaching strategies developed to cope with teaching the less able in the comprehensive school he studied: *adapting the rules* – smoking/swearing, etc. were overlooked or allowed, and some teachers indulged; *flexibility* – alternation between work and play in class, coffee drinking, cards and so on, the latter sometimes taking over and becoming essential elements; *developing relationships* – swopping of gossip and stories, joking, overt friendship and flirting.

Pollard (1980, 1982), whose work is in primary school, has argued that coping strategies must be conceptualized much more fully at the micro level. His analysis is based on teachers' primary and secondary 'interests-at-hand'. Primary interests are facets of 'self': maintaining self-image; controlling work load; minimizing stress and protecting health; deriving enjoyment; sustaining autonomy. Secondary interests are order and instruction, which he sees in the role of enabling survival, defined as a balance of interest satisfaction. Achieving interests-at-hand is dependent upon obtaining compatible pupil behaviour. There exists a negotiated system of behavioural understandings associated with particular times, places and personnel in the classroom, which offer differing opportunities for particular interests-at-hand. Teachers therefore juggle their strategies and interest priorities to optimize their satisfaction.

So far we have identified some of the ingredients in, and varieties of, teachers' coping strategies. Choosing and using them is the essence of teaching. As we saw above (5.3), decisions on how to deal with deviants have to be carefully considered and related to specific contexts. Being dominant and strict or avoiding confrontation are not simple alternatives, nor are their outcomes necessarily predictable. The range of considerations is complex: short-term, long-term, individual, and class objectives as well as teacher interests and aspects of context are all involved. A further dimension is the level and type of commitment and the identity concerns of the teacher. Woods (1981) has used Hammersley's (1977) ideas to construct what might be seen as two types of teacher: idealist and pragmatist. The first is orientated towards the ideals and principles of teaching; adaptation to, or compromise with, educational situations is resisted or rejected. The second is orientated to what is, or what is not, possible in given circumstances and the strategies for achieving that, involving opportunism. Teachers are likely to vary between these two extremes and may well change in the course of their career.

Clearly, this approach emphasizes both the element of choice and the variety of constraints which contextualize teachers' coping strategies. To some it may be an over-active view of the typical teacher in a typical lesson. Certainly, the basis of much teaching practice appears to be handed down, substantially ready-made, from heads, senior and other staff, LEA advisory staff, teacher education courses, literature, curriculum packages and teachers' social and educational backgrounds.

Perhaps because of differences in their nature and problems of research, pupils' coping strategies have received less attention and have been approached differently to those of teachers. The basic and enduring characteristics of pupil strategies are assumed to be responses to teachers and to teachers' presentation of school, and to be group rather than individual undertakings. Pupil response is clearly what is demanded and expected in classrooms and reflects differences in the power distribution there. A further assumed characteristic is that of at least initial basic goodwill; Delamont (1976), for example, writes, 'the pupils' first strategy is to find out what the teacher wants and give it to her – assuming that they can see a payoff for themselves, in terms of grades, eventual jobs, or peace and quiet. When there is no discernible benefit to be had by giving the teacher what she wants, "disruptive behaviour" is likely to become the major strategy.'

As we saw (5.6), initial classroom encounters are actively used by pupils to 'suss out' what teachers want. Giving it to them, however, does not necessarily imply serious attempts at pleasing the teacher and/or learning. Tuckwell (1982) observed infant school pupils not seriously tackling problems but searching for cues from teachers' and pupils' responses, faking attitudes and hedging bets. A common coping strategy for instance is, when put 'on the spot', to make a gesture, hoping that teacher will correct or direct, hence avoiding being properly shown up! Some commentators, for example Holt (1982), stress that pupils' strategies are short-term, relating to the here and now, while teachers' are long-term and future-orientated. While a basic instrumentalism can be recognized in pupils' strategies this is also true of many teachers; pupils have less opportunity and social 'need' to express long-term goals than teachers do.

Most of the work in this field has followed the adaptation model, using variants of the pupil culture approach (see 4.6, which might usefully be reviewed here). There is general agreement that pupils can be broadly classified into three groups according to their orientation to school. In respect of secondary school pupils, Hargreaves (1972) and Woods (1983) use: pleasing teacher/ supportive; indifferent/detached; delinquent/oppositional; Pollard (1979) uses goodies, jokers and gangs for junior school pupils. These are categories of basic disposition rather than strategies which relate to specific behaviours. For example, working in class may appear supportive, but can arise from detached 'time passing' or ritual. Denscombe (1980) points out that many pupils' strategies are 'counter-strategies' in response to teachers, rather than creations to further pupils' aims and intentions. Hence, it is useful to review Woods' list of teacher strategies above in this respect. Readers will easily be able to relate corresponding aspects of pupil behaviour to fraternization, absence or removal, ritual and routine, or occupational therapy. An important and very popular coping strategy is having a laugh/mucking about (see 5.9 on humour). Woods points to the complexity of its motivation – subversion, confrontation, identification with teacher or peer group, an antidote to fear and boredom, relief, enjoyment – or just fun!

Underlining our consideration of coping strategies is the fundamental and the most common pupil and teacher strategy – that of negotiation. Faced with pupils' conflicting interests and strategies, teachers have some logical choices. They can adopt what Hargreaves (1979) has called 'policing' – vigorously and systematically controlling pupils, making explicit the rule system and power differences between them and pupils, and giving priority to moral rather than cognitive aspects of the classroom. Alternatively, they may indulge in avoiding confrontation, refusing or minimizing the response to challenges. Both Woods and Ball (1980) have suggested that these two strategies are likely to produce and develop deviancy. Or teachers may indulge in negotiation in an attempt to arrive at a shared understanding with the class. Pupils face similar choices, both corporately and individually. It is obvious, however, that all three strategies both imply and involve negotiation, even though its 'rules' and extent may vary. Because of the centrality of negotiation in social life the next section takes a look at it in action in classrooms.

## 5.8 Negotiation

Pupils and teachers share the need to cope, or survive their daily classroom experience and accomplish something, and they provide for each other a significant part of that social reality. I used to ponder on how wonderful school would be without teachers, since when I have day-dreamed about life in school without pupils! Most classrooms can be seen as having a working agreement/regime, the result of an adaptation by, and negotiation between, the two parties. Here we concentrate on the latter, although adaptation (discussed in 4.6) is clearly related. In a real sense negotiation is composed of the meeting of the strategies just reviewed in 5.7. For some people the idea of negotiation in the classroom suggests either an unflattering picture of teachers' ability or authority, or a balance of power between teachers and pupils. In absolute terms at least, both these ideas should be rejected. What is clear is that teachers do not have much which most pupils urgently need and they yet are judged, and judge themselves, on the extent to which they succeed in getting pupils to perform and behave in fairly specific ways. Teaching is considerably more than controlling pupils, so the latter have considerable potential power – from the withholding of goodwill to complete destruction. While the concept of negotiation holds good even in what might be considered the ideal educational setting of tutor/research degree student, what emerges from that relationship has been negotiated in a not dissimilar fashion to that of the classroom. A further factor is that teaching and learning appear to be based on values of unachievable perfection, but practised quite pragmatically. Pupils' and teachers' performance could always be better – hence no 'could not do better' or 'perfection' comments on school work or reports! Comparative, negotiated performance and evaluation are the norm.

Our consideration of classroom negotiation is limited to two aspects – order and work – which are central to teaching and learning. We start with Pollard's (1979) work in primary schools, where he sees a 'working consensus' operating for most of the time. Negotiation in the primary school typically involves one teacher and one class, whereas in secondary school it involves a series of each. As Pollard points out, however, this does not simplify the situation since greater intimacy and different organization imply a range of working consensuses or rules related to the teacher's mood, the task involved (written work, craft, drama), the time of lesson or day (beginning, working, clearing up), and the area of the classroom (craft or wet area, near teacher's desk, etc.). These rules involve complex understandings and both pupil and teacher 'deviancy' is related to them. Pollard usefully distinguishes pupil and teacher acts within a framework – see Table 5.3. Routine deviancy (having a laugh, talking, fidgeting, and so on) and censure (mild rebuke, restatement of rules, etc.) are taken for granted by both parties. Unilateral acts (severe misbehaviour or teacher losing temper) are problematic and disruptive. However, Pollard (as we have seen in 5.7) avoids treating pupils as homogeneous, seeing groupings differently disposed to school which he labels goodies, gangs and jokers (but without the polarization of secondary school pupils). Goodies had greater deference to the teacher even when unilaterally censured, gangs had limited respect for teachers whom they saw as unfair, and jokers were inclined to view and judge teacher behaviour in its context. As you can see from the table, they also varied in the range of their behaviours. To this analysis he adds that pupils were defending their 'self' – self-image, enjoyment, control of stress, retention of dignity (compare with teachers' 'self', 5.7), which were pursued differently according to disposition. Pollard sees the jokers as crucial in negotiation, since they were the mediating, majority force, and therefore useful to the teacher. He concludes with the implication, 'if a teacher establishes negotiating relationships with a wide range of children and is perceived as 'fair' and 'reasonable' in his dealings with them, then he reduces the number of children who will tend to become involved in unilateral acts of disorder.'

**Table 5.3**
Teacher and pupil actions within classroom working consensus

| TEACHER ACTS | | | PUPIL ACTS | |
|---|---|---|---|---|
| Unilateral act | Acts within parameters of working consensus | | | Unilateral act |
| non-legitimated censure | legitimated routine censure | conformity | legitimated routine deviancy | rule-framed disorder |
| Pupil groups' parameters of action | Goodies ⟶ | | | |
| | Jokers ⟶ | | | |
| | Gangs ⟶ | | | |
| | | Action derived from working consensus | | Action derived from peer culture |

(Devised from diagrams pp. 84 and 90, Pollard 1979)

126

As has been suggested, underlying negotiations are sets of expectations and values about schooling and life. To some extent these have been viewed above (5.2 and 5.3) but are further explored in 6 with respect to cultural and professional differences. It is also important to appreciate that negotiation and working consensus are essentially dynamic and developing processes.

Woods (1983) has approached negotiation in respect of school work, which he identifies as the 'central official activity of school life'. His view is derived from observation in a secondary modern school. He distinguishes between types of work and relates them to pupil adaptations (see 4.6), as shown below, arguing that 'command of the process of negotiation is at the heart of teaching'.

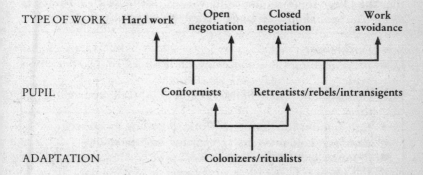

Hard work might be thought to indicate agreement rather than negotiation; pupils vary, however, in what they regard as hard – copying, creative writing, PE all vary in this respect. Even among well-disposed pupils (and even some of my students!) it can be a challenge to overcome their disinclination to do what they regard as hard work. Consequently, it merges into open negotiation in which teachers attempt to sell or disguise hard work. They carry pupils along, with promises of relief and reward, do some of the work for them (notes and teacher talk), attempt to make it fun or a game, or compensate for it with other activities. Pupils play a responding role – you have almost certainly experienced it all yourself. Closed negotiation in contrast contains little goodwill or belief in consensus, though it stops short of the open conflict of work avoidance, resulting in a semblance of work. In closed negotiation the teacher tries continually to impose the traditional lesson structure, despite failure, while pupils pretend to learn, but are mainly concerned with playing their own version of the game. Both accept the situation with resignation, avoiding confrontation and indulging in time wasting and ritual (for example, distribution of equipment, settling down, gearing work to time, etc.).

The techniques involved in negotiation are numerous and difficult to convey outside the classroom. Turner (1983) has constructed a list from which the following examples are drawn. These arose from his work in a comprehensive school and you will notice that they bear some similarity to Woods' list of teacher strategies (5.7). You will almost certainly be able to add to them.

- *Persistence*
- *Brinksmanship*: not conceding until forced to, or concession made
- *Comparison*: 'Miss Smith lets us . . .', 'call yourself an A form . . .'
- *Justification*: for having to work, or failing to do so
- *Reminders*: of previous agreements or happenings
- *Promises* and *threats*
- *Vehemence*: feigned loss of temper, or looking cool
- *Appeals*: to tradition/higher authority: 'it's always been . . .' 'it's not fair', reference to senior/headteacher
- *Adopting an extreme position*: but being prepared to settle for less
- *Mobilizing support* from another party: classmates, other teachers
- *Cajolery* and flattery
- *Friendship* and *collaboration*
- *Humour* and *play*

## 5.9 Humour

Readers of much sociology of education might well be led to conclude that schools and classrooms are rather grim places of conflict, confrontation and discipline. There is a neglect of the enjoyment and laughter of which many have fond memories. Perhaps this neglect reflects the almost total dearth of jokes about sociologists! In featuring humour here, we are recognizing its actual as opposed to its research importance. Unfortunately, space and the nature of classroom humour and jokes – they are very situationally specific and context-bound (most do not bear telling outside) – preclude proper illustration. The analytic approach adopted here can easily be 'fleshed out' by readers' reflections upon their school days. Here we concentrate on classroom humour; staffroom humour is discussed at 4.8, and playground humour has yet to be addressed by researchers.

Walker and Goodson (1977) make a useful analytic distinction between jokes and comedy as related to formal and informal classrooms. Formal classrooms create teacher and pupil roles as joker, while informal ones tend to produce joking relationships. The latter may thrive in formal situations but will primarily be found among teachers and pupils separately and outside, not inside, the classroom. Jokes are often about negotiation, about the boundaries between personal and social identity. Teachers' jokes are bids for increased control, those of pupils challenge it, and the two reflect the imbalance of classroom power. Comedy is more the humour of equals (though often based on utterly fictional equality) and is not only sensitive to personal identity but stresses this over social identity.

The control function of humour takes several forms. Walker and Adelman (1976) see it as a means by which teachers who have strong positive relationships with their pupils maintain control in class. In the strawberries incident (see 5.5 above), 'the class is signalling to the teacher that they know what he wants and the quoting becomes a joke'. In marked contrast, Woods (1975) shows that sarcasm is used by teachers as a form of class control in the process 'of showing up' individuals or groups. 'The lowest form of wit', as we used to tell our English teacher, who was a master of the art. 'But the most useful', he used to reply. Measor and Woods (1984) draw attention to how teachers can use the comedian role (pantomime and silly voices, for example) to hold pupil attention, defuse explosive situations, aid discipline and humanize school rules. Overall, such humour contributes towards developing the middle ground between teacher and pupil interests, or cultures.

Stebbins (1980) distinguishes between intentional and unintentional humour. The first, like all humour, has its serious side, or as he puts it, carries messages. While humour designed to promote consensus indicates, at least temporarily, a degree of equality, that for control (putting down/showing up) reinforces status differences and teacher authority. Unintentional humour functions and is used as a safety valve. In open (informal) classrooms Denscombe (1980) sees teachers as using humour to reinforce and further friendliness and collaboration within the class and its activities. A further aspect is the way teachers use humour to 'humanize' classrooms and themselves. Stebbins draws attention to how teachers provide comic relief which offers respite from the seriousness of classroom work and is designed to reduce fatigue which would otherwise threaten performance and motivation. Research has yet to establish whether humour assists learning (other than adding to its pleasure or relieving its tension) – maybe we just remember the funny bits! Teachers also use humour to display aspects of their human side in order to correct or supplement pupils' knowledge about them in their role. Like pupils, teachers seek, though not necessarily expect, enjoyment and laughter in the classroom. Pollard (1980) argues that teachers' humour is perhaps related to the desire to be liked – as we saw above (5.2), pupils use humour as a criterion by which they judge teachers, even if being human is a bit of a bonus!

Pupils' use of humour is similar to that of teachers. Woods (1976) recognizes 'having a laugh' as a central and natural part of pupils' way of life. He argues that there are two forms of what he calls institutionalized laughter: 'mucking about' – rather aimless behaviour often called 'silly' by teachers; and 'subversive laughter', aimed at undermining the authority of the school or teacher. The amount to which these are indulged in is related to the degree of commitment to school. Achieving pupils, being more committed, were less involved in both types than pupils in non-examination classes. 'Mucking about' was associated with boredom at class and school felt by the latter group of pupils. Subversive laughter was more political in nature and was directed against the authority and routine of school and teacher while serving to maintain the interests of pupils' peer groups. As Pollard (1984) points out, however, not all laughter is oppositional; some supports and develops classroom relationships and culture. In open classroom situations, Denscombe identifies its use by pupils to avoid the short-term attention and control of teachers and to provide light relief and legitimate breaks in activity. For pupils, as for teachers, humour can be viewed as a means of coping with the classroom situation and can be used to influence both the progress and control of lessons.

It is of interest to note that nearly all writers draw attention to the inherent dangers of humour in the classroom: it can misfire, be misunderstood, be difficult to control or require techniques to move into and out of. These cautions are surprising, since they apply to nearly every aspect of classroom social interaction within the use of which the arts of teaching and learning lie.

## 5.10 Composite views

In 3, 4 and 5 we have reviewed a range of the insights to be gained through sociological perspectives into the nature of classrooms and schools. As I have previously emphasized, despite the apparent separation of topics and approaches covered, they have to be appreciated as a whole. Each represents a view gained at a particular level of abstraction and each inevitably fails to capture the atmosphere and complexity of the real-life classroom or school. Indeed, that is not the intention: observations have been extracted from social reality and modelled into generalization. The end product provides structure, language and knowledge of value in understanding the social reality of schools and their classrooms. However captivating that reality may be, it is clear – from our considerations here and throughout this book – there is an intimate relationship between it and social life outside school. So we turn our attention in what follows to tracing aspects of that relationship.

# 6

# Educational Differentiation

## 6.1 Differentiation in school and society

Here we are concerned with the whole range of differentiations found in our schools and their classes. Differentiation is used here in its literal sense – a noun from the verb 'to differentiate', meaning 'to constitute a difference; render unlike; recognize differences between; distinguish, discriminate' and even 'develop characteristic differences'. Note that these dictionary definitions clearly suggest an *active* process. In our present context the word refers to a whole range of factors – the separation and segregation of children into different schools, within schools into different classes and ability groupings, the categorization of children in the same class into separate groups and, at the micro level, verbal and non-verbal differentiation by teachers in their interaction with individual pupils. Before looking at these processes in detail, we return to the question discussed in 4.2, namely the extent to which educational practices and processes are unique and based on pedagogical principles as opposed to being more directly related to practices and processes in society at large.

There is considerable agreement among macro/structuralist sociologists, whether of the consensus or conflict perspective, about the intimate relationship between education and society, and its direction (see 4.5iii, 8, 9.1). Hence Durkheim is quoted here as illustration of, rather than justification for, the arguments put forward. He wrote, 'Education is only the image of and reflection of society. It imitates and reproduces the latter in abbreviated form, it does not create it' (1952). Hence knowledge of the features of the societal/cultural context of schools is essential to an understanding of school-based phenomena. A further assumption made here is that weight must be given to both '*Manifest functions* . . . those objective consequences contributing to the adjustment or adaptation of the system which are intended and recognized by participants in the system' and '*Latent functions* . . . those which are neither intended nor recognized' (Merton 1957). So, for example, it is necessary to view ability grouping not only in terms of its basic rationale – that it produces groups of pupils with reasonably similar ability, which make viable groups for teaching – but also in terms of its more hidden (unfortunate?) outcomes – it leads to social as well as ability segregation, forms the basis for friendship grouping, and children appear to live up, or down, to the labels they are given (see 6.4).

Differentiation and segregation are, of course, characteristics of society at large. Few would refuse to accept that there are differences in the general population in terms of wealth, power and prestige or, to use a simpler term, social class. A whole welter of data on social class (based on occupation) shows that differences exist between classes in income, employment, health, housing, family structure, child rearing, education, politics, religion, leisure and opinion (for a review, see Reid 1981). Moreover, classes tend to be segregated in terms of where they live and where they work, and display differences in attitudes, beliefs and behaviour. The residential segregation is pretty obvious in any journey across one of our cities. It can be argued that this form of segregation works towards the perpetuation or maintenance of differences and inequalities. Thus poor people's actual knowledge of the wealthy's homes, way of life, schools, local services, and so on, let alone the unequal distribution of society's resources used to maintain them, remains relatively limited, certainly at the experiential level. The converse is also true, the wealthy having only a sketchy idea of life in the slum areas of our cities. Other forms of social stratification (see 7) – sex, ethnic group and age – operate in similar fashion.

As in society so in education, the segregation of children into schools hides from pupils, parents and even teachers any real knowledge of the differences between types of school. LEA school pupils have hazy and often inaccurate knowledge of the facilities in other schools, particularly independent ones; while the converse is also true. Differences which exist within and between LEAs (see

7.10b) and within particular categories of school are thus hidden. In further and higher education there are clear distinctions of provision, facilities and expenditure between universities, polytechnics, colleges of higher education, technical and further education colleges, together with differences within types. Scholastic or academic and social class differences often come together. The social class composition of types of school and educational institution varies very considerably (6.3, 6.4 and 7.2). In general terms, the higher the status of the institution the higher the proportion of middle-class pupils or students. In the same way forms of in-school segregation, like ability grouping, often hide the unequal distribution of staff, facilities, curriculum and expenditure from pupil and parent eyes, especially because of the relationship between social class and school class or position in it. In general terms, the working classes are over-represented among those deemed to be less successful in school (see below and 7.2), while their parents are less knowledgeable about schooling (3.4). Once ability groupings have been made, their subsequent performance can be used to justify them, and even where such grouping does not exist formally similar processes can take place (see 6.4).

A further functional aspect of differentiation can be developed from the ideas of Durkheim (1956) and Hopper (1971). Durkheim argued that education had the job of fitting out children not only for society but also for that particular level of society in which they were to operate as adults – that is, their occupational role. Hopper wrote about the 'warming-up' and 'cooling-out' processes in education. Since it is neither feasible nor desirable initially to select those children who are destined for high-status jobs, schools need to 'warm up' and keep warm the aspirations and endeavour of all children; but education has also to 'cool out' unrealistic aspirations. Presumably the latter process partly accounts for the fact that very few overweight, myopic, low-achieving school children aspire to be airline pilots! The two processes are 'designed' to produce in children aspirations that are realistic in terms of their own ability and of the ability/willingness of society to provide such occupational roles for them.

These processes are not, of course, precise, as the over-production of schoolteachers in the 1970s and school-leaver/graduate unemployment in the 1980s witnessed. Ability grouping typically affords the most able the highest status: if you like a feeling of superiority, the 'comfort' of groups below them. Generally this status in school is a reflection of the status of their family origin in society at large, and is even more likely to reflect the status of the occupational life to which they will progress after leaving school. The experiences of the lower streams are similar but reversed. The suggestion is, then, simply that the divisions between schools, and within them, reinforce and indeed increase initial differences between children (6.4b). Collins (1971) suggests that such processes produce two groups: the carriers of élite knowledge – the minority who are successful in education; and those who have a respect for, or acceptance of, the first group – the majority who are not successful in education. Schools can then be seen to pave the way for, and legitimize, the long-term separation and differential reward system operating in society at large (see 8.2). In their structural arrangements, schools fulfil Durkheim's (1956) claim that 'Education is, then, only the means by which society prepares, within the children, the essential conditions of its very existence' – which is almost identical to the views of Marxist commentators (9.1).

A further insight can be gained from Durkheim's lectures to student teachers. Here he drew an analogy between education and hypnotism, arguing that if the teacher could hypnotize pupils into a state of blank consciousness and exceptional passivity then pupils would have maximal receptivity for assimilating the teacher's ideas. However, Durkheim saw that this ideal condition (from the teacher's point of view!) was never wholly achievable and therefore that the teacher must always play a dominant role: 'one can say that education must be essentially a matter of authority' (1956). The centre of a teacher's power would seem to be the ability to differentiate between pupils in terms of interaction, the marking of written work, and so on, and their part in differentiation within the school – helping to determine pupils' futures, which class they will be in, whether they sit examinations, etc. Forms of differentiation also reflect the relationship between passivity and educability, or ease of teaching.

A large number of participant studies of secondary schools have shown that as one moves up the ability range the pupils become more in accord with the values and interests of teachers, the school and education (Hargreaves 1967, King 1969, Lacey 1970, Ball 1981). Those towards the bottom, lacking passivity, are often contained rather than taught and in general are avoided by experienced teachers. The school system treats them as relatively unimportant and keeps them in ineffective situations where they won't disturb the status quo or the real purposes of the school. In many ways, it can be suggested, schools exploit them as society will when they enter the adult world. They are the ones who run messages and help the caretaker; their treatment and lack of status is a direct and anticipatory socialization for life after school. 'Just as the priest is the interpreter of his god, the teacher is the interpreter of the great moral (social) ideas of his time and of his country' (Durkheim 1956). One basic means by which this is achieved is the separation and segregation of children within and between schools, thus avoiding the problems caused by 'warming up' or 'cooling out' the wrong individuals or groups of children; or teaching inappropriate parts of the curriculum, values and interests to those who are destined never to need them.

The argument so far – that differentiation in education reflects and is related to differentiation in the social structure of society – can be tested by reviewing the controversy around three possible educational innovations: (1) the abolition of independent schools; (2) the introduction of real and full comprehensive schools; (3) the introduction of mixed ability teaching. Whatever educational principles are involved in these controversies, they are not the main feature of the arguments of lay or professional supporters and opposers. The debates are all centred round social as opposed to educational principles and concerns. This is not particularly surprising, since these innovations are no mere tinkering around with the educational system but are challenges to the social fabric of society. The net result of such changes would be to cause groups who have beliefs in their justified or desirable separation to mix. At one level, this would be seen to cause clashes of values, beliefs and behaviour; a common assumption is that human beings gravitate towards the worst. More important, however, such changes would greatly increase competition and hence the possibility of social and occupational mobility. For example, the 'public' school-pupils' monopoly of élite jobs (see 6.3) might be broken or affected. Probably a larger proportion of the children of those parents comfortably established at the top end of the social structure would find themselves faced with a decline in status. Nor would it be one-sided, since the increased potential for upward mobility might well be resented by those who have been successfully socialized to accept and value their place in the social order (see, for example, Jackson and Marsden 1962/1966 and Willis 1977).

These arguments bring into focus the question of the relationship between education and society. What is suggested here is more than the common assumption that they are related (which nearly all sociology of education texts point out). Here they are seen as the products of each other, with the implication that the stronger (society) will believe that the weaker (education) should not be allowed autonomy in any more than an apparent sense because of the seriousness of the issues involved. In other words, education is far too serious a matter to be left either to educationists or to teachers. Under the guise of such ideologies as academic freedom and the power and authority of headteachers lies a very real force of social control. This has been well illustrated at two London schools – Risinghill in the mid 1960s (Berg 1968) and William Tyndale in the 1970s (Dale 1981) – and, at the time of writing, Ray Honeyford at Drummond Street school in Bradford. The relatively small part played by schoolteachers in educational policy-making at government, LEA and even school level is further evidence.

A number of objections can be made about the picture presented so far. In particular it can be argued that it is far too comprehensive and generalized. Pupils succeed and fail in school and afterwards both because of, and in spite of, the educational system and its relationship with the social structure. Many teachers fail, through enlightenment or inability, to process their charges adequately in the manner outlined. These limitations can be accepted, particularly since they do not refute the argument. It is the subtlety of social institutions that makes them effective. The blatant and absolute use of power always runs the danger of evoking powerful reactions. In the present case, as in many others, exceptions to rules are commonly used to justify whole systems. Implicit in this thinking is the justified assumption that all human institutions are imperfect, and that if individual cases of justice can be demonstrated, any underlying fundamental injustice fades into unimportance. If our educational system allows John or Joan Bull, who come from disadvantaged home and school, to be successful, then if Joe or Jill Soap are not successful it is obvious that the fault lies with them and not the system. Clearly, while this line of thinking is common, it is faulty. It is at this stage that quantitive analysis becomes vital. We need to know not so much of the Bulls and Soaps but of their relative proportions in the population at large. Alongside this we need to know similar factors about the other groups, composed of Jeremy and Samantha Bypass-Symthes and their ilk, who also inhabit our society. This has been, and should remain, a major role for macro-sociology, and some of its evidence is presented below (7.1 to 7.5).

Our discussion here has concentrated on a single form of social differentiation, that of social class and education. While this is the best rehearsed form it is important to realize that other forms – sex and ethnic group – are also vitally involved in educational differentiation (see 7.3 and 7.4). Broadly speaking, sex differentiation in social life generally, and in education specifically, can be seen in terms of the assumed primary adult roles the sexes are expected to occupy – wives and mothers on the one hand and breadwinners on the other. Most commentators point out that the social role differences of the sexes are established very early in the family, and that schooling, along with other social processes, reinforces them (see Sharpe 1976). Likewise, school plays a part in the achievement differences between ethnic groups. 'Just as the educational system has in a sense failed to meet the needs of the child from a working-class background, so now, to an even greater extent, it is failing to meet the needs of the child from a different cultural background, and this is demonstrated by differences in mean levels of attainment.' (Little 1975).

These concerns are more fully developed in 7. Here the major emphasis of the argument has simply been that social differentiations in society are of importance in educational situations. And, indeed, that the educational system cannot be fully understood without such an appreciation, since explanations along pedagogic lines, or in individual terms, are unsatisfactory. Having suggested a causal direction – from society to education – we now turn to the major forms of differentiation in schooling before continuing a discussion of their implications (6.6).

## 6.2 Schools

The existence of different types of schools and educational institutions in a society implies that groups of children will be segregated from others and receive different education. Traditionally, this segregation has been uncontroversial in respect of those with special educational needs – ESN, mentally handicapped, blind, deaf and so on. The Warnock Report (*Special Educational Needs* 1978) and the Education Act of 1981 severely challenged this view and aimed to integrate many children with special needs into ordinary schools – an objective currently pursued. For a sociological treatment of special education see Tomlinson (1982). In respect of the general population, segregation by school is particularly controversial when viewed within a cultural value set that emphasizes equality or equality of opportunity, and within a society in which education is directly related to occupation, life chance and lifestyle opportunities (see 7 and 8). In Britain the segregation of groups of children into separate types of school has to be viewed in a historical context. Prior to the nineteenth century, education was really only for the rich, who had tutors, and a very few others who attended charity schools. The development through voluntary educational institutions, mainly provided by the churches, to compulsory education for all (Forster Act 1870), has been marked by segregation and differentiation. A number of criteria have been used for differentiation.

*Religion.* Interestingly enough, it was only in 1871 that religious considerations were abolished for entry to Oxford and Cambridge universities; before that, atheists, Jews, nonconformists and Roman

Catholics could be denied such education on the grounds of their inability or unwillingness to swear to the 39 Articles of the Church of England. The majority of the early nineteenth-century Sunday schools and church day schools, the only education available for most, made denominational subscription a factor. Denominational schools and colleges exist today. In 1983 over a million (22 per cent) of maintained primary school pupils in the UK attended voluntary schools (almost two-thirds of which were Church of England and one-third Roman Catholic). Almost 14 per cent (634,000) of secondary school pupils attended voluntary schools (about half Roman Catholic and a quarter Church of England) (*Social Trends 15*). Such schools remain then a significant part of the educational system, especially in Northern Ireland, although their distinctiveness from LEA-maintained schools varies considerably. Many independent schools are similarly Church-founded and run. In the late 1970s/early 1980s eleven independent Muslim schools were founded, together catering for about a thousand pupils (*Social Trends 15*). The churches' traditional major contribution to higher education has been in teacher education colleges, which are now diversified into institutions of higher education.

*Sex*. Originally real education was for males only. Vestiges of this still exist, notably in curriculum differences between the sexes and lower female entry into degree courses (see 4.5, 7.3, 8.2a). Single sex schools, once the norm, have become quite rare except in the independent sector, where the most prestigious are boys' schools – though these mostly now have nominal numbers of girls, usually in the sixth form. Sex as a criterion of segregation by school has become very much less important.

*Age*. Early schools catered for all ages and often taught them in classes of mixed age. Age segregation became much more prevalent with the development of larger schools, the identification of infant, primary, secondary and tertiary stages of education, and the institution of streaming (see 6.4). There was a minor counter-trend in infants' schools, some of which introduced vertical-age or family-grouping teaching units. This form of organization, criticized by

HMI, increased with the decline in pupil numbers in first schools (Barker Lunn 1982).

*Ability.* Early schools generally taught children of all abilities, as do first, primary and most middle schools. The establishment of secondary schools, particularly the tripartite system which followed the 1944 Education Act (see below) segregated pupils of different ability into particular types of school. The introduction of comprehensive schooling has in many areas removed segregation by ability between LEA schools.

*Social class and/or wealth.* This has remained a constant and central factor, and is our main concern.

The 1870 Education Act created two types of education – elementary for working-class and secondary for middle-class children (Silver 1973). The former provided suitable education for the manual worker and the latter education for non-manual occupations and for entry into higher and further education. A major factor here was the way powerful sectors of society used schools to maintain or enhance the status and prospects of their children. Thus alongside the elementary and secondary schools were the 'public' schools, so called because most were originally charity schools for the poor – as were many of the older grammar schools. These were suitably revamped by the emerging upper middle class of the Industrial Revolution for their children. Such schools became increasingly exclusive by charging fees, becoming boarding establishments, teaching idiosyncratic curricula like the classics, and establishing special relationships with universities, the civil service, church and commerce (see Table 6.1). They remain an important and divisive element in education today.

   The most significant historical change came with the 1944 Education Act, which abolished fees for secondary schooling. This was seen as removing the last economic barrier to schooling and making a significant contribution to equality of opportunity for all, regardless of class or wealth. The Act had as its aim the provision of education for each child according to its age, aptitude and ability.

Efforts were directed mainly towards the secondary-school stage, establishing the tripartite system – grammar schools for the academically able, technical schools for those who, while not particularly able, could be taught a trade or skill, and secondary modern schools for those who were not examinable. The Act did little about 'public' and independent schools, which remained outside the LEA system. Since there were few technical schools the system is best viewed as bipartite – grammar and secondary modern. Government research in the late 1950s revealed that the social-class composition of the types of school were quite different (*15–18* 1960). While 71 per cent of the male children of professional workers went to selective (49 per cent) or independent schools (22 per cent), only 18 per cent of semiskilled and 12 per cent of unskilled workers' male children attended selective and none independent schools. There had been little change. In much the same way as the system that it had replaced, the new one, with minor regional variations, functioned so that grammar and independent schools catered for the middle and secondary modern schools for the working class.

While there were earlier examples, it was really in the 1960s that the first unsystematic local moves were made to introduce comprehensive secondary schooling – simply a school for all children. Many supporters saw this as a major step towards a less socially divisive and more equal system. By the early 1980s comprehensivization was still incomplete. In Scotland and Wales in 1982/3 the percentage of pupils in maintained secondary schools which were comprehensive was 97, in England 84 and in Northern Ireland nil (*Education Statistics for the United Kingdom 1984*). There was also pronounced LEA variation in both the extent and type of comprehensive schooling. Some LEAs have only comprehensive schools, for example Leeds, Waltham Forest (London), Sunderland and Suffolk; in others only a small percentages of children attend such schools: in Buckingham 25, in Kingston-upon-Thames 8 and in Trafford 8 (Hansard 1984). In the latter case, for instance, the age range was catered for by 16 varieties of schooling not counting sixth-form/tertiary colleges (*Comprehensive Education* 1977) making it a nonsense to talk of *a* system of secondary schooling. In some areas, because of residential segregation or the development of community schools (drawing all the children from the immediate area around a school), the social-class segregation in schools may be even starker than before. The coexistence of grammar and independent schools means that the middle-classes and some children of ability may be 'creamed off' the comprehensives. The introduction in the early 1980s of the government's assisted places scheme, providing taxpayers' money for independent school fees has probably increased this. Nationally, the impression gained is that these changes result in more middle-class children attending 'non-selective' schools – from about a quarter in the mid 1950s to more than half in the mid and late 1970s. This was largely due to comprehensivization, although of course it did not necessarily entail any greater mixing of the social classes within particular schools. The remaining grammar schools stayed basically middle-class and the secondary moderns working-class. Comprehensive schools were attended by similar proportions of every class but class 1, of whom 30 per cent attended independent rather than LEA schools (*General Household Survey* 1972, 1976 and 1978).

## 6.3 Divisive schooling

Whether intentional or not, the effect of our present like our past educational system is to keep apart children from different sections of the social structure and to treat them to educational fare of differing types. This is most potently illustrated by independent, fee-paying schools, which include the so-called 'public' schools. The term independent refers to independence from the LEA system and not, as many suppose, to financial independence. While parents pay fees, it has been estimated that various forms of state subsidy for such schools in 1979 amounted to between £350 and £500 millions – comparable to the sums received by either British Leyland or British Steel (Rogers 1980). And this was prior to the Conservative Government's introduction of the assisted places scheme.

143

## The Sociology of School and Education

In the UK in 1983 some 5.9 per cent of children of all ages attended independent schools – in Northern Ireland the percentage was more than double, while in Scotland it was much lower than the national figure. Just over one per cent more male than female children attended them (7.6 compared with 6.4) (*Education Statistics for the UK 1984*). We shall concentrate on independent secondary schools, attended by 8.5 per cent of UK secondary pupils in 1983 (*Social Trends 15*). These are clearly middle-class institutions; while 30 per cent of children from social class 1 attended them only one per cent from classes 4, 5 and 6 did so (see 10.2, *General Household Survey 1976*, 1978). Most research has been on 'public' schools, defined by the Public Schools Commission (1968) as those independent schools in membership of HMC, GBA and GBSA. While difficult to define or characterize accurately, they are the longer-established, most prestigious independent schools and are mainly boys' and boarding schools. In 1984 4.4 per cent of males aged 14 attended HMC schools compared with only 0.5 per cent of females (based on information supplied by ISIS). Hence such schools are almost exclusively male and middle-class; the PSC reported that only one per cent of pupils were from the working classes while 85 per cent were from classes I and II, which comprised but 18 per cent of the male population at the time. It would be difficult then to disagree with the Commission's finding that 'public' schools are 'socially divisive', in that they recruit and segregate a very particular group of children from the majority. Similarly, Halsey, Heath et al (1980) conclude from their survey of male education, 'the private schools represent a bastion of class privilege compared with the relatively egalitarian state sector'. The significance of 'public' schools lies not only with their almost exclusively middle-class intakes but also with the destinations of their output. Public school products are remarkably successful in securing élite jobs in our society. This is clearly demonstrated in Table 6.1. When looking at the proportion of public school-educated holders of these positions, it should be remembered that only 2.5 per cent of the school population aged 14 were so educated. Of particular note is the very high proportion of MPs who have served the DES whose own education was at HMC school.

## Table 6.1

Percentage* of public school** and Oxbridge educated holders of
various élite positions in Britain in the 1980s.†

|  | Public School | Oxbridge |
|---|---|---|
| **The establishment** | | |
| Civil service (under-secretary and above) | 50 | 61 |
| High court and appeal judges | 83 | 83 |
| Law lords | 89 | 89 |
| C. of E. bishops | 59 | 71 |
| Ambassadors | 69 | 82 |
| | | |
| **Commerce and industry** | | |
| Directors of major life insurance companies | 92 | 50 |
| Directors of clearing banks | 70 | 47 |
| Chairmen of clearing banks | 83 | 67 |
| Directors of Bank of England | 78 | 89 |
| Chairmen of merchant banks | 88 | 59 |
| Directors of 40 major industrial firms | 66 | 40 |
| | | |
| **Politics** | | |
| Conservative MPs | 70 | 48 |
| Labour MPs | 14 | 15 |
| Alliance MPs | 52 | 30 |
| Parliamentarians serving DES 1964–84†† | | |
| Conservative | 79 | 63 |
| Labour | 31 | 34 |

* Rounded, of total of group whose education was known.
** In membership of HMC, GBA and GBSA, generally excluding other independents.
† Dates: for establishment 1984; for commerce 1981, for industry 1971; for politics 1983.
†† In addition a further 3% Labour and 4% Conservative attended other independent schools.

Compiled and devised from, *Who's Who* (1984), *Whitaker's Almanac* (1984), Sampson (1982),
Whitely (1973), Butler and Kavanagh (1984), *The Times House of Commons* (1964–84).

The table also indicates the strong relationship between
attendance at Oxford and Cambridge universities and élite positions
in our society, and suggests a powerful relationship between
attendance of independent school *and* Oxbridge. This is spelt out in
Table 6.2, which shows that the independent school minority constitutes over half of those admitted to Oxbridge.

Given that there is a relationship between parental class and
children's educational achievement (see 7.2), the question arises as
to whether independent schools provide a superior and advan-

**Table 6.2**

Percentage* of 14- and 17-year-olds and university entrants educated at LEA, independent and HMC schools, UK 1983.

|  | LEA schools | Independent schools** | HMC schools |
|---|---|---|---|
| 14-year-olds | 93 | 7 | 2.5 |
| 17-year-olds | 82 | 18 | 9.5 |
| University entrants | 75 | 25 | na |
| Oxbridge entrants† | 48 | 52 | na |

* Percentages other than HMC are rounded.
** Includes HMC schools.
† LEA figure includes FE, Oxbridge figures are 1984/5.

(Devised from Table 12, *Education Statistics for the United Kingdom 1984* (1985), Table G9, *UCCA* (1984), information provided by ISIS, *Cambridge University Reporter* (1985) and *Oxford University Gazette* (1984))

tageous education or merely reinforce the educational and social advantages of middle-class children. Would these children be equally successful in ordinary schools? Like many other education questions there are no simple answers. The educational achievements of independent school leavers are clearly superior to those of LEA schools. In 1982/3, 75 per cent of independent compared with 23 per cent of LEA school leavers gained five or more O level GCEs, and the respective percentages for one or more A levels were 63 and 14 (*Hansard* 1985a). Independent school pupils are much more likely to enter sixth forms – as can be seen in Table 6.2 – and to enter university or undertake degree courses as shown in Table 6.3. At the other extreme, earlier studies (Masters and Hockey 1963 and Kalton 1966) showed that of public school pupils known to have failed the 11+ selection examination (though we don't know how badly), 70 per cent went on to pass four or more O level GCEs. Such higher educational achievements in these schools may, of course, merely reflect their social-class composition. The only really pertinent study is that of Douglas, et al (1968) who matched boys in their survey on social class and compared the achievement of those at public and LEA grammar schools. Grammar out-performed public schoolboys at 16+ examinations, 66 compared to 55 per cent gaining at least four passes including three from English, maths, science, and a foreign language. The study also revealed that girls in independent schools were considerably less successful and left school earlier than those at LEA grammar schools. Despite their over-representation at Oxford and Cambridge, public school-educated males have been shown to be less likely than LEA grammar school products to gain 'good' honours Oxbridge degrees (Glennerster and Pryke 1973), while maintained school male undergraduates gained a higher percentage of Firsts at Tripos examinations in 1984 than did those from independent schools (*Cambridge University Reporter* 1984). While limited in scope, such findings suggest there is no clear-cut evidence for an overall educational superiority of public and, probably, independent schools – which vary greatly. Given the very real differences between, and within, the types of school and their catchment areas, much fuller and deeper research would be needed to prove the case.

### Table 6.3

Percentage* of 18+ year-old school leavers from maintained and independent schools entering university and degree courses,** England 1983/4.

|  | University | Degree course |
|---|---|---|
| Maintained school leavers | 23 | 35 |
| Male | 26 | 38 |
| Female | 20 | 32 |
| Independent school leavers† | 44 | 54 |
| Male | 49 | 58 |
| Female | 38 | 49 |

* Percentages are rounded.
** At university/polytechnic/other institutions (including teacher education).
† Who were 18% of all leavers of this age, 21% of male and 15% of female leavers.

(Devised from Table C2, *Statistics of School Leavers, England 1984* (1985) )

Much the same conclusions can be drawn from the educational provisions of public schools. At the time of the PSC, the proportion of staff in such schools who had degrees, whose degrees were of first class honours standard and had been obtained at Oxford and Cambridge, was higher than in LEA schools. It would be more than a bold claim to suggest that the teaching they gave was superior, especially since a lower proportion had undertaken teacher education courses. There were more teachers to pupils in public schools: the ratio in 1967 was 1:12 compared with 1:23 in LEA schools, although the grammar school ratio was 1:17. In 1982/3 UK independent schools had a teacher/pupil ratio of 1:13, maintained secondary schools 1:16 and maintained primary schools 1:22 (*Education Statistics for the UK 1984*). Given the extra duties and proportionately larger sixth forms in public schools, the difference is perhaps not large. Teaching groups do appear to be smaller in independent schools, and typically the length of the supervised day and week are much longer. Overall, the facilities of such schools, other than libraries and playing fields, have not been shown to be consistently superior to those of other schools.

It is in those aspects of education which most defy measurement that the advantages of independent schools can be seen to lie. First, and in contrast to other schools, they have considerable control over pupil entry, recruiting pupils whose parents have a firm commitment to this particular type of education and over half of whom were themselves so educated. We can suspect, then, that the congruence between home and school is quite direct and shows much less variation than is the case with other schools, as indicated by the parents' willingness to support the schools financially – in addition to paying fees – and the higher rate of entry into the sixth form and higher education. Maybe Burt (1961) correctly summed it up when he wrote, 'Professional parents want the training in character, manners, speech and social ideals which, with few exceptions, only the better type of public schools at present seems able to impart.' The PSC was almost sceptical (perhaps because of its evidence) when it reported, 'Public schools claim to provide a better education whether it is on better facilities, better teachers or the advantages of boarding. Parents presumably accept this and anecdotal evidence to the Commission suggests that employers do (e.g., public school boys have more self-assurance).' Here, once again, is a clear message that education is vitally important in the social sense; it is the confirmation of a status culture, the legitimization of privilege (see 8.5b). It is probable that embarrassment over these associations with background, exclusiveness and privilege was behind the decision of the HMC in 1985 to drop the term 'public', and to adopt 'independent', for their schools. Overall, the general public has been shown to approve of public schools (55 per cent) – although support was much more pronounced in the middle than in the working classes – and only about a quarter of those surveyed thought they should be abolished (Gallup Polls 1973). Interestingly enough, however, a bare majority of parents interviewed thought fee-paying schools provided better education than maintained ones and less than half would send their children to them if they could afford to do so (NOP 1980).

It is, of course, the boarding element of public and some independent schools which is their most distinctive feature. This together with the home backgrounds of the pupils and control over entry are probably the key to the schools' success in socializing a recognizable standard product with a real market value. Attempts have been made, via Goffman's (1962) concept of 'total institutions', to liken the processes in such schools to those in prisons and mental hospitals. Pupils are similarly supervised for twenty-four hours a day, learn respect for their superiors (masters and prefects), allegiance to the rules of the organization over their personal desires, and loyalty to their peers and the ideals of the institution which mirror those of their parents and the status group to which they belong. The continuous and protracted experience of a school run by teachers for parents, both of whom share the same values, and supported by the informal culture of the pupils (see 4.7), is in some contrast to the regime of most LEA schools. Quite apart from the existence of any 'old school tie' type of recruitment into the élite jobs by well-placed 'old boys', the social rather than necessarily the educational advantages of an independent-school education are most likely to appeal to some parents and employers (see 8.5) and be relatively unavailable in LEA schools.

While public and independent schools are the most blatant examples of differentiation and segregation in education by school, numerous other examples exist. Some of these can be seen as chance happenings and others as partly or wholly contrived. As pointed out in 7.10b, there appears to be a relationship between the socio-economic-cum-geographical situation of a child and the schooling it receives. Within this overall relationship there are, of course, further variations. Schools are not good, bad or indifferent *only* because of the age and extent of their buildings and facilities, their situation, the children they contain and their ability to attract able staff and keep them (see 4.9). However, a general association may be observed in that the older, poorer schools, with staff recruitment and turnover problems (at least until the over-production of teachers) and with low academic achievement of pupils are to be found in inner-city areas serving predominantly working-class clientèles.

While it is possible to argue that the effects of separate and different education of children from differing social-class backgrounds is functional – it is part of the process of the reproduction of the existing social structure and order – it can also be seen as undesirable. Such separation can be viewed as contributing, for example, to industrial and political problems in that those in control of resources and those who work, or provide resources have little understanding of each other as they experienced quite separate schooling and education. There have also been more immediate concerns; for example, that the continued separation of the social classes in education produced continual inequality in educational provision and also that the absence of middle-class and able children adversely affected the achievements of other children and the ability of schools to realize the untapped talent which was assumed to exist. Although the most common belief about the move towards comprehensive secondary education is that it was to end the selective examination at 11+, the authors of the scheme were also interested in ending social separation and segregation. 'It is the government's declared objective to end selection at eleven-plus and to eliminate separatism in secondary education' (*Organisation of Secondary Education* 1965). Marsden (1971) declared that, in the same year, Labour Party policy presented comprehensive reorganization as a response to 'overwhelming technological and popular demands' together with 'research evidence of waste and social divisiveness in the bipartite system', and the Public Schools

Commission was set up to advise on the best way of integrating public schools with the state system of education. No real moves followed, though the semi-independent status of direct grant schools was abolished in 1977, whereupon all those other than the Roman Catholic ones went fully independent. Such considerations and the reality of the mid 1980s clearly underline the arguments presented in 6.1. With regard to public schools they suggest the obvious political power of those involved in maintaining them intact. The independent sector not only survives but is growing in terms of the proportion of children it caters for. Alternatively, they point to the political naivety, lack of power or even insincerity on the part of the politicians and others who framed the policies of change; or again, some compromise or negotiation between conflicting views.

With regard to comprehensive schools the situation is far more complicated. The variation in their implementation is vast. While definitions of what constitutes a comprehensive school vary similarly, it is true that its pure form – a school for all – has only exceptionally been achieved. The salient questions here are: is a school comprehensive when it is single sex? – when it is denominational? – when it is in competition with independent/public/grammar schools? – when it caters only for children up to the legal minimum school-leaving age? – when its catchment area provides an intake limited in respect to social class or ethnic group? – when it operates ability grouping or segregates pupils, in much the same fashion as under the bipartite system? At this point it becomes necessary to consider what could be done to end social segregation and differentiation in schooling. Logically it would call for a single system of schools, the intake to which would reflect in the correct proportions the social composition of the surrounding area according to the criteria of ability, social class, ethnic and religious background and sex. However, a city school could recruit *all* the children in the area surrounding it and yet not be representative of the social structure of the city as a whole, the region or society. Given the extent of residential segregation in the UK, some social segregation through schooling may be inevitable, but with little effort and planning it could be markedly less than at present. More important, the implications and results of it are far from inevitable. Schools in poor areas do not have to be poor schools; the gap between best and worst does not have to be so great. To be otherwise, though, would require planning and expenditure on a scale hitherto not yet undertaken, involving positive discrimination for some areas or parts of the social structure and possibly the establishment of national standards and policy.

Having looked at some of the factors contributing to differentiation in education by schools and its implications, we turn now to consider differentiation within schools.

## 6.4 Ability grouping

As we have seen (3.4), an obvious and major function of schools is the differentiation of pupils by ability. Together with age, ability is a fundamental aspect of the organization of schools, hence ability grouping in a variety of forms has been and is characteristic of British schooling. Definitions of these major forms are as follows:

*Streaming*. The placing of children of the same age into different classes on the basis of ability, normally involving one or more of the following: performance on a school-based attainment test; performance on an external intelligence and/or attainment test; teacher's personal and/or professional assessment; the child's age.

MIXED ABILITY. This takes two forms

 *indirect or random*; the placing of children into classes, say, by name, alphabetically; and
*direct*: the forming of *parallel groups* by first ascertaining the ability/attainment of the age group and then ensuring that each class has representative numbers across the range.

*Banding*. Some large schools, mainly secondary, do not stream but divide pupils into, say three, ability groups – above average, average and below average. This can result in a number of classes composed of pupils from each band (a loose form of streaming) or can be the basis for direct mixed ability grouping (each class containing the three bands).

*Covert streaming*. The allocation of children in an overtly non-streamed class to relatively closed groups.

*Setting*. The allocation of children to classes for particular subjects on the basis of their ability in that subject. Although this system is more likely to occur in a non-streamed school, it can operate to an extent in a streamed one.

*Grading*. The allocation to a class according to children's attainment and progress, and not to their age or measured ability. It is widely used in American and Soviet schools but not in British ones.

These definitions are not to suggest that pure forms of ability grouping commonly characterize our schools. As we shall see, combinations and variations are possible and frequent, and there is considerable variation with age of pupil, and type and size of school.

Since streaming was until recently the major form of ability grouping in British schools and remains an important form, with aspects of it (banding and covert streaming) forming part of current practice, it is the best researched and the most suitable basis for our consideration. The rationale of streaming is firmly set in the psychological tradition of education, with its belief that a child's ability is measurable and remains fairly constant over time. The origins of streaming, as we know it, can be traced to the evidence that Burt gave to the Consultative Committee on the Primary School (Hadow) in 1931: 'By the age of ten, the children of a single age group must be spread over at least three different standards. And by the age of twelve . . . children need to be grouped . . . not merely in separate classes . . . but in separate types of schools'. The British use of streaming is unique, particularly with regard to its extent – it is illegal in Norway, was abolished in the Soviet Union (1963) and is not used in the United States or France (Jackson 1964).

Streaming rests on two simple beliefs: that since children vary in their ability (however defined) they learn best in classes of children with similar ability, and such classes are more easily, or better, taught. In contrast, mixed ability classes are believed by some to hamper the learning of the least and most able and make teaching more difficult. It is important to appreciate that these views, expressed by large majorities of teachers in studies by Daniels (1961) and Jackson (1964) and a good proportion of those in Barker Lunn (1970), have to be seen in context. Streaming had been a characteristic of primary-school organization since the 1930s, and most of the teachers were the products of such schools, and had trained and worked in them. We might expect people so involved in an organization to have some acceptance of it, but the situation has been and is dynamic. Nearly all primary schools with more than one class per year were streamed in the 1960s (Jackson 1964), but during the 1970s surveys showed that the majority had adopted mixed ability (Bealing 1972, *Primary Education in England* 1978). More recently, Barker Lunn (1982) found two-thirds with mixed ability, and a quarter assigning pupils to classes according to some assessment of ability or attainment. The situation, however, was complex: some setting featured in a third of large schools, almost all of which had remedial groups, while a third of all schools had enrichment groups for the most able – resulting in streaming for some part of the curriculum. A substantial minority of schools had shifted away from full mixed ability classes to what might be seen as part- streaming – the result, Barker Lunn suggests, of concerns about primary schooling raised by the Great Debate of the mid 1970s and the HMI. Secondary schools have sustained streaming to a greater extent. Tibbenham et al (1978) report that of NCDS children aged 12–13 attending comprehensive schools, 44 per cent were streamed, 41 per cent were setted and 16 per cent were mixed ability. Interestingly enough, while almost half the Scots pupils were in mixed ability classes, elsewhere in Britain the percentage was less than 10. In many secondary schools, option 'choice' two years before 16+ examinations effectively streams or bands pupils according to type, subject and number of examinations. In contrast, small schools, with no more than a single class for each year group, will by definition have mixed ability classes.

Such views are limited to the way in which classes are constituted and reveal nothing of how they are taught; mixed ability classes do not ensure mixed ability teaching/learning. Indeed, these activities may well be organized round ability groupings within the classroom, and these can also feature in streamed or banded classes (see 6.4b).

## 6.4a THE COMPOSITION OF ABILITY GROUPS

Given their rationale, we would expect these to be differentiated in terms of ability. With regard to streaming in primary schools, this expectation has been borne out overall. Douglas (1964), using common attainment tests (standardized so that the average score of all children was 50), showed that pupils in the upper streams of two-stream primary schools had higher scores than those in lower ones (55 marks compared with 45); there was, however, a considerable overlap between streams. Similarly Barker Lunn (1970) found that 15 per cent of the children in her sample were, according to either their English or arithmetic scores, in the wrong stream. This could mean either that the assessment of ability was not as accurate as it could or should be, or that factors other than ability were being taken into account. In the first place psychologists only claim 90 per cent accuracy for the best tests, so that even when these are used, 10 per cent of pupils may be misplaced. Further, the 'averaging out' of ability, by the use of either IQ/VRQ tests or a series of subject tests (which are averaged together) to produce a list of children in ability order, may clearly disguise or enhance some pupils' particular strengths or weaknessess. In fact, allocation to ability groups may be based on less objective measures, such as teachers' reports, which may produce greater vagaries. Second, considerable research exists to suggest that ability grouping appears to favour children with certain ascribed (as opposed to achieved) characteristics. The most famous of these is social class. Douglas found that on the basis of their performance on standardized tests, 11 per cent more middle-class children were in upper streams and 26 per cent fewer in lower streams than would be expected. He also found that children who had poor maternal care, or who came from large families, were more likely to be in lower streams. Jackson and Barker Lunn support the social class finding and further suggest that children born in the autumn are favoured. An underlying reason for this is likely to be their longer infant school careers (see also 7.6). Barker Lunn shows that girls fared better than boys: they were more often found in the upper stream and boys in the lower than would be expected. Troyna (1978) found in an ILEA comprehensive school that the proportion of West Indian pupils ranged from 14 to 78 per cent between the top and bottom streams (a tendency also illustrated in Coard, 1971). The over-representation of middle-class pupils in the upper, and working-class in the lower, ability groupings has been found in secondary modern, grammar, and comprehensive secondary schools (Hargreaves 1967, Lacey 1970, Ball 1981).

Such ascribed factors (all of them forms of social stratification, see 7.1) can, of course, be seen as related to ability. The value of much of the research reported here lies in the fact that when ability is held constant, ascribed factors still operate. To some extent ability grouping involves social as well as academic differentiation. There is, as we have seen, evidence to suggest that teachers, consciously or unconsciously, discriminate among pupils according to social criteria (see also 5.3 and 6.5a). With regard to the most obvious, neutral and educational factor – the length of infant schooling – it is surprising that many schools fail to make age allowance in grouping children by ability (Barker Lunn).

Ability grouping of pupils, then, appears endemic in schooling. While this process is clearly related to teacher type/attitude/practice, as we shall see below, there is also a real sense in which schools reflect societies and most other social groups, in that forms of stratification are almost universal, if not inevitable. Ball (1981) reports that mixed ability groupings appear to condense and reproduce the stratification of pupils previously found in banded classes and that these were essentially similar to those reported by Sharp and Green (1975) in mixed ability groups in a primary school: bright, normal, and problem.

## 6.4b THE EFFECTS OF ABILITY GROUPING

There is a good deal of evidence to show that ability grouping is a self-fulfilling prophecy – that the original decision to put children into groups is proved 'right' by their subsequent performance.

Douglas, for example, showed that children in upper streams improved their attainment test scores between the ages of eight and eleven, the less able improving most. Between the same ages the scores of children in lower streams deteriorated, those of the most able among them deteriorating the most. The net effect was that the two streams had a larger difference between them at the end than at the beginning. Marginal children in both streams had moved towards the stream's norm. An important contributory factor here is likely to be the lack of movement of children between groups. Barker Lunn pointed out that over a three-year period 75 per cent of the children who were in the wrong stream (according to their ability) remained in the wrong stream. Those who were promoted tended to make good progress while demoted children tended to get worse. Of course it is probable that other factors are at work alongside. In the last example, it could be that promoted and demoted children differed in personality and motivation as well as in ability and stream. Douglas demonstrated how social class and stream can operate together. While middle- and working-class children in upper streams both improved their scores, it was the middle-class ones who improved the most. In lower streams, middle-class children's scores improved (although not as much as in higher streams), while working-class children deteriorated.

A notable effect of ability grouping is that it helps to structure pupils' friendships and the development of informal cultures (see 4.7). These effects have been extensively explored, particularly in regard to streaming in secondary schools (Partridge 1966/8; Hargreaves 1967; Ford 1969; King 1969; Lacey 1970). All these showed that friends tended to be chosen from within the same stream, for the obvious reason that streaming results in limited interaction with pupils in other classes. The studies also revealed that as one descends streams, so commitment to school declines and distinctive 'anti-school' informal cultures become more apparent and common. Lacey (1970) points up the role of ability grouping in this, by looking at it in action. In the mixed ability first year of the grammar school he studied, all boys displayed a high commitment to the norms of the school. In the second year came streaming, the differentiation of pupils and, progressively, their polarization into pro- and anti-school subcultures. This differentiation and polarization has been recognized and illustrated in a banded comprehensive school by Ball (1981), who also observed that in mixed ability groupings the increased face-to-face interaction of social classes and differing levels of achieved ability did not increase social mixing/friendship, although it did appear to lower antagonism between differently achieving pupils. Troyna (1978) found that within-stream friendship choices were 73 per cent in the top stream and 88 per cent in the lower. He further found that black pupils in lower streams immersed themselves in racially exclusive peer groups and ethnic culture (see also Driver 1977). Black pupils in higher streams were less commited to 'in-group' culture and friendship choice. Ethnicity may then have been used as a further defence against the structural position imposed by schooling and its organization. This is similar to Willis's (1977) suggestion that 'shop-floor' culture may operate for low-achieving working-class pupils (see also 4.7).

Staff can in effect become streamed themselves, by association. In primary schools the older, more experienced teachers normally teach older children and higher streams/bands, where they exist. In secondary schools those with most experience, qualifications and the highest graded posts tend to spend more of their time teaching the most able. Young, inexperienced, low-status staff tend to be associated with the less able. While this state of affairs may be seen to reflect the salary and rewards structure of the teaching profession and, to an extent, its value system, it can be seen as influencing the effect of ability grouping. It would be a bold claim that the evidence shows that the 'best' teachers teach the 'best' children. But even if it were only partly true, it may go some way to explain the growing separation in terms of performance of different abilities through the school system. It is, then, interesting to speculate what the net effect would be if the situation were to be reversed – if the less able received the best teaching.

The effects of ability grouping on children's learning has received a good deal of attention, although research in the field has tended to be inconclusive. Studies can be quoted which support the superiority of streaming and others of non-streaming. Much of this research has shortcomings, using small samples, being limited in time, span and scope and failing to be properly comparative. The largest British study in primary schools (Barker Lunn 1970) found that comparable pupils made similar progress in streamed and non-streamed schools. Fogelman et al (1978a) found no differences in measured reading or mathematics attainment test scores between NCDS pupils at secondary schools which were streamed, setted, or mixed ability – having taken account of measured ability at entry to the school and other related background measures. However, in mixed ability schools a larger proportion of pupils with relatively low ability took public examinations than in differently organized schools (though this may merely reflect examination entry policy differences).

A particularly interesting finding of Barker Lunn was that the actual teachers involved were more important than the organizational basis of ability groups. This will, of course, not surprise readers intimately involved in schools. She identified two types of teacher, based on their attitudes and teaching methods. One type (we shall call 'streamers') believed in streaming, were less interested in the slow learner, were not permissive, had low tolerance of noise and talking, favoured physical punishment, and used traditional lessons more frequently than progressive; the other type, 'non-streamers', had opposing beliefs and practices. The sample of schools was balanced – 36 streamed/36 non-streamed – and overall two-thirds of all the teachers were found to be streamers and were only just the minority (48 per cent) even in non-streamed schools. Implicit here, and explicit in the research, is the fact that some classes in non-streamed schools are non-streamed in name only. This limits the value of comparing the progress of children by school type.

In the study no differences were found in the average academic performance of pupils of comparable ability and social class taught in streamed or non-streamed schools. Neither did teacher type seem to affect academic outcomes, though this could have been blurred by children changing from one type to another, year by year. Similarly, in more general aspects, neither school nor teacher type had any noticeable affect on children of above-average ability.

However the social, emotional and attitudinal development of average and below-average pupils was affected by both, and particularly by teacher type. Such children, taught by non-streamer teachers in non-streamed schools, had better relationships with their teachers and held higher academic self-images than other children. The poorest attitudes to school were found among children taught by streamer teachers in non-streamed schools. Pupils in non-streamed schools had better images of their class and also thought that others had a better image of it, than their counterparts in streamed schools. While in both types of school, ability and social class were factors in pupils' friendships, there were more mixed ability friendships in non-streamed schools. Below-average ability children taught by streamer teachers were more likely to be friendless and neglected by their peers (perhaps reflecting the attitudes of their teachers). In non-streamed schools a greater ability range of children participated in non-academic school activities than in streamed schools, where those of high ability tended to monopolize such pursuits. Parents, too, appeared to be affected by school organization. Streaming was interpreted as an indication of their children's future. Parental aspirations for children in non-streamed schools were less linked to the child's ability than to parental hopes.

In secondary schools the findings are more mixed. For example, Essen et al (1979) found hardly any evidence of differences in pupil self-ratings, motivation towards school, plans for the future and school behaviour at 16 for those attending schools which had streams, sets, or mixed ability classes for their 12- to 13-year-olds. However, Ball (1981) identified an 'improvement' in the social control and socialization of comprehensive school pupils in mixed ability classes in comparison with those in bands. To date, such evidence as we have suggests that formal ability grouping used in schools has little if any effect on academic achievement, but that it may affect other aspects of school life.

The organizational and educational importance of ability grouping, like other organizational aspects, is clearly mediated by the teachers who operate the system. The crucial factor here is the involvement and commitment to a particular form of ability grouping in operation. Abolishing streaming does not end selection, categorization and differential treatment of pupils of differing ability; if anything it places the teacher in a more significant role in these respects and is probably more challenging. Mixed ability teaching, as opposed to organization, calls for commitment and the use and development of different skills. Organizational change in British schools is rarely, if at all, achieved by popular acclaim. Reid (M.) et al (1981) found that in two thirds of the schools they studied, the initiative for the introduction for mixed ability grouping came in a directive fashion from the head teacher. Noting that such changes have far reaching implications for teachers' roles and methods, they argue that successful reorganization is unlikely to be effected without 'extensive consultation, discussion, persuasion and support'. In noting the absence of radical change in classroom methods following the move from banding to mixed ability, Ball (1981) argues that this 'may be linked to the lack of ideological commitment to the innovation by teachers, though organizational and social constraints, as well as the teachers' residual attitudes, play their part . . .'; which echoes Barker Lunn's comment on de-streaming in primary schools. The deployment of teachers and school resources, together with teachers' behaviour and attitudes, appear to some extent fortuitous or accidental to the ideas behind forms of ability grouping. We can reasonably conclude that teachers behave and operate in particular ways in spite of, as well as because of, the organization of schools.

We turn next to a form of differentiation which appears to be characteristic of, or lie beneath, teaching and learning whatever its context.

## 6.5 Categorization

Here we are concerned with the less formal processes involved in the differentiation of children in class and school. While these are related to the structure and organization of schools and education in society, they are also related to personal and professional aspects of teachers' role performance, and, in turn, to a fundamental fact of social life. In everyday life we all constantly categorize (label or classify) people, events and situations, which is to say we make generalizations about them from limited information. Where people are concerned, categorization involves having expectations and making predictions about their behaviour, attitudes, interests and reactions. Reflection upon our everyday life quickly brings to mind the whole concept. We would find life intolerable without categorization; each new encounter would have to be built up from scratch. Teachers are continually faced with large groups of children; the secondary school teacher may teach, say, 150 or more individuals in groups of 30 in the course of a single week. Not surprisingly, then, teachers categorize their pupils using a variety of criteria along a number of dimensions, basically related to the extent to which pupils within them allow teachers to get on with the job of teaching (see 5.3).

There are two consequences of this. First, since teachers (like us) are likely to resist having to recategorize, pupil behaviour that is contrary to prediction is likely to be accommodated as out of character (or category); for example, bad behaviour by the school captain is differently perceived and dealt with from that of the most consistent miscreant of 4G, whose good behaviour is similarly likely to be overlooked. Second, teachers directly, or indirectly, are likely to communicate their categorization to the pupil(s) involved. This, in turn, is likely to affect the pupil's own self-image and behaviour, since the balance of power in schools and classrooms creates pressures to accept teachers' definitions.

We have touched on this process in various places; in 6.4, and in 3, 4 and 5, it is suggested that formal aspects of the school, ability grouping in particular, provide a certain institutionalized categorization of pupils. Further, that in the process of educational selection, ranking and segregation are endemic and that these depend not only on academic but also on social criteria, which can rarely be separated. Here we review some of the criteria used by teachers to categorize and subsequently to differentiate their pupils.

It is possible to identify two major types of differences which form the basis of teaching categorization – group differences and individual differences (Brophy and Good 1974). In following this 'convention' it will be plain that these differences are intimately inter-related.

## 6.5a GROUP DIFFERENCES

### i *Social class*

There is ample evidence, as we have seen, that teacher categorization results in differentiation of pupils broadly along social class lines and that this takes place from the infant school onwards. This reflects King's (1978) finding that 'in terms of teacher-child relationships, models of behaviour and forms of knowledge, infant education has a closer affinity to their equivalents in the families of the middle classes than those of the working classes'. While the work of Rist (outlined at 4.2) illustrates the process, a significant and specific British study is that of Goodacre (1968), which evolved from an earlier observation (Goodacre 1967) that, while infant school teachers' estimates of children's reading ranked in order of merit – middle class, upper (skilled manual) working class and lower (semi- and unskilled manual) working class – this was not reflected in the children's performance on standardized reading comprehension tests. These tests failed to display the superiority of the middle-class, showed the upper working-class children performed better than was suggested by their teachers' evaluations, and confirmed that lower working-class children were the poorest readers. Briefly, the investigation revealed that teachers regarded pupils' home backgrounds as an important factor in learning to read and that they frequently categorized pupils as coming from 'good' or 'poor' homes. While able to give detailed and complex descriptions of these home backgrounds, it is clear that teachers had little first-hand knowledge since few had ever visited homes. Teachers gained their 'knowledge' of pupils' homes from a range of indirect clues – pupils' self-presentation, behaviour and self-reporting. Goodacre suggests that there is strong evidence that differentiation is based upon well structured stereotypes, dependent upon such clues. She writes: 'These findings suggest that teachers tend to think of the "good" home as one which facilitates their task ... teachers of young children may be equating the "good" home with middle-class values, and therefore discriminating against working-class children and their parents. . . .' Similarly, Nash (1973) reported that some teachers thought, quite wrongly, that less able and attractive children were from poor homes. It has to be appreciated that this categorization takes place at an early and crucial period in a child's education – while learning to read in infant school. Such early categorization can be seen to affect not only initial but also subsequent school experiences, through the passing on of school records, their incremental affect on pupils' progress, and the continued categorization by subsequent teachers. Social class or background categorization appears to be a very general phenomena in schools. Delamont (1976) reports that even in the fee-paying upper-middle-class girls' school she studied, the staff differentiated between pupils from intellectual homes and those from merely wealthy ones!

Teachers certainly have been shown to use direct and indirect social class references when talking about their schools, pupils and jobs (Reid 1980). Generally speaking they view education as an important aspect of social class and life, seeing the social structure in terms of a large central group (with which they identify) cut off from a 'real money and exclusive' upper group and a 'poor and uneducated' lower group. There remains, however, a good deal to discover about teachers' awareness of social class and how if affects their practice. In the same study I recount a considerable range of teacher reaction to my teaching of class – rejection, accommodation, neutrality, assimilation and conversion. In general most teachers and sociologists accept, understand and live with class (and other forms of stratification) while resisting many of its implications in their work and lives.

ii *Sex*

Given the nature of sex differences and the sex stratification of our society and its educational system (see, Reid and Wormald 1982 and 7.3), it would be surprising if teachers did not categorize on this criterion too. In 5.3 we looked at research which indicated that in general teachers appeared to have preferences, particularly in primary schools, for female rather than male pupils, and that this resulted in different evaluations and treatment of the sexes. It would appear that the explanation for this preference goes beyond teachers' sexual prejudice and lies with their reaction to differing pupil behaviour and attitudes along sex lines. An illustration of the depth of the problem is that boys gain some two thirds of teachers' attention and dominate pupils' talk in classrooms, as elsewhere (see Spender 1980). As French (1986) concludes from her observations in a variety of schools, this is not simply because they are boys and treated as such, but because their activity and behaviour demands response from teachers.

If, as seems the case, the ideal pupil role is more congruent with the female than the male role in our society (see 5.3 and 6.5c) then this would explain both teachers' general preference for female pupils and their stronger reaction against deviant ones (see Davies 1984). The apparent shift in teachers' preference towards male pupils in the later stages of secondary schooling and in higher education might then be explained in terms of changing pupil role demands and performance (see 7.3), rather than a shift of prejudice. Such reasoning does not mean that teachers are free from sexism, any more than the curriculum they teach (5.5) and the rest of society.

## iii *Ethnicity*

British research in this area is far from extensive and relates only to the relatively unhelpful categories of Asian, West Indian and Other (see 7.4). Comments made about this further obvious form of social stratification are similar to those made about sex. Ingleby and Cooper (1974) report that ethnic minority pupils received poorer ratings from reception class, infant school teachers than did other pupils and that this gap did not close over a year. Ethnic minority boys emerged as a particularly ill-favoured group. In 5.3 we reviewed other research which indicated that teachers in general hold less favourable or negative attitudes towards West Indian pupils than towards both white and Asian pupils. Indeed, studies have suggested that teachers have positive stereotypes of Asian pupils as industrious, responsible and keen to learn, without the behaviour problems associated with West Indians. Once again this categorization, or stereotyping, can be seen as related to group differences in pupil role performance and educational achievement (7.4). Hence it is difficult to disentangle teachers' reactions to ethnic differences in pupil behaviour, attitudes and performance from forms of racism. Recent research has provided some view of this interaction and its educational outcome. Wright(1985), from a study of two schools, concludes that teacher/West Indian pupil, relationships were often antagonistic, and that this influenced teachers' professional judgements about pupils' ability and, hence, ability group placement and examination entry, which effectively restricted their educational opportunity. There were no marked differences between the ethnic groups on standardized reading test scores at time of transfer to secondary school, but in 16+ examinations, West Indian achievement was markedly lower than Asian and white, especially in respect of gaining five or more O level GCEs. A cautious view of the dynamics of interaction within multi-ethnic classrooms is provided by Green (1985). He found that pupils of different sex and ethnicity were likely to receive 'widely different educational experience' related to their teachers' educational attitudes and ethnic tolerance. Ethnic minority pupils taught by highly intolerant teachers had lower self-concepts than those of European origin. Highly intolerant teachers responded less positively to the ideas and feelings of pupils than did those who were highly tolerant. Green found that in classrooms with intolerant teachers it was West Indian pupils who were most seriously affected and had the lowest levels of self-concept.

## 6.5b TEACHER PREJUDICE AND ETHNOCENTRISM

In reviewing teachers' categorizations with regard to forms of social stratification we are touching upon two aspects of human social behaviour: ethnocentrism – belief in the intrinsic superiority of the nation, culture or group to which one belongs; and prejudice – literally, opinion formed beforehand based on inadequate facts.

Both these are extremely common, though they clearly vary in extent among teachers as among the population. We recognize the extreme cases of racism quite easily and are becoming sensitive to those of sexism, if not classism, but it is important to fully appreciate that very few, if any, people can be said to be without prejudice. The importance of prejudice lies in the likelihood that such attitudes become expressed in discriminatory behaviour (some forms of which are now illegal, see 7.1) which has detrimental effects upon certain groups. As we have also seen (4 and 5), the institutions of education, as well as those who work them, are actually or unintentionally prejudiced. Teachers, it can be argued, have then an obligation not only to examine their own prejudices, behaviour and practice, but also those of their pupils and colleagues. They have the wherewithal to affect to varying degrees the regime and climate of their classrooms, staffrooms and schools, to make them as free as possible from the sinister aspects of prejudice and discrimination. In so doing they would be moving towards a bold and socially desirable objective: '. . . the key to understanding the concept of racism [sexism, classism] lies in creating a situation where people are willing and able to examine and appraise attitudes and practices, both their own and other peoples', free from preconceived notions of superiority and inferiority, or "guilt" and "innocence" . . .' (*Education for All* 1985; my insert).

## 6.5c *INDIVIDUAL DIFFERENCES*

### *Achievement*

Given the overriding importance of attainment in education and the existence of ability grouping in British schools, it is no surprise that achievement or ability plays an important part in teachers' categorizations. Indeed, it can be recognized as the most important, though it is often confused with other factors, particularly behavioural and social ones. As we have seen (5.3), teachers display a preference for able pupils and where schools have streams, bands or sets, teachers tend to apply 'appropriate' group stereotypes to classes, adapting curriculum and teaching methods in 'suitable' ways and probably helping to produce a self-fulfilling prophecy (4.2 and 6.4b). In non-streamed situations many teachers continue to categorize and differentiate their charges along similar lines (5.3). Wittingly or otherwise, teachers communicate their categorization to the pupils, so that there is a relationship between teachers' perceptions of children and the children's self-perception and between teacher expectation and outcome. What such research at least indicates is that teachers, quite correctly, adapt their approaches to what they assume to be the ability of those they teach. Not to do so would be absurd. However, problems arise when, or if, their assumptions are incorrect, inaccurate or result from categorization based on inappropriate clues, many of which are identified here. It is, perhaps, hardly surprising, given their job, that teachers have a preference for more able children and display this in classrooms and school. It may also be argued that it is not surprising, given the evidence of the relationship between social factors and achievement (see 7), that teachers are more favourably disposed towards children from particular types of home background and that they often see ability and home background as synonymous (6.5a).

## Physical appearance

This is the most obvious clue on which to base categorization and there is some experimental evidence to suggest that teachers (like others) will form opinions on appearance. Teachers presented with eight photographs of children were asked to put them into two groups – bright and dull (Brynner et al 1972). Some were always categorized correctly in relation to measured IQ and ability, others incorrectly and others inconsistently. The consistently wrongly categorized boys were a very smart and bright-looking chap with low measured IQ – categorized as bright – and a less smart, rather dull-looking chap with high measured IQ – categorized as dull. A further study used a larger number of photographs balanced in terms of social class, sex, and ethnic group and asked teachers to estimate school adjustment and performance, aspiration, attitude to homework, and parental involvement (Harvey and Slatin 1976). Working-class children were rated lower, especially when black; the

most experienced teachers were the firmest in their characterizations. Asked how they made the categorizations, the teachers
identified similarity with pupils they had taught and facial expression. It is perhaps surprising that teachers are prepared to make
judgements based on photographs.

## Speech

There is considerable evidence that a person's speech characteristics
affect the way in which they are perceived and evaluated by others
along a whole range of criteria including ability, attitude, social
class, prestige and personality (Giles and Powesland 1975). There is
a considerable range of speech characteristics but we concentrate
here on accent or dialect. Despite the fact that regional, class and
ethnic variations from Received Pronunciation or Standard English (mostly related to south-east English/BBC accent) are not
linguistically inferior or inadequate (Trudgill 1975), they are
typically viewed as being just that (Labov 1969, Giles and Powesland 1975 and see 7.9b). This has educational significance to the
extent that teachers categorize pupils according to their accent or
dialect and allow their judgements concerning pupils' abilities to be
affected. Edwards (1978) experimentally explored this area by
having student teachers and pupils listen to recordings and assess
the speech, behaviour and academic ability of speakers with Received Pronunciation (middle-class), working-class and West Indian accents. There was considerable evidence of stereotyping. The
student teachers assigned highest status to the speech, behaviour
and ability of RP accented speakers, the lowest to West Indian, with
working class in-between. Working-class pupils made very similar
evaluations, while middle-class pupils did not distinguish between
working class and West Indian. A further group of West Indian
pupils gave the RP accented speakers highest place in terms not only
of speech, behaviour and ability, but also in terms of desirability as a
member of the class. They ranked West Indian accented less
favourably on behaviour, but the same on other counts as working-
class ones. Teachers who listened to tapes of unidentified, disadvantaged and middle-class Irish children reading, gave less

favourable ratings to the former on 17 dimensions, some related to speech – vocabulary, fluency and reading ability; others based on inference – intelligence, writing, disposition and family background (Edwards, J. 1979).

## Personality

Although there is little specific research on this in Britain, it would appear that teachers have preferences for pupils with particular types of personality. In general, they prefer conforming and acquiescent pupils and reject active and assertive ones (Brophy and Good, 1974). Not only can this choice be related to teachers' preference for pupil behaviour which assists their role performance (5.3) but also to pupils' sex differences (5.3 and 6.5aii), to the extent that the former qualities are normally associated with the young female and the latter with the male role in western society.

## First names

Teachers have been shown to hold stereotypes about first names, three quarters seeing some as desirable and others as undesirable (Garwood and McDavid 1975). Pupils with 'desirable' names scored higher on self-concept and achievement (Garwood 1976). Harai and McDavid (1973) found that teachers formed more favourable judgements of essays which were apparently written by children with common names (which had in fact been randomly assigned) and less favourable opinions of ones bearing unusual names. I suspect that this may partly explain some of my experiences as a pupil!

## Writing

Yes, teachers do knock off marks for sloppy presentation, poor handwriting, and so on! Teachers' essay marking is affected by the style of handwriting used, even where the essays are otherwise identical and teachers requested to mark for content only (Briggs 1971, Soloff 1973, Bull and Stevens 1979). Briggs (1980) used some actual 16+ examination answers written in five different hand-writing styles. At the pass/fail borderline *how* the essay was written was found to be almost as critical as its content.

## 6.6 Educational and social reflections

Having reviewed some forms of teachers' categorization of pupils, certain implications and considerations need to be identified. Clearly, the most important implication is that categorization leads to differentiation of pupils by teachers and that this in turn affects pupils' learning and achievement, their self-image, attitudes to school and education and probably, eventually, their prospects and views of the world in adult life. It can be argued that, for those who are categorized in undesirable directions the whole process is disastrous, and even that it involves unprofessional behaviour on the part of teachers. On the other hand, those favourably categorized benefit from the process.

We must remember that teachers are human, and it is difficult for them either to avoid categorizing pupils or to treat pupils as identical units. Indeed, as has been suggested, in some cases the latter would be equally undesirable. Two important factors must be borne in mind. First, teacher/pupil relationships are clearly two way processes. Pupils affect teachers' behaviour in much the same way as teachers affect their pupils. As we saw in 5.2, pupils categorize their teachers – often very cruelly. This is likely to affect both pupils' behaviour towards their teachers and that of the teacher involved. It can, then, be very difficult to love 4G who have you down as an élitist, academic, 'square' bore, whose major interest in life is their discomfort, or to avoid loving 4A who see you as a young, dashing, 'with-it', brilliant historian, their gateway to O level! Second, it would be false to assume that categorization necessarily involved the conscious recognition of differences and the application of varying treatments. As we have seen, categorization is a normal and constant part of social life. Clearly, both these factors must be viewed within the context of the classroom, the heady and demanding reality in which the drama is played out. Teachers' preferences for middle-class, bright, able and co-operative children can then be seen in behavioural and situational terms. It is simply easier, and possibly more rewarding, to teach them. Hence, whether teachers consciously discriminate in favour of particular groups or types of pupils, or whether the preference arises from the coincidence between ideal pupil-role performance and ascribed factors is open to debate. Sociologists, in general, are more concerned to illuminate processes than to impute motivations to social actions. Hence the material reviewed here is not necessarily critical of teachers as individuals (not *all* of whom fit the description), but it does suggest the importance of a knowledge and awareness of categorization for those wishing to understand schooling. In particular a developed sensitivity towards categorization – both institutional and individual – is a professional prerequisite for the concerned teacher. Obviously, racism, sexism and classism have no legitimacy in classroom or school.

Three main considerations arise, and, since the evidence is far from conclusive, these are best viewed as relatively open-ended questions.

*What is the role of knowledge in the formation and reinforcement of categorization?* The existence of records and information about, and the institutional categorization of, pupils would appear to structure teachers' categories. As we have seen, schools are persuasive in inducting members of staff into this aspect of their role. We have also seen that, quite independently of such 'official' sources, teachers have access to 'knowledge' or form opinions about their pupils. Since this was shown to happen in reception classes of infant schools, it seems unlikely that categorization would not be characteristic of teaching even if teachers were ignorant of their pupils. In turn, this raises the question as to whether full and accurate knowledge of pupils would enhance teachers' categorizations and hence their teaching, the progress of their pupils, and the fairness of schooling. This would, of course, involve considerable data collection and teacher education and probably cause widespread reaction from parents, the public and social agencies.

*Does categorization reinforce existing differences between children, or is it instrumental in creating differences?* The evidence suggests that its role is more towards reinforcing existing differences than towards creating them. However, it is also true that over the school career categorization widens, as do differences between pupils. In terms of ability, achievement, behaviour and motivation, infant school children are more alike than those in the final year of a secondary school. In this sense, it could be argued, supposed initial differences have been intensified so that they become enlarged, or real ones.

*Are the categorizations especially professional (products of teachers and teaching) or are they reflections of public and generally held views?* While explanations can be sought in terms of teachers' role performance and schooling practices, the coincidence between teachers' categorizations and those in society at large cannot, and should not, be ignored.

The structure and content of the main forms of differentiation in schooling have demonstrated that differentiation in the social structure is mirrored by that in schools and classrooms. The implied direction of influence illustrated here can be questioned, however, although the reverse could hardly be argued – that differentiation in the classroom directly produced the same in society. It is more reasonable to accept, as was argued at 6.1, that school and society are intimately related and therefore that the forms of differentiation are very similar, if not the same, in both. However undesirable – educationally, morally or ideologically – the affects of differentiation in and between schools may be, it is probably unrealistic to expect schools and teachers to change radically the facts of social life; other, that is, than in the important sphere of individuals. This may go part way to explaining the limited success of educational changes, which often appear to be only partly or poorly implemented, in changing society. It suggests that in general, social change precedes educational change.

So far our considerations, while centred on the school, have also clearly moved beyond those walls and into society. The picture that has emerged is that education can – indeed must – be viewed as a social enterprise. Our concerns now broaden out to consider the relationships between education (mainly schooling) and the family, the economy and industry, the social structure, government, politics, and religion. Given this subject matter – macro-social factors – what follows relies almost exclusively on structuralist perspectives.

# 7

# Social Stratification and Education

## 7.1 Basic social divisions

One of the most obvious facts about society and social life is the existence of major divisions between people based on, or related to, differences and inequalities. We are all conscious of our sex and age and aware of social class and ethnic group differences. Sociologists use the term social stratification to denote these major groupings in society, which are, with variations, found in almost all societies. The term suggests not only the division of society into layers, but also some form of differentiation between, or comparative evaluation of, the layers – a hierarchy or ranking. This hierarchy is related to the ownership of, or access to, social wealth; a term used here to refer to any scarce and valued commodity in society. Consequently, it refers not only to the ownership of property and wealth, the receipt of income and different life chances and styles, but also to more ephemeral aspects such as power, prestige and status, together with our central concern – education.

A further, and important, characteristic of social stratification is that members of each strata are given and expect differential treatment; they have different rights, privileges and duties, and hold views of the world, others and themselves which are related to those differences. These aspects are most easily appreciated in reflecting upon the differences between the sexes or age groupings in our society, though they are equally apparent within, and between, social classes and ethnic groups. For example, there are objective, clearly distinct differences between the sexes in a range of factors, including wealth, rights, and opportunities, which cannot be denied and are currently under some revision. It was in an attempt to overcome some of the perceived disadvantages of women in our

174

society that the Equal Pay Act, 1970, Sex Discrimination Act, 1975 and the EOC were introduced. Earlier but similar legislation and organization exists in respect of what we shall refer to as ethnic minority groups – the Race Relations Acts, 1965 and 1968, and the CRE.

In the first sub-section below a review is presented of some of the research data which illustrates the relationship between different forms of social stratification and education. Like all types of data, that from large-scale surveys has limitations. Of particular concern are the definitions used. While sex as a research variable is unproblematic, social class and ethnic group are not, both varying in definition and being to some extent contentious. The definitions used in the research reported are given below and in 10.2/3, but it is important to appreciate from the outset that the groupings used are large and mixed. So while emphasis is placed on overall differences between groups, it must be appreciated that these are relative and not absolute – not *all* middle-class children succeed nor do *all* working-class children fail in schools! Similarly, measures of educational achievement are limited to achievement tests, examination performance and entry into further or higher education, which some would argue is a limited view of the benefits of schooling. However, given the clear relationship between such performance and subsequent occupation/lifestyles (see 8), they may be seen as crucial.

Traditionally, a major (perhaps *the*) concern of the sociology of education has been with the relationship between social class and education. This means that it has by far the largest research base and, since class is also the fundamental form of stratification in society, it is where we begin.

## 7.2 Social class

The interest in the relationship between class and education is, of course, not only sociological. It has its roots in the whole philosophical and political question of equality (or rather the legitimate criteria for inequality) in education – a question that has characterized much of our education history (see 7.7).

While the concept of social class is very complex, for our present purpose we can accept the way it is operationalized in empirical

175

research: 'a grouping of people into categories on the basis of occupation' (Reid 1981, and illustrated in 10.2). Class is used in educational research in two main and distinct ways – as an individual characteristic and to characterize a geographical or other area. Our initial view is of the first and most common approach, the relationship between parental class and child's achivement (8.2a deals with adult class and education), while 7.2b illustrates the second – areal class.

## 7.2a PARENTAL CLASS

The main weight of research and concern has been with social class and terminal educational qualifications (O and A level GCE/further and higher education). It is possible, however, to trace class differences in participation and performance throughout the educational system. In the early 1970s access to pre-school education was clearly related to class. At the extremes, twice the percentage of children of 'professional' fathers went to nursery school than those with unskilled manual fathers (14 compared with 7 per cent) and nearly three times the percentage attended day nurseries or playgroups (18 compared with 7 per cent) (*General Household Survey, 1972* 1975). Following a government White Paper in 1972 (*Education: a framework for expansion*), there was some expansion of provision which, together with a drop in the number of children in the relevant age group and a spread of part-time places, brought the class differences in respect of the chance of pre-school education much closer (*General Household Survey 1977* 1979). Whether, and how, such experience affects subsequent performance at school is not clearly indicated by research. What can be shown, however, is that by the age of seven, the differences in performance of the social classes in infant or first schools in the essentials of reading and arithmetic are marked (Davie et al 1972). Table 7.1 contains figures based on the test scores of some 15,000 children, showing that those from social class V were six times more likely to be poor readers than those in class I (see top row of table). The study reveals even greater differences in respect of children who are 'non-readers', class V being fifteen times more likely than class I to be in that category. The table also shows similar differences for mathematics. Note, too, the clear divide between the middle (I, II, III nm) and the working classes (III m, IV, V) and how class I stands out as being better in terms of performance than the other middle classes while social class V performs correspondingly worse than the other working classes.

## Table 7.1
Reading and arithmetic attainment test scores of 7-year-old children by social class of father* (percentages)

| | Social class* | | | | | | |
|---|---|---|---|---|---|---|---|
| | I | II | III (nm) | III (m) | IV | V | All† |
| Grouped Southgate reading-test scores | | | | | | | |
| 0–20 | 8 | 15 | 14 | 30 | 37 | 48 | 29 |
| 21–28 | 37 | 39 | 43 | 41 | 38 | 34 | 39 |
| 29–30 | 54 | 47 | 43 | 29 | 25 | 17 | 32 |
| Grouped problem arithmetic-test scores | | | | | | | |
| 0–3 | 12 | 19 | 19 | 30 | 34 | 41 | 29 |
| 4–6 | 38 | 39 | 43 | 42 | 42 | 37 | 41 |
| 7–10 | 50 | 42 | 38 | 28 | 24 | 22 | 31 |

* For definition, see 10.2.
† Of whole sample, including those without father or social class information.

(Derived from Reid 1981, devised from Tables A165 and A168 Davie et al 1972.)

These early class differences increase with further schooling. Commenting later on the same children, Fogelman and Goldstein (1976) wrote,

For a given 7-year score the children whose fathers were in non-manual occupations are, at the age of 11, about 1.0 years ahead of social classes III manual and IV, who in turn are about 0.4 years ahead of social class V. This, of course, is additional to the pre-existing differences at the age of 7, which were respectively 0.9 years and 0.7 years. Thus the overall differences at 11 have increased to 1.9 years and 1.11 years respectively.

Very similar results were found for arithmetic. Douglas (1964) in a similar longitudinal study using a battery of standardized tests including intelligence, reading and school attainment, showed that between the ages of 7 and 11 middle-class children's scores increased, whereas working-class children's scores declined, so that the difference between them increased. Both these longitudinal studies found that the divergence of attainment test scores between the social classes observed at ages 7 and 11 continued through secondary school. So the overall picture is one of a widening gap between children from different social classes, which is greatest at ages 15 and 16. Fogelman et al (1978b) comment that their figures imply that at 16 years only about 15 per cent of children in social class V could be expected to score above the mean of non-manual children. These findings are perhaps surprising. It could be held that schools ought to operate so that at least initial differences are not heightened while it might be argued that their purpose should be to equalize differences by improving the performance of weaker pupils.

The most crucial stage of schooling is clearly the leaving examinations. Burnhill (1981) provides a dramatic view of the relationship between social class and secondary school examination achievement among Scottish school leavers. Table 7.2 shows that at each level of achievement the percentage passing declines across the social classes from I to V, and this can be compared with the overall percentage (the hatched line) which neatly divides the non-manual from the manual classes. As can be seen, at the extremes 95 per cent of children from class I left school with at least some qualification and 58 per cent had three or more higher SCE passes, compared to only 45 and 4 per cent respectively of those children from social class V. A more general view of the relationship is provided by the *General Household Survey 1982* (1984). Table 7.3 shows, by sex, the highest educational achievements of a large sample of adults related to the social class of their fathers. The expected pattern – the

178

**Table 7.2**

School examination* performance of leavers from Scottish schools,
1975/6, by social class of father† (cumulative percentages)

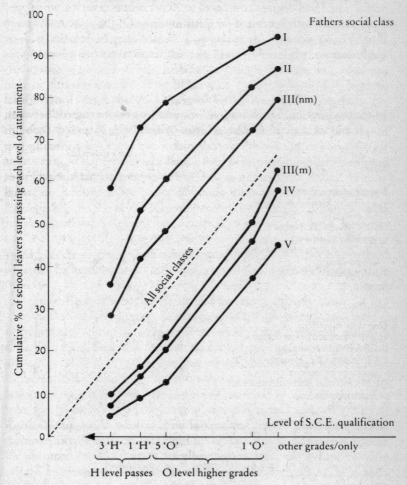

* For definitions, see 10.3
† For definition, see 10.2
(Derived from Figure 1, Burnhill 1981.)

'higher' the class the larger the proportion with qualifications – is sustained together with very clear indications of differences between the sexes (see also 7.3 and 8.2). Some 40 per cent of females with fathers in social class I had degrees compared to 23 per cent of females, while only 7 per cent of both sexes had no qualifications. Of those with fathers in class VI, 60 per cent of males and 75 per cent of females had no qualifications, while only 4 and 1 per cent respectively had a degree.

**Table 7.3**

Highest educational qualification* attained by persons,† aged 25–49, by sex and social class of father,‡ Great Britain 1981/2§ (percentages)

| | | | Father's social class | | | | |
|---|---|---|---|---|---|---|---|
| **Males** | 1 | 2 | 3 | 4 | 5 | 6 | ALL |
| Degree or equivalent | 40 | 20 | 22 | 6 | 5 | 4 | 10 |
| Higher education below degree | 17 | 15 | 13 | 10 | 7 | 8 | 11 |
| GCE A level or equivalent | 13 | 12 | 12 | 9 | 8 | 6 | 10 |
| GCE O level/CSE, higher grades or equivalent | 16 | 20 | 17 | 15 | 11 | 8 | 15 |
| GCE/CSE other grades/commercial/ apprenticeship | 2 | 6 | 8 | 13 | 12 | 12 | 11 |
| Foreign/other | 5 | 6 | 5 | 4 | 3 | 2 | 4 |
| None | 7 | 22 | 22 | 44 | 55 | 60 | 40 |
| **Females** | | | | | | | |
| Degree or equivalent | 23 | 8 | 9 | 2 | 1 | 1 | 4 |
| Higher education below degree | 27 | 15 | 15 | 7 | 5 | 4 | 9 |
| GCE A level or equivalent | 9 | 8 | 6 | 3 | 3 | 1 | 4 |
| GCE O level/CSE, higher grades or equivalent | 22 | 25 | 22 | 17 | 13 | 8 | 17 |
| GCE/CSE other grades/commercial/ apprenticeship | 6 | 11 | 14 | 12 | 11 | 9 | 12 |
| Foreign/other | 6 | 6 | 4 | 3 | 3 | 3 | 4 |
| None | 7 | 27 | 30 | 57 | 64 | 75 | 50 |
| Social class of sample | 3 | 17 | 10 | 44 | 19 | 7 | 100 |

* For details see 10.3 (in respect of A and O level, etc. = one or more passes).
† Not in full-time education.
‡ For definition see 10.2.
§ Data for 1981 and 1982 combined.

(Devised from Table 7.5(a) *General Household Survey 1982* (1984).)

Elsewhere in this book we review evidence that children from different social classes inhabit different schools and different positions within them and receive different teaching and education, and that such differences affect school performace (see 6). These factors are clearly important when viewing the terminal education achievements of the social classes. So, too, is the question of intelligence or ability (see 7.8). Consequently, although the data in Table 7.4 is dated, it is particularly valuable for our purpose since it holds constant the type of school attended and the measured IQ ranges of the children studied. The table shows that, other than for children of the highest IQ range (130 or more) at the O level stage, differences in achievement existed between middle- and working-class children in distinct favour of the former. In the middle IQ range (115–29) a quarter as many more middle-class children gained five or more O levels than did the working-class, two thirds as many more gained two A levels, and more than twice the number entered degree-level courses. Note, however, that these are not measures of pure achievement. They also involve staying on at school and using educational qualifications to enter higher education rather than employment. Hence part of the difference in A level success between the classes was due to differences in entry to sixth forms. Even at the highest IQ range the percentage of those who actually gained two A levels and subsequently went on to degree courses was 86 per cent for the middle and 60 per cent for the working class. Very similar results were obtained in a study some six years later (*Statistics of Education 1961*, Supplement) which held constant the type of school and the grade of 11+ secondary school selection examination. Here, although the overall achievements at O level were higher, the social class differences remained. They are again revealed in the cohort from the study mentioned above (Douglas 1964). The follow-up study, in which ability measured at age 15 was held constant but not the type of school attended (Douglas, et al 1968), revealed that the percentage of the top-ability group (16 per cent) who had gained five or more O levels (including at least three from English language, mathematics, science and a foreign language) varied from 77 per cent for the upper-middle-class children across the classes to 37 per cent for lower-working-class

children. These findings are broadly supported by Rutter et al
(1979) who, having controlled for verbal reasoning, found parental
occupation to be related to the examination performance of children
in their sample of London schools. The relationship was particularly strong among children in the middle band of ability and
slightly less so for those in the higher ability band.

### Table 7.4

Academic achievement by pupils* at LEA grammar schools, by
grouped IQ scores at age 11 and social class of father,† England and
Wales‡ (percentages)

| | | Social class | |
| IQ score | Achievement | Non-manual | Manual |
| --- | --- | --- | --- |
| 130+ | Degree course | 37 | 18 |
| | At least 2 GCE A levels | 43 | 30 |
| | At least 5 GCE O levels | 73 | 75 |
| 115–129 | Degree course | 17 | 8 |
| | At least 2 GCE A levels | 23 | 14 |
| | At least 5 GCE O levels | 56 | 45 |
| 100–114 | Degree course | 6 | 2 |
| | At least 2 GCE A levels | 9 | 6 |
| | At least 5 GCE O levels | 37 | 22 |

* Born in 1940–1
† For definition, see 10.2.
‡ Figures for degree course are for Great Britain.

(Derived from Table 5, *Higher Education* (1963), Appendix 1, part 2.)

Post-school education presents the starkest picture of the relationship between social class and education. The most comprehensive research was that of the Robbins Report (*Higher Education*
1963), which surveyed about one in every 200 people born in
1940/1. In terms of full-time degree-level courses the survey revealed that while a third of class I entered such courses, only one per
cent of classes IV and V did so. In other words, a person from social
class I was 33 times more likely to end up on an undergraduate

course than someone from classes IV and V. At the other extreme, only 7 per cent of social class I failed to gain any educational qualification compared with 65 per cent (nearly two in every three) of classes IV and V. An interesting aspect of this research was that it also looked at the relationship between *mother's* social class (occupation before marriage) and children's educational achievement, with very similar results to those of father and child. The study did not, however, consider mothers and fathers together.

The evidence is brought more up-to-date in Table 7.5 which shows the social class profile of university and advanced further education students. The bottom line of the table gives the overall distribution of the population by social class for comparison (though see footnote). There is a clear over-representation of the middle classes – who are only 35 per cent of the population, but 80 per cent of university undergraduates – and under-representation of working classes – 65 per cent of the population, only 19 per cent of undergraduates. The figures for advanced further education (which includes public sector undergraduates, see 10.3) are only slightly less pronounced at 69 and 31 per cent for middle and working class respectively. Class differences are stark at the extremes: 22 per cent of university undergraduates came from class I, one per cent from class V, despite the latter being larger in the population (7 compared to 5 per cent).

### Table 7.5

Percentage distribution of full-time university entrants, UK 1984, and advanced FE students, GB 1977, by social class*

|  | I | II | III(nm) | III(m) | IV | V | Middle | Working |
|---|---|---|---|---|---|---|---|---|
| University | 22 | 48 | 10 | 12 | 6 | 1 | 80 | 19 |
| Advanced further education | 13 | 37 | 19 | 20 | 9 | 2 | 69 | 31 |
| 18-year-olds† | 5 | 20 | 10 | 40 | 18 | 7 | 35 | 65 |

* For definition see 10.2.
† Based on 10–14-year-olds in 1971 Census.

*Note*: the UCCA social class classification is based on occupational information provided by candidates and does not always include employment status.

(Devised from Tabulation 1, p. 7, UCCA 1985; Table 2.18, Farrant 1981 and Table 46, *Household Composition Tables* 1975.)

This type of evidence (see also Reid 1981 Chapter 6) suggests that any view of the social origin of groups of students in higher or further education reveals an over-representation of the middle classes and under-representation of the working classes compared to the classes' distribution in society at large. There is, however, one sector of the educational system in which social class appears to have no effect on performance. In spite of the powerful association between social class and entry into higher education, studies of university students have failed to show any consistent relationship between parental class and the class of degree obtained (Brockington and Stein 1963: Kelsall 1963).

There is a certain crudeness in the normal use of fathers' occupation as the single criterion of a child's social class. Not only has mothers' social class been shown to be related to educational performance, but we can suspect that fathers and mothers are important in combination. Moreover, it is obvious that aspects of social class beyond occupation have important effects, or are related to, such performance. Particularly important here, and as has been demonstrated in research, is the educational level of parents. Certainly adult social class and occupation are related to educational level (see 8.2a). So occupation is a proxy variable or a shorthand reference to a large number of factors of class, many of which have to be found to be related to educational performance. Studies with more information about their subjects reveal interesting insights. One of my own (Reid 1969), for example, identified some sixteen 'family characteristics' related to both educational success and to 'middle-classness'. Detailed analysis revealed a small number of working-class children (defined by father's occupation) who had *more* of these characteristics than many of the 'middle-class' children. They had, for example, middle-class, educated mothers and grandparents and came from educationally responsive and supportive, materially well-off, small families. These children were among the most successful in the whole sample and were the most successful working-class part of it. The reverse was also true: some middle-class children had few of the 'family characteristics' and were not successful. The use of the simple occupational definition of class could be seen to misplace some success and failure. What is being argued, therefore, is that the class chances in education, as outlined above, may in fact be more blatant than they appear. More sophisticated criteria of social class than fathers' occupation might well reveal much greater differences in educational performance between the classes.

## 7.2b AREAL SOCIAL CLASS

Anyone travelling in Britain will have recognized that the social class composition of areas shows marked variation, indicating a degree of residential segregation. Here we limit our attention to areal class differences between LEAs, although variation in school catchment areas is also of interest (see 4.9 and 7.10). LEAs display a wide range in the percentage of pupils living in households whose heads have non-manual occupations: from 50 per cent in Surrey to 11 per cent in Knowsley as compared to the average for all English LEAs which is 28 per cent. The DES *Statistical Bulletin 13/84* (1984) related these differences to the proportion of age groups gaining GCE and CSE qualifications and found a very strong relationship. For example, the percentage of pupils gaining one or more A level GCEs in Surrey was 22, in Knowsley 8 and overall 15. The comparable percentages for five or more O level GCE higher grades or equivalent were 33, 12 and 23 respectively. The survey included a number of other socio-economic factors – measures of population density, household amenities and over-crowding, non-white children, unemployment, supplementary benefit payments, infant mortality and family size – which all to varying degrees displayed a relationship with educational achievement, though none matched the statistical significance of the social class measure in respect to attainment at A and higher grade O level GCEs. Several educational and resource variables, together with overall expenditure, were also associated with attainment but were 'of small degree' and much lower than the socio-economic variables. As the Bulletin clearly indicates, any comparison of the educational attainment of LEAs 'would be seriously misleading if the socio-economic background of pupils were not taken into account'. Of course, it has to be recognized that the LEAs are large and diverse, displaying considerable intra-area variation. However, this type of research reinforces that on parental class in identifying social class as an important and fundamental variable in educational performance.


## 7.3 Sex

The achievements of boys and girls in school are not as markedly different as those between the social classes and have more to do with different performance in areas of the curriculum. At primary school, girls display an early superior ability in reading which decreases between the ages of 8–9 and 11. The large-scale survey, *Primary Education in England* (1978), found girls to have slightly higher reading test scores at 9 years than boys and the difference between the sexes to have decreased by the age of 11. In Scotland, Maxwell (1977) found the difference among 'boys and girls at the same age . . . who had received the same teaching' to have disappeared by the age of 11 years. In mathematics the differences between the sexes are less clear-cut. None were discovered in the *Primary Education in England* survey, although boys displayed an edge on items concerned with graphical presentation. There are some indications that the sexes have particular strengths within mathematics. Ward (1979) recorded better computation skills for girls whilst Schuard (1981) found girls' scores higher on verbal items, and boys' on spatial items. The *APU Mathematical Development Primary Survey* (1980) found 11-year-old boys scored higher than girls in the categories of length, capacity, rate and ratio. Overall, there would appear to be no outstanding differences in the performances of the sexes at the primary school stage.

Despite entering secondary schools at a more or less equal level, the sexes become differentiated in terms of the subjects they study, success in public examinations and destination on leaving school. All subjects on the curriculum are nominally available to all, although the study by HMI (*Aspects of Secondary Education in England* 1979) found that the opportunities to study craft and science subjects were different for the sexes. This fact, together with aspects of subject choices, is related to the clear sex differences in the subjects passed in the 16+ examinations. For example, more boys than girls gain higher grade GCE/CSE/16+ passes in science (36 compared with 25 per cent) and mathematics (31 and 44 per cent), while more girls pass in English (44 compared with 33 per cent) and foreign languages (20 and 12 per cent) (*Statistics of Education 1982* 1984). Overall, girls were more successful than boys in 16+ examinations, 57.8 per cent gained one or more higher grade pass compared with only 51.7 per cent of boys and only 8 as opposed to 11 per cent failed to gain any leaving qualifications. Girls also out-perform boys at the traditional yardstick of academic achievement at 16, namely five or more higher grade passes, 27.1 compared with 25.5 per cent in 1982/3 (*Statistics of Education 1983* 1985). Recently a higher proportion of girls than boys have stayed on in sixth forms. In England and Wales in 1982, 33 per cent of girls and 30 per cent of boys stayed for a year and 22 per cent of both sexes for two. In Scotland, girls were more likely to have stayed both for one year (48 compared with 40 per cent) and for two (21 compared with 18 per cent) (*Social Trends No. 15* 1985). Marginally more (0.5 per cent) of male than female UK scholl leavers in 1981–2 gained matriculation (two or more A levels on equivalent), while the percentage gaining one or more were almost identical (see Table 7.6). The only marked difference between the sexes is in terms of passing three or more A levels – the English figures for 1982–3 were: male 10.4 and females 8.8 per cent of leavers.

It is on leaving school that the largest differences between the sexes occur. While a larger proportion of males leave for employment (66 compared with 57 per cent) and women are more likely to continue their education (33 compared with 24 per cent), fewer women enter degree courses than men (6.9 compared with 9.1 per cent) (*Statistics of Education 1982* 1984). There is considerable variation in the type of higher and further education undertaken, and in the subjects studied. Vocational courses such as teaching, catering and nursing are predominantly female. Of those going on to degree courses men are more likely to attend university – in 1983 59 per cent of undergraduates were male, although change is taking place, in 1971 the figure was 68. Women are over-represented in arts, language and education degrees and under-represented in those

## The Sociology of School and Education

in science and particularly engineering (*University Statistics* 1982). Women are slightly more likely to enter polytechnics and twice as likely to enter other institutions of higher education to read for degrees.

The sex pattern of post-school destination reflects not only school experience and achievement, but other factors too. While women are more likely to delay their entry into employment than men, their heavier use of vocational courses may indicate a more instrumental view of education in that they decide upon an occupational role earlier. This is probably related to differing occupational opportunities for the sexes and the anticipation of the female sex role in respect to marriage and child bearing.

In straightforward terms we can conclude that sex is clearly related to educational achievement. It is true that many educational differences between the sexes are closing – for example, the proportions at university, and levels of school achievement. Table 7.6 shows the gap in the percentages of male and female school leavers with A levels to have closed almost completely between the mid-1960s and early 1980s –

### Table 7.6

Percentage of school leavers by highest qualification* and sex, United Kingdom 1965/6 to 1981/2

|  | 1965/6 | | 1975/6 | | 1981/2 | |
|---|---|---|---|---|---|---|
|  | *Male* | *Female* | *Male* | *Female* | *Male* | *Female* |
| 2 or more GCE A levels 3 or more SCE H levels | 12.9 | 9.1 | 14.4 | 12.3 | 14.8 | 14.3 |
| 1 or more GCE A/SCE H level | 16.1 | 12.2 | 18.0 | 16.3 | 18.5 | 18.6 |
| 5 or more GCE/SCE O levels/CSE higher grades only | 7.0 | 8.8 | 7.3 | 9.5 | 8.8 | 11.0 |
| No higher grades/ and no passes at GCE/SCE/CSE | 62.7 | 63.1 | 51.1 | 47.5 | 49.9 | 42.5 |

*For definition see 10.3

(Devised from Table 29, *Education Statistics for the United Kingdom 1984* 1985.)

despite a higher percentage of females than males continuing to leave with five or more higher grade O levels only (row 3). This latter difference together with increased female participation in sixth-forms suggests that females may soon outperform males in gaining any qualification. Similarly, some changes towards greater equality may be detected in subject choice and type of further and higher education. To what extent these changes herald a future lack of differentiation between the sexes in educational achievement is, of course, open to speculation. What is clear is that the past and the present have resulted in men in the population being more likely to have educational qualifications, and markedly more likely to have higher educational qualifications (particularly degrees), than women (see Table 8.1).

## 7.4 Ethnic minority groups

Britain has a good number of such groups, but interest and research have been almost exclusively concentrated on the most easily recognized, the large ethnic minorities of Asians and West Indians. Others, such as Jews, Poles, the Irish, and other Europeans have barely been recognized, though the recently published *Education for All* (1985) does make mention of Chinese, Cypriot, Italian, Ukranian, Vietnamese and Travellers' children as 'examples of particular types of communities whose needs we considered to be particularly deserving of attention in their own right'. Educational and governmental research typically treats Asians and West Indians as if they were single and homogeneous communities. In fact, each is composed of groups which display wide variation in terms of culture (including language and religion), origins, background and residence in Britain. Research into ethnic disadvantage in education has been more limited than that into housing and employment. No official educational data in respect of ethnic minorities has been collected by the DES since 1972, and while collection was restarted in 1983, none has yet been published.

The general picture to emerge from research is that Asian children perform similarly to, or somewhat better than, their white classmates, while West Indians perform less well, in both primary and secondary schools. Little (1981) surveyed performance in ILEA schools at the point of transfer from primary to secondary. He found New Commonwealth immigrant children a year below the age norm in reading, and under-represented by about half in the top 25 per cent of the ability range in verbal reasoning, English and mathematics. In comparing Asians and West Indians who had received all their education in Britain, it was found that Asians performed similarly to whites in mathematics and verbal reasoning, and only slightly less well in English, while West Indians performed markedly less well on all three measures. In fact, West Indian children have been shown to 'under-perform' in comparison with socially disadvantaged white children in ILEA education priority area infant and primary schools (Barnes 1975, see also Mabey 1981).

Taylor (1976) found Asian boys doing better than whites in 16+ examinations in Newcastle, and similar achievements for the two groups have been recorded in Leicester (Brooks and Singh, 1978) and the Midlands (Driver and Ballard 1979). The most extensive surveys of this stage of education are those undertaken for the Rampton and Swann Committees (*West Indian Children in our Schools* 1981 and *Education for All* 1985). The main findings are presented in Table 7.7, which shows West Indian GCE O level/CSE performance to be markedly lower than that of Asians and Others in five LEAs. Note that the overall performance in these LEAs is lower than for the whole of England (compare columns 4 and 5). While Asian achievement of higher grade passes in mathematics matched that of Others, in English it was lower (21 compared with 29 per cent) and in A level attainment , the West Indian score was the lowest. The data, however, reveals significant increases in the latter's attainments between 1978/79 (figures in brackets) and 1981/82; the percentage gaining five or more higher grade GCE O level/CSE passes doubled and that for A levels increased by two and a half. It is interesting to note that the percentage failing to gain any graded examination result is identical for all groups and that at 19 per cent it is greatly in excess of the 11 per cent for all England. Essen and Ghodsian (1979) presented similar findings from the NCDS study. Standardized test scores in mathematics and reading of 'first generation immigrants' were lower than white children's, but among 'second generation immigrants' only West Indians scored lower. A survey of 16 schools in an outer London borough found Afro-Caribbean pupils performing less well than others at 16 and 18+ (Craft and Craft 1983).

**Table 7.7**

Educational attainment of Asians, West Indians and Others in five English LEAs, 1981/82* (percentages)

|  | Asian | West Indian | Others | 5 LEAs | All** England |
|---|---|---|---|---|---|
| 1 or more GCE A level† | 13(12) | 5(2) | 13(12) | 12(10) | 14(13) |
| 5 or more higher grade GCE O level/CSE | 17 | 6(3) | 19(16) | 18(15) | 23(21) |
| 1–4 GCE O level/CSE | 64 | 75 | 62 | 63 | 66 |
| No graded results | 19 | 19 | 19 | 19 | 11 |
| **English GCE O level/CSE** |  |  |  |  |  |
| Higher Grade | 21(22) | 15(9) | 29 | 26 | 36(34) |
| Other Grade | 51(47) | 60 | 46(41) | 48 | 47 |
| **Mathematics GCE O level/CSE** |  |  |  |  |  |
| Higher Grade | 21 | 8(5) | 21 | 20 | 26(23) |
| Other Grade | 46(41) | 47 | 47(42) | 46 | 47 |
| **Destination on Leaving School** |  |  |  |  |  |
| Degree course | 5 | 1(−)‡ | 5(4) | 5(4) | 6 |
| Any full-time education course (includes degrees) | 34(21) | 27(16) | 17(12) | 21(13) | 26(19) |

\* Figures in brackets refer to 1978/79 and are shown only where markedly different from 1981/82.
\** Maintained Schools only
† For definitions see 10.3.
‡ (−) less than ½%.

(Derived from Tables 3, 4, 5, 6, and 7, *Education for All* 1985 Annex B.)

This overall picture is well supported in general terms. Tomlinson (1980) has reviewed some 33 studies of ethnic performance in our schools, of which 26 showed West Indians scoring lower than whites on individual or group tests, over-represented in the ESN category, or under-represented in the higher streams of school. This general view of low West Indian performance is challenged, however, by Driver (1980). In the five multi-racial schools he researched, West Indian children did better overall in 16+ examinations than did whites. The largest difference was between the two sets of girls. Among West Indians, girls did better than boys; among whites, the boys did better than girls. He suggests that the explanation may lie in cultural differences, namely the female focus of Jamaican/West Indian life and English working-class attitudes towards the education of girls.

His research, like most in the field, has received a good deal of criticism (for example, see Troyna, 1984). Many of the studies are dated and limited, and there is considerable variation in the type and size of sample used. While some of these criticisms can be made in general terms about much educational research, certain ones are particularly important in this field. The most serious limitation is that most studies ignore social class as a factor. Failing to hold class constant raises the question as to whose performance is being compared with that of ethnic minorities. Because of the residential segregation of social classes and ethnic minorities in our society the comparison will often be with white children from semi- and unskilled manual backgrounds. Hence the often quoted similar performance of Asian children might well be limited to a similarity with white children of particular social classes.

Roberts, et al (1983) have claimed that black under- achievement might be attributable to the fact that they reside in districts and attend schools where the attainment of all pupils is below average. Ethnic groups are known to have different occupational/social class structures (see, for example, Reid 1981) which also vary in different parts of the country. Some ethnic group differences in educational achievement may be attributable to class or class in combination with ethnicity. Some ethnic minorities are over-represented in semi- and unskilled employment, and suffer higher unemployment, lower incomes and poorer housing than whites (see Brown 1984) but such differences have not been taken into account in research. Craft and Craft compared Asian, West Indian and white, middle- and working-class educational performance and found that the class differences at 16+ were similar within each ethnic group. The lower performance of West Indians in both social classes begs the question as to whether their location within the classes was the same as that of other groups. Further analysis, including sex, was thwarted by the fact that only 9 per cent (257) of their sample were West Indian – of whom only 31 were middle-class. Failure to analyze ethnic educational performance by social class and to use scales sensitive enough to locate properly ethnic minorities is likely to lead to à confusion between ethnicity and class. Before assuming ethnicity to be the central variable it would be prudent to examine the role of class, not only for our understanding but also since otherwise educational policy and strategies designed to combat the problem may prove inappropriate or inadequate (Reid 1986a). As is the case with class, the definitions of ethnic groups used in research disguise or ignore important cultural variations, including values relating to education, concepts of sex roles, occupational and familial aspirations and the like, all of which are probably related to educational performance. Thus, the lack of full and proper social class and cultural identification in the research in this area means that our view and understanding of the relationships between ethnic group membership and educational performance and achievement is not as clear as it might, or should be.

Data is not generally available on ethnic minority participation in further and higher education, but as in the case of other forms of social stratification, degree course entry appears the sharpest differentiator. As Table 7.7 indicates, the *Education for All* survey found 5 per cent of Asian and 1 per cent of West Indian school leavers compared with 6 per cent of all leavers in England bound for degree courses. In some contrast both Asian and West Indian pupils are more likely to stay at school beyond the age of 16 and to enter full-time post-school education (see also Craft and Craft). In the latter case the overall rate in the five LEAs was 20 per cent, with West Indian, Asian and Others at 28, 33 and 17 per cent respectively. Apart from cultural factors it is likely that differing levels of school achievement and opportunities to enter employment are involved.

Notwithstanding the reservations about research outlined here, it is clear on the evidence to date that ethnic group, like sex and social class, is clearly related to educational experience, attainment and outcome.

## 7.5 Cumulative stratification

Our review of the evidence so far has reflected the tendency of research to treat forms of social stratification as if they were separate entities. In fact, as has been indicated, social class, sex and ethnic group act in combination to produce cumulative educational advantage or disadvantage. This is clearly shown in Table 7.3 in respect of class and sex, and well illustrated by Edwards and Roberts (1980), who produced what amounts to a pecking order with regard to higher educational chances – middle-class male/middle-class female/working-class male/working-class female. They calculated that social class I males had a 58 per cent chance of going to university and 85 per cent chance of some form of higher education, while females of similar class had chances of 38 and 56 per cent respectively. Social class V male chances were 1.4 per cent for university and 2.1 for higher education and those for females 0.8 and 1.2 per cent. Between class I and V the class/sex chances declined at a regular rate. As we have seen, it is almost certain that a third element of ethnic group should be added to the pecking order – white, Asian, West Indian. A detailed order would be difficult to define because the research provides only glimpses of the nature of the role of class and sex in the achievement of ethnic minorities. There is little doubt, however, that white, male and class I would be at the top!

Such consideration underlines the importance of treating social stratification as a single, composite phenomenon. Failure to do so not only detracts from explanations of educational achievement but is also likely to flaw policies designed to alleviate inequality. Tackling any single form in isolation is extremely unlikely to relieve educational inequality in the others and may merely result in its redistribution. What is called for is more detailed, extensive and protracted research, for which at present there seems to be little enthusiasm and even less political will and resources.

## 7.6 Age

In many ways age is the least straightforward form of social stratification to relate to education. We can recognize that society views education as being firmly associated with childhood and early adulthood. This is clearly reflected in the comparatively less than generous provision for adult and continuing education, despite the development of such institutions as the Open University. More fundamentally, age forms the basis of school organization and is an important criterion of performance. Children progress from class to class on the basis of their age and are judged according to age-based standards, or the average performance of their peers. Thus O level GCE and CSE are 16+ examinations; passing them at other ages has implications concerning the person's ability. This emphasis on age and stage in schooling reflects, or contributes to, the competitive nature of our educational system, which has relatively less provision for those who might take longer to achieve given levels. This can be seen in some contrast to competence-based systems, where progress from class to class is based more on performance than solely on age – for example, the grade systems of the USA and the Soviet Union, and, historically, of Britain. A movement of children at critical stages because of age – from infant to junior school, for instance – may in some instances (for example, for those who have not mastered reading) have long-term implications for their subsequent achievements. The recent development of open entry sixth forms indicates that some pupils whose performance at 16 was not good achieve well given an extra year – a fact recognized by many 'public' schools which arrange for their pupils to take three rather than two years over A level GCE courses.

There is also evidence to suggest that children born in autumn perform better in school than those born in spring and summer, mainly because the former are likely to receive longer schooling in infant or first school (up to two terms more), and remain the eldest in their school classes throughout their careers. Evidence from the NCDS indicates that length of schooling is the crucial factor, since all the children surveyed were all born in the same week of a year, yet roughly equal proportions started school before the age of five and after it. 'Early starters' were more likely to be middle-class and attend small schools – nevertheless, after holding constant these and other variables, test results in general ability, reading and mathematics at age 11 showed that 'early' performed better than 'late' starters (Fogelman and Gorbach 1978). While such factors can easily be seen as advantageous in the early years of schooling, it is perhaps surprising that they have been found to operate throughout the school career (Thompson, D. 1971, Barker Lunn 1972). ESN pupils have been shown to include an over-representation of younger children in each age group (Pumfrey 1975).

No relationship between season of birth and social class or ethnic group has been established, and there probably is none. The importance of ages and stages in schooling may, however, be indirectly related to differing performance along social stratification lines. Such a system is to the advantage of those best equipped, able and willing to tackle schooling as presented, and to the disadvantage of others. From our considerations so far, and those below, it is easy to align such differences with class and ethnic groups.

## 7.7 Towards an explanation

So far, 7 has merely described, in some detail, the relationships between forms of social stratification and educational achievement. Explaining those relationships, as will be seen, is both difficult and unresolved. If there were adequate and ready explanation(s), then the solution would be to hand and the problem potentially solved. A number of approaches have been adopted, each of which is best seen as an avenue of potential explanation, and they are in need of being viewed together. Again, because of its importance and fuller treatment in literature and research, social class will be our major concern, though sex and ethnic group will not be neglected.

Attempts at explanation assume the existence of a problem or situation which requires solving or changing. Social problems do not, however, exist in themselves, but only when they are recognized as such. There are then those who would see no problem within the data we have reviewed and be unmoved by its implications. They would say, well, life is unequal or unfair so why not education? Or they would indulge in social Darwinistic thinking: the fittest survive, others do not and it matters little therefore what is done for either. Attempts at explanation and policy designed to change the situation must therefore be premised on ideas of equality or equality of opportunity. Within education such ideas display considerable range, from the *minimal* – a lack of structural barriers in schooling and education which prevent members of social groups gaining access to any given level, to the *maximal* – equal opportunity is only achieved when the proportion of each social group gaining each level of attainment is identical to that group's proportion in the population (equal opportunity equals equal attainment). We have minimal opportunity; maximal opportunity may be utopian; actual opportunity lies between. In Britain there have been sustained, if not significant, efforts towards greater equality of opportunity, which have fuelled, and been fuelled by, much of the research reviewed in this book and the endeavours of many involved in education. They have been sustained not only by desires for greater social justice but also (and some would argue, more important) by assumptions about the economic desirability of an educational system efficient in releasing available talent wherever it occurs, and about aspects of social control and legitimation.

## 7.8 The question of intelligence

If it could be conclusively shown that middle-class male and white pupils were actually and innately superior in an educational sense, then there would be little need for further concern. The educational achievements of the classes, sexes and ethnic groups would be a straightforward reflection of their different abilities. Of course, in the case of the sexes this could hardly be sustained. Not only is there *no* evidence that women are by nature less intelligent than men but it would be a curious type of intelligence that allowed them to outperform the other sex at 16+ but not to do so at 18, and that ignored the fairly rapid closing of differences in achievement over the last few decades (see 7.3). Rejecting ability or intelligence differences between social classes and ethnic groups is less straight-forward, but no less necessary. As we have seen, part of the complexity arises from the fact that the performances of ethnic groups

197

vary considerably in relation to that of the majority. At the same time there is evidence that, in general, middle-class children perform better in the school and also on intelligence tests than do working-class children. There are also the claims of scientific racism, epitomized by the work of Jensen (1973) which argue that the performance of black ethnic groups is due to biological factors rather than social ones. The crucial question is whether or not there are social groups which have innately or genetically different levels of intelligence. Initial considerations are, then, what is meant by intelligence, and what is the relationship between that definition and IQ tests?

Any argument that middle-cass children perform better in school than working-class children because of superior genetic intelligence rests on several more than questionable assumptions. First, that the middle class is a readily identifiable and stable group. This is basically untrue. It has during this century grown at a rate, and in a manner, which cannot be accounted for by human reproduction (see Table 8.6). In fact the size and composition of social classes are determined by the structure of occupations in society and the occupational definitions used by social scientists to identify them. Further, the composition of classes is affected by social mobility into and out of them (see 8.6).

Second, the argument would assume that it is possible to distinguish between innate and environmental factors in intelligence. A pertinent question here is, where do environmental factors begin to affect, or interact with, the genetic structure of a human? At birth? No, since the environment of the foetus in the womb has already affected its development and is itself related to the incidence of certain characteristics. The moment of conception? What about the preconceptual environment of the sperm and egg? The problem of being unable to distinguish neatly between the innate and the environmental is linked to a third assumption concerning measurement. Obviously intelligence can be recognized only when it is expressed, and in order for that to take place learning must have occurred. Learning is not a spontaneous happening in human beings. Babies are born knowing how to suck but need to be shown where in order to survive. Hence, whenever measurement is made, it must include learning as well as, or rather than, the innate or unlearned. It would appear futile, then, to pursue the separate identification of the two contributory factors, since these are, for such purposes, inseparable. Note that it is not being claimed that innate factors are not involved, merely that they cannot be operationalized. Perhaps intelligence is best viewed as a potential which a baby has along with many others – for example, to reach a certain weight, strength and life expectancy. Whether these potentialities are realized, or rather to what extent they are, depends on environmental factors. If the baby is kept in a box, has its feet bound up, lives in an unhealthy environment or is fed incorrectly its performance will be affected. The same is true of intelligence.

A further assumption is that IQ tests measure a general capacity rather than something that is culturally produced or learned. Although a claimed strength of the tests is that they predict educational performance, although not particularly well, this could simply mean that they measure identical or similar things. Verbal tests clearly depend on knowledge of, and ability and willingness to use, language in particular ways, which are of course learned and vary culturally. Thus the fact that urban children perform better on such tests than rural children (or white than black) almost certainly points to environmental rather than innate differences. A further consideration here is that most tests have, for convenience, been standardized on urban school populations, and it would be easy to produce a test based on rural phenomena which would leave urban children baffled! Non-verbal tests work on the assumption that all children have the same familiarity with the manipulation of shapes, figures and blocks, etc. – more than a bold claim. Finally, test performance is normally dependent to some extent on speed, and can to an extent be improved by learning and practice.

It could be that real intelligence (not necessarily that which IQ tests test) is randomly distributed through society but that its application and expression in the form which shows up on tests is not. It is worth bearing in mind that psychologists tell us that intelligence, like many other genetic characteristics, returns towards the mean over generations. Very intelligent parents generally have children who are intelligent but not aggressively so – their IQ will be closer to the average for the population than that of the parents; similarly, but in the opposite direction, for the children of parents with low, but normal, intelligence.

The intention here is not to imply that psychologists are unimpressed with the interplay between innate and environmental factors. A very interesting, classical exposure of the importance of the environment on intellignce is that of Hebb (1949), who cites an experiment with white rats from the same litter bred from the same stock – that is, their heredity has been held constant – which were exposed to widely different environments. One group was put at birth into stimulating cages, full of things to do, the others into non-stimulating, plain cages. On maturity both groups were put into maze-solving situations (a common end for psychologists' rats!). The first group, as might be expected, performed much better than did the second. The experimenters then gave all the rats maze-learning instruction. Not only did the first group learn more quickly than the second, but the latter group never managed to match the performance of the first group. From the same stock, then, were produced 'intelligent' and 'unintelligent' rats. While there are dangers in translating 'facts' from rats to human beings, the possible relationship is there. Indeed, the initial differences can be accepted in the human case.

A further consideration must be of the whole concept of intelligence and ability in terms of its psychological as opposed to its everyday meaning. While it is true that the psychological view of intelligence – that it is measurable and fairly constant over time – has become part of the way we think of intelligence, this is a comparatively recent concept. In previous centuries the word 'intelligence' was used in a different sense – surviving today only in the armed forces – as knowledge. In times past, for example, people went to university to 'increase their intelligence' rather than as now 'because they are intelligent'. This is closer to how in everyday situations we 'recognize' intelligence – through people's actions and the display of their knowledge and/or experience. I used to sit in awe of the 'intelligence' of some of my university tutors as they dealt brilliantly with difficult questions in class. After a few years of teaching I realized my awe was of their experience, not their intelligence. Having been struck dumb by a question, I found an answer so that next time around it was a different story. Similarly, I may now appear more intelligent than when I started to teach, not for any change in my basic ability but because of the opportunities and time I have had to acquire knowledge together with an ability to display it. These experiences enable me, in some situations, to appear more intelligent than I would do otherwise.

Probably the most telling criticism that can be made in the present discussion is that even where 'ability' or intelligence is held constant social-class differences are still apparent and therefore remain to be explained (as we saw in 7.2). Kamin (1974) raised a further and important aspect, the cultural/political implications of belief in inherited ability differences. Having reviewed the empirical evidence on IQ he concluded:

There exists no data which should lead a prudent man to accept the hypotheses that IQ test scores are in any degree heritable. That conclusion is so much at odds with prevailing wisdom that it is necessary to ask, how can so many psychologists believe the opposite? The answer, I believe, is related to the second major conclusion of this work. The IQ test in America, and the way in which we think about it, has been fostered by men committed to a particular social view. That view includes the belief that those on the bottom are genetically inferior victims of their own immutable defect. The consequence has been that IQ tests have served as an instrument of oppression against the poor – dressed in the trappings of science, rather than politics.

Following an extensive survey of what they see as 'very imperfect' evidence on IQ differences between ethnic groups, Mackintosh and Mascie-Taylor (1985) conclude that the evidence is not compelling but points in the direction of IQ and school performance being the result of the same social factors in white and ethnic minorities. For example, they show that when social factors (parental occupation, income, family size, overcrowding and neighbourhood) are matched, differences in IQ between West Indians and whites are sharply reduced to inconsequential levels.

Similarly, the work of Stones and Bagley et al (Verma and Bagley 1979) on black minorities in Britain contradicts the ideas of Jensen, and leads to the conclusion that 'there are no intellectual differences between black and white children in British schools which cannot be accounted for by social factors'.

Our considerations then lead to the rejection of any idea that differences in the educational performance of social groups are the result of different levels of inherited ability or IQ. Put another way, explanations for such differing educational outcomes must be sought in social and not in individual terms. It is to the examination of social factors that we now turn.

## 7.9 Cultural approaches

This approach starts from the facts that different social strata display different cultures, or subcultures, together with differing levels of educational achievement, and leads to the investigation of cultural differences in order to identify those aspects related to educability. The basic modelling used, or employed, is that middle-class culture/home background enhances the educability of children, while working-class culture detracts from it. As we shall see, because of the class-relatedness of many of the variables used, an inherent danger in this approach is that it may simply re-measure social class differences.

### 7.9a POVERTY

The most obvious and fundamental difference between social classes is their relationship with social wealth, and there is a long history of the identification of poverty as a factor in educational achievement. Any contemporary neglect of poverty as a factor in social life and education appears to rest on the false assumption that poverty is an abject condition which has been almost entirely removed from our society. Anyone who harbours this view should read Townsend's (1979) comprehensive account of poverty in the UK, which estimated that around 3.3 million persons lived in households which

Social Stratification and Education

by the state's standards (based on supplementary benefit rates plus
housing costs) were in a state of poverty. It is also important to
appreciate fully that poverty is a relative and dynamic condition.
The poor may have got wealthier but the differences between poor
and rich have been sustained, while items once regarded as luxuries,
like baths, hot water systems, telephones and televisions, etc.,
quickly become so common as to constitute the basic necessities of
life in a society such as ours.

A comprehensive view of poverty and disadvantage is provided
by the NCDS which found that 6 per cent of British children
fulfilled all three criteria of disadvantage, in experiencing family
incomes low enough to receive supplementary benefit/free school
meals; homes which were overcrowded/lacked hot water systems;
families with one parent/five or more children. Such disadvantaged
children – only one in 25 of whom were middle-class – were, as a
group, less likely to have pre-school education and more likely to be
older starting school; to experience larger classes; to have parents
less likely to visit school; to experience poor levels of health; to be
absent more frequently from school; to receive lower behaviour
ratings from teachers; and to gain low maths and reading scores at
11 years – on average three and a half years behind the others
(Wedge and Prosser 1973). At the age of 16, those from families
receiving supplementary benefit or family income supplement
gained lower scores on standardized tests and higher deviant behaviour ratings from teachers, even when social class was held constant
(Essen and Ghodsian 1977). While these accounts catalogue some of
the main disadvantages of poverty in respect to education, we need
to keep in mind that disadvantage did not in itself explain lack of
attainment: some disadvantaged children were found at the highest
levels, while not all the low scorers were disadvantaged, and an
analysis of 40 factors revealed that in general terms those found to
be relevant to the educational attainment of *all* children were
similarly relevant to the disadvantaged.

This is in no way to dismiss poverty as an important, adverse
factor in educational achievement, any more than to fail to recognize that it exists predominantly among the semi- and unskilled
working classes, which contain relatively high concentrations of

ethnic minorities (Smith 1977). Not only may relative and actual poverty affect progress in school to 16+, but it is likely to be critically related to extending schooling beyond that age – for which there are no mandatory grants – or into further and higher education for which the inadequate grants also presuppose family ability and willingness to forego income, if not to provide extra support. This is to concentrate on costs in economic, rather than social terms (see 7.9b).

Poverty is an educational problem not only at the individual but also at the social level, since it is concentrated particuarly in inner city areas. This was clearly recognized by the government in the mid 1960s following the Plowden Report (*Children and their Primary Schools*, 1967) and DES circular 11/67 which stated, 'The government believe that better educational provision can, by compensating for the effects of social deprivation and the depressing physical environment in which many children grow up, make an important contribution to overcoming family poverty.' This led to the establishment of EPAs, involving elements of positive discrimination towards schools in socially deprived areas, with a view to the relief both of educational under-achievement and some aspects of poverty (for a review, see Robinson 1977). We take up the issue of educational and social ecology at 7.10.

## 7.9b LANGUAGE

### i *Social class*

Language, being at once an obvious cultural product – varying between and within cultures – and playing the key role in education, has received a great deal of attention from a wide spectrum of those concerned to explain educational performance. The field of sociolinguistics is clearly multidisciplinary (Trudgill 1974, Giles and St Clair 1979) and concerned with language as social behaviour in its social and cultural setting. We concentrate on the work of Bernstein because it is preeminently a sociological approach and has been particularly influential in British education and sociology. His considerable publications extend over more than two decades, during which his ideas have been modified and developed, aroused considerable controversy, and been misrepresented and over-simplified. The latter is a danger here, though we concentrate on his central statements which are readily available (Bernstein 1971, 1973, Hymes and Gumperz 1971).

In essence Bernstein has attempted to relate the social structure to educational achievement via language. An early realization of the difficulty of communicating with working-class children in formal classroom language, and the greater discrepancy between working-class scores on verbal and non-verbal IQ tests than middle-class, appear to have given rise to his concept of two linguistic codes – the *restricted* and the *elaborated*. Put as simply as possible, the restricted code is a form of speech that can be predicted by an observer; is basically simple, involving a limited range of alternatives; is descriptive and narrative rather than analytical and abstract; relies on a common understanding between speaker and listener; some of its meaning is implicit; and the manner and circumstance of speech are of importance as well as its content. In contrast, the elaborated code is more difficult to predict; is more complex, involving a wide range of alternatives; is analytical and abstract; does not rely on a common understnading of meaning; has an explicit meaning; and extra-verbal factors are of little importance to it.

Bernstein's thesis is that these codes are the products of distinctive social situations associated with social-class differences. In the case of the working class, it maintains that if the factors of similarity of occupation, status and residence, strong communal bonds, work relationships, little individual decision making in work, poor homes and little intellectual stimulus all come together, 'it is plausible to assume that such a social setting will generate a particular form of communication which will shape the intellectual, social and affective orientation of the children'. The resulting communciation or code will 'emphasize verbally the communal rather than the abstract, substance rather than the elaboration of processes, the here and now rather than the explanation of motives and intentions, and positional rather than people-orientated forms of social control.' Readers will recognize that he is referring to the restricted code and appreciate that the contrasting work, life and social situation of the middle class, by the same reasoning, give rise to the elaborated code.

It is important to understand what Bernstein is *not* saying. There is *no* claim that people speak the codes, any more than they speak grammar; both are underlying, abstract principles which regulate communication and generate speech (Stubbs 1983). *Nor* is there a claim that the codes are mutually exclusive or that they are the exclusive property of one social class. The restricted code arises wherever the culture of a group emphasizes *we* rather than *I* and occurs to reinforce social relationships and create social solidarity. Hence it is characteristic of many groups such as prisoners, adolescents, members of the armed forces, friends, and husband and wife. The elaborated code, in contrast, is found where the culture emphasizes *I* rather than *we*, whenever, that is, common identity and understanding cannot be anticipated. In general terms, then, *all* people have access to restricted codes, but parts of the working class do not have the same access to an elaborated code as do the middle class. As a simple illustration I may, according to the argument, switch from a restricted code over breakfast with my family to the elaborated with, say, my students at work; whereas, if I worked at a local factory or coal mine among people I had grown up with, I might stay within a restricted code. To recap, the linguistic codes exist to reinforce the social relationships of a group or situation, and they are related to that group's position within the social structure.

Bernstein does not rest his case on social class, stating that 'as the connection between social class and linguistic codes is too imprecise' it is necessary to make a further consideration, that of family role systems. He distinguishes between *positional families* in which decisions are made according to the formal status of a person's role (father, mother, child). Such a family system gives rise to 'closed' communication which is less likely to encourage the verbalization of individuals' differences, intentions and motives since they are prescribed by the family. Social control relies upon the relative power of the people involved rather than on speech. On the other hand, *person-orientated families* occur where decisions are made on the grounds of the psychological and individual differences of members rather than their formal status. This involves 'open' communication which is likely to encourage discussion rather than legislation and to support expression of the individual differences of members. Social control, here, will be through verbal elaboration. These ideas provide a complex theory involving a number of variables which can come together in any combination and in varying degrees. Bernstein maintains, however, that access to the codes is broadly related to social class – that is, there is a relationship between the working-class, positional family and the restricted code; between the middle-class, person-orientated families and the elaborated code. The theory allows for exceptions and variation. Some working-class families in non-traditional settings (through rehousing, employment, and so on) who move towards person-orientated family systems may also display movement towards the elaborated code. However, as Bernstein states, the literature strongly suggests that the traditional working-class family is of the positional type and that while the conditions now exist for more individualization of relationships it is not possible to claim that working-class culture has been eroded and replaced by middle-class culture.

The thesis is presented diagrammatically in Table 7.8; the vertical arrows are the expected links, the other arrows possible ones. As readers will appreciate from the table, the thesis is some way from a theory in the classical sense, while a further distraction is the absence of any detailed examples of the linguistic differences between the users of the two codes (Stubbs 1983). There are two further considerations. First, the codes reflect and in turn support differing views of the world. The restricted code is related to a view of the world as something which has to be responded to in which the subject (person) is passive. The elaborated code relates to a view of the world as something capable of being manipulated, where the subject is active. These can be seen as related to social-class differences in work situations and having consequences for attitudes towards and use of education (see also 7.9c). Second, the codes are about performance not competency – that is, language use, not language knowledge. They do not imply differences in vocabulary or even necessarily in understanding, but refer to differences in normal linguistic performance and usage.

## Table 7.8
### Bernstein's thesis of restricted and elaborated codes

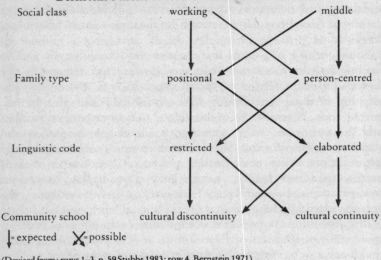

(Devised from: rows 1–3, p. 59 Stubbs 1983; row 4, Bernstein 1971)

Bernstein sums up the relationship between the codes and school performance:

> It happens, however, that this communication code [restricted] directs the child to orders of learning and relevance that are not in harmony with those required by the school. Where the child is sensitive to the communication system of the school and thus to its orders of learning and relation, then the experience of school for this child is one of symbolic and social development; where the child is not sensitive . . . then this child's experience . . . becomes one of symbolic and social change. In the first case we have an elaboration of social identity; in the second case, a change of social identity. Thus between the school and community of the working-class child, there may exist a cultural discontinuity based upon two radically different systems of communication.

This statement is sometimes taken to mean that Bernstein is implying that working-class children fail at school because of their restricted code. However, in reality he writes in terms of tendencies, not absolutes, and refers to 'different social and intellectual orientations and procedures despite a common potential'. As we shall see below, these considerations have serious implications for schools and teachers.

Some critics have argued that the code thesis has contributed to the relatively common view that the language and thought of the 'lower' classes suffers from verbal deprivation and that they are inferior, illogical and limited in comparison with those of the middle class. Edwards (1976) has argued that Bernstein has wanted it both ways – that at the same time as rejecting such criticisms he claims a profound educational disadvantage for restricted code users. Before commenting on the criticism it is as well to look in more detail at its substance. Labov (1969) is one of the best-known commentators to reject the superiority of Standard over non-Standard English.

His account is very detailed but his ideas are easily illustrated by two pieces of recorded speech. The first is by Larry, a loud and rough black gang member, who is asked what colour God is.

*Larry* He'd be white, man.
*Interviewer* Why?
*Larry* Why? I'll tell you why. Cause the average whitey out here got everything, you dig? And the nigger ain't got shit, y'know? Y'understan'? So – um – in order for *that* to happen, you know it ain't no black God that's doin' that bullshit.

The second is of a college-educated upper-middle-class black who is asked whether dreams come true.

*Charles* Well, I even heard my parents say that there is such a thing as something in dreams. Some things like that, and sometimes dreams do come true. I have personally never had a dream come true. I've never dreamt that somebody was dying and they actually died, (mhm) or that I was going to have ten dollars the next day and somehow I got ten dollars in my pocket. (Mhm) I don't particularly believe in that, I don't think it's true.

As Labov points out, and as will be obvious to readers, Larry's statement is a complex of ideas, orderly and effectively presented, even though its style may be unfamiliar and far removed from that of Charles. The latter's statement is much simpler but the language more conventional. In fact the full text (the above is only the first third) reveals that Charles uses words unnecessarily (verbosely), some modifying and qualifying, others repeating or padding the main argument. Our reaction to the two speeches is by way of a 'firmly fixed social convention' of preferences for one over the other. Of course we have no way of knowing how typical these two speakers are of their peers, but we do now have the suggestion that language codes or forms can be viewed both as inferior or superior to each other, depending on whether content or style is being considered. Certainly we must be impressed that they are different, as both Bernstein and Labov are. It is, however, fairly apparent that whether or not one code or form is intrinsically superior to the other is quite superfluous to the argument here because of the importance of the social setting of language use. As Labov writes, 'The initial impression of him [Charles] as a good speaker is simply our long-conditioned reaction to middle-class verbosity.' If, then, teachers and the educational system recognize Standard English or the elaborated code as the superior or the only acceptable form of expression, it follows that in this situation non-Standard English or the restricted code is viewed as inferior or unacceptable.

It would appear likely that that is how teachers in general do react; indeed they have been shown to have preferences for accents and dialects (6.5c). While there is a danger that some teachers may use the codes thesis to 'explain' the failure of some children in terms of their language, this would appear to be redundant to Bernstein's argument which is in basic agreement with that of Labov. Both recognize differences rather than deficiencies. The important contribution from Labov is the illustration of the dangers of assuming too much or too little about the thought, ideas and ability of a person from the 'appearance' of their language and speech.

It is now possible to turn this criticism of Bernstein around – instead of seeing his thesis as a criticism of the restricted code, to view it as one of schools and education. This is precisely what he has done by criticizing compensatory education (1969). 'If the culture of the teacher is to become part of the consciousness of the child, then the culture of the child must first be in the consciousness of the teacher'; or, as the DES would have it, the teacher 'should start where the child is and should accept the language he brings to school' (*A Language for Life* 1975).

There is, however, a distinct lack of knowledge as to the extent to which teachers and schools use or favour the elaborated code and the consequent process by which restricted code users are discriminated against or under-perform. While we do have indications that teachers control the language and language use in classrooms (5.5) and that there and in assessment and examinations Standard English is rewarded, the extensive and intensive classroom observation necessary to judge the importance of codes has yet to be undertaken on any scale. Bernstein's research team has concentrated on investigating the part played by the family and socialization in the development of the codes.

Finally, in common with many users of the term 'social class', Bernstein's work can be criticized for omitting any clear or precise definition. In many instances, he is careful to describe restricted code users as 'lower-working-class' or as inhabiting 'traditional working-class areas', and his treatment of the elaborated code users suggests the upper and educated end of the middle class. This, of course, leaves the majority of society outside the clear class categories of code users. While, as we saw in 7.2, the two groups identified are at the polar ends of the scales of social and educational achievement, such treatment clearly limits the explanatory power of the thesis. Explanation of the variable achievements of the large soft-centre of the social structure awaits better social class and code definitions, better class location of the codes and hence finer delineation of the relationship between the two. The present crudeness is, of course, conceded by the addition of certain factors: orientation of the family role system, the mode of social control and the resultant linguistic relationship. However, these do not provide a useful operationalization, since the measurement of such factors, if possible, would be laborious in the extreme.

To conclude, what Bernstein has provided is an intriguing and plausible association of factors which, while holding out the possibility of helping to explain the relationship between social class and education, awaits demonstration.

## ii *Ethnic minority*

Language differences are an obvious factor in the educational experience of ethnic minorities, especially among those whose native language or that of the home and community is other than English. While this applies to members of many groups, concern has centred almost exclusively upon Asian and West Indians, who face very different language situations, and whose performance in education is also differentiated (7.3). While many of our considerations in (i) above are relevant here, it is necessary to appreciate that the degree of language difference is not only greater, but also ranges from those whose English while fluent is a dialect such as West Indian Creole, which may interpose problems for teacher and pupil in terms of listening, interpreting, reading and writing, to those who have no, or very little, English, and whose own language is not only completely different but is written using a different script – which is true of some Asians (Taylor 1974).

In one sense the situation faced by many Asian children appears to be straightforward: in order to learn at school they first need to master English. This need is obvious to pupil, parents, teacher, school and LEA, and, as a consequence, fairly structured attempts are made to teach and learn it. Some LEAs, like Bradford, have run schemes aimed at ensuring that children about to enter school have a sufficient command of English to benefit from the experience. There has also been the development of specialist language courses and teachers, together with some experimentation in mother-tongue teaching. To judge by examination results (Table 7.7) such efforts appear to be successful in that overall 16+ results of Asian pupils match those of their white classmates, and a similar proportion pass in English language, though the percentage with a higher grade is somewhat lower at 21 compared with 29.

The language differences of West Indian children are of a different order and complexity. While ostensibly English-speaking, what Edwards (V.) (1979) has termed 'Creole interference' appears to play a crucial role in the relative under-performance of some West Indian children. Again, it needs to be stressed that there is a continuum from broad Creole through to Standard English, the use of which varies according to social class and the social situation of speech – in both the West Indies and Britain. While Creole and English share a good deal of vocabulary, they differ in grammar, sound, sentence construction and the meaning and use of words. As we have seen in (i) above, there is nothing to suggest that Creole, or any other language or dialect, is inferior, faulty or unstructured; but Edwards argues that, despite evidence to the contrary teachers commonly hold the view that West Indian pupils are inarticulate and non-verbal. She describes in detail, for which we lack the space, how Creole interferes in speech, comprehension, writing, grammar and reading, placing some pupils at a considerable disadvantage when instructed in Standard English. Unlike a foreign language, however, there is a lack of common recognition of a 'problem'. Consequently, and in some contrast to the case of the Asians, there is less, if any, effort by all involved to deal with it. As we have seen (6.5c), teachers may incorrectly apply stereotypes of lack of ability from the appearance of such language, and hence wrongly categorize West Indian pupils. Low teacher expectations and differential treatment are likely to lead to low performance. The process appears so effective that Edwards (1978) found that West Indian pupils tended to undervalue the speech and speakers of their own group. Experience of discrimination in school and society may be encouraging some West Indians consciously to re-adopt, or develop, their Creole (Troyna 1978).

However important and obvious language may be as a factor in educational attainment, two things are clear from our review. First, we have a long way to go in terms of research to a proper understanding of its role and to devise strategies aimed at enhancing the attainments of those whose language differs from Standard English. Second, and related to the first, there is a clear danger in treating language as if it were a free-standing factor. Clearly it is inter-related with a host of further cultural variables and only derives significance within the context of schooling where particular linguistic and cultural assumptions are made.

## 7.9c VALUES, ATTITUDES, INTERESTS AND ASPIRATIONS

The relationship between these factors and differing educational performance has been a traditional, if somewhat fragmentary, concern. A common sociological and everyday assumption is that a person's behaviour is affected by the values he/she holds relating to the situation in question. Such values are not invented by the individual but are clearly related to the social reality in which he/she is brought up and lives. As we have seen (4) such an approach shows that groups inhabiting the same position in a social structure or system share a common culture or subculture – a sort of corporate kit for survival in social life. Clearly, social classes and many ethnic minority groups can be viewed as subcultures. Squibb (1973) has shown how important it is to view subcultures in relation to each other. In other words, to see how, together, the various cultures in a society tend to give cohesion and stability to the social structure as a whole. Culture – through values – defines and legitimizes both one's own group's position, behaviour and relationship and that of others (this has been discussed with respect to education, see 4 and 8.5). It is also necessary to appreciate that the history or past experience of a group is a vital consideration in understanding its culture. A change in circumstances does not necessarily bring about a change in values or attitudes, while the latter may only be explicable in terms of the past. In the educational context, then, we can suspect that social class, ethnic and sex differences in social and educational experience – past, present and anticipated – are associated with differing values. Indeed we witness this throughout this book. That social-class differences in values exist is not in question. What must be discussed is whether such differences can be related to differing educational achievement, and, more important, whether they have any explanatory power.

It is possible to differentiate between *manifest values* – those relating directly to education – and *latent values* – those relating to areas which have only a tenuous or indirect relationship with

214

education. Similarly, the literature deals with parental and child values. While parental values are the most researched – note the parallel here with the greater research on teachers than pupils in 4 and 5 – they are clearly more problematic. In asserting the effect of values on behaviour we are assuming rather than demonstrating an influence, while probably ignoring intervening variables; in imputing effects of parental values on children's behaviour we are compounding that assumption. Further, there are quite severe methodological problems involved in identifying and measuring values, problems that much of the research has ignored or made light of. Similarly, as the title of this section indicates, it is concerned with a whole variety of factors which can only be very loosely referred to as values – though the term is used here for the sake of brevity.

*Manifest values.* There is a good deal of research that shows that parents of children who are successful in school take a greater interest in their education, visit school more often, provide greater encouragement, value education more highly, want them to have a better and longer education and have higher occupational aspirations, than do parents of less successful children. Such findings have a long and consistent history in the literature. To quote an influential large-scale government research survey:

> ... associations were found between social class and the responsibility and initiative taken by parents over their children's education, in the interest shown and support given by fathers over their education and upbringing, in the time and attention parents devoted to their children's development and in their interest in and knowledge of the work their children were doing at school. In respect of each of these factors the home situation was likely to be more favourable the higher the social class of the home (*Children and their Primary Schools* 1967).

In relating such factors to school performance the report concluded: 'The variation in parental attitudes can account for more of the variation in children's school achievement than either the variation in home circumstances or the variation in schools.'

Now, since social class is related to educational achievement, if achievement were related to certain parental values, then a potentially powerful explanation could have been identified. To work it would demand that the relationship was direct and causal, as follows:

Parental values $+ \rightarrow$ child's educational achievements $+$
Parental values $- \rightarrow$ child's educational achievements $-$

The value of this explanation would be that it might explain achievement variation not only between social classes and strata but also within them. Success at school would be due to having certain values, lack of success to being without them.

Such ideas need to be treated with caution, however, since this type of research has been severely criticized on a number of counts. First, it fails to see that the holding of values is a process. Values arise from cultural settings but they are also dynamic, being shaped and affected through experience, in this case by the child's educational experience. Bynner (1972) in her follow-up study to *Children and their Primary Schools*, shows that the marked social-class difference in aspiration is dependent partly on the fact that more middle-class children than working-class get into secondary schools which provide an opportunity for further education – since differences in parental aspirations were of the same order across the types of schools as across the social classes. Within NCDS, middle-class children were more likely than working-class ones to attend schools with established parent-school relationships (Davie et al 1972).

Finlayson (1971) challenged the suggestion that because parental attitudes were a better predictor of achievement than home circumstances there was hope that unfavourable attitudes might be affected, leading to an improvement in children's achievement. He sees a dynamic between the normative (initial parental attitudes) and the informational (feedback from the school). As parents gain more information, so their attitudes and aspirations 'get more realistic' – that is, more closely related to the child's actual performance. This appears a plausible explanation of the survey's finding that the strength of the relationship between parental attitudes and child's achievement was greater among children at the top end of primary schools than among those in infant schools. Clearly involved here are aspects of school organization, particularly ability-grouping. As Barker Lunn (1970) has demonstrated, streaming can affect parental aspirations in both directions, upwards for working-class parents with children of above-average ability and downwards for middle-class parents of average-ability children.

Second, there is some evidence that working-class parents are socially ill at ease in school and with teachers (Halsey 1972) and may avoid them for this reason rather than lack of interest; also that they have less knowledge of the system (Midwinter 1977 and see 3.4) or not share teachers' interpretations of children's activities and their value (Tizard et al 1981).

Third, as Acland (1980) has illustrated, the measures used often combine attitudes with circumstance (for example, family outings clearly involve both) and fail to consider differences in schools' efforts to involve parents. In re-analyzing the data he concludes that the independent effect of parental values was weak and uncertain.

Such concerns call for further research that is more sophisticated in a number of directions, mainly in being more detailed and truly longitudinal. On the parental side an obvious lack is our knowledge of their educational experience, both direct and indirect. We can suspect that people's valuation of education is related to their assumptions about its utility to them, their observations of its utility to others, and their anticipation of its value to their children. We also need more information about children's actual educational experience. Together with this we require an exploration of the mechanisms whereby experience and values are articulated and communicated and their relative effects on the people concerned – all this over the time span of a child's career in school. Such gaps in knowledge (and there are others) serve as a caution to the utility of most research to date based as it is on answers to bland questions – the answers to which may be socially affected – and on other gross assumptions.

Precisely the same observations can be made about the research findings on children's manifest values concerning education.

Briefly, these present much the same picture and have been illustrated earlier (see 4 and 5). Children who were successful, or in the process of being successful, in school, have been shown to value education more highly, be in greater accord with the school's regime and teachers' values, more diligent in study and behaviour and have higher educational and occupational aspirations, than their less successful peers. Here again we may question the methods and collection of this information and the causal direction of values. Are values the cause of achievement or the effect of it? At the moment it is only safe to accept that they are associated.

*Latent values*   are more general, perhaps more basic, and assumed to be culturally distributed and related to educational achievement. A commonly used conceptualization is that of Kluckhohn and Strodbeck (1961), who suggested five value orientations. Three of these have been used to investigate both parents' and children's values and relate them to educational performance. They are:

| | |
|---|---|
| ACTIVITY | passive ————— active |
| TIME | present ————— future |
| RELATIONS WITH OTHERS | famialistic ———— individualistic |

The right-hand column is that which, it is argued, corresponds to the middle class's value orientation and therefore to the assumption that such values are of benefit in educational situations. Value orientation is measured by questionnaires containing a number of statements to which people respond on a 5- or 6-point scale ('strongly agree' to 'strongly disagree', sometimes with a 'no view' category). Here are some examples:

ACTIVITY 'You must accept life as it is for there is nothing much you can do to alter things.' (disagreement equals active orientation)
TIME 'You have to give up having a good time now to do well later on.' (agreement equals future orientation)
RELATIONS WITH OTHERS 'Keeping in contact with friends and relations is more important than moving up in the world.' (disagreement equals individualistic orientation)

A survey of London secondary-school boys found high scores on the three value orientations (that is in the middle-class direction) related to school achievement (holding IQ constant) and teacher-rated conduct (Sugarman 1966). Interestingly enough, there was no significant relationship between the boys' values and their fathers' social class. Within each social class, however, the under-achievers (relative to IQ) were more often low value scorers and the over-achievers were more often high scorers. This fact was most striking in the working classes. In other words, Sugarman suggests, these values are middle-class in the sense that they separated out those boys who were bound, via school achievement, for middle-class jobs. Both this study, however, and that of Banks and Finlayson (1973) failed to find the relationship among grammar school pupils.

Sugarman claims that there is an association rather than a causal relationship between values and achievement, which presents three possibilities: achievement and conduct affect values; values affect achievement and conduct; all three are related to a further factor. His study supports the third possibility and identifies the factor as the 'intellectual quality' of the home – which principally affects values and, in turn, school achievement and conduct, though with intervening school and peer group factors.

Craft (1974) used these value orientations in Dublin, with the parents of a group of children, of whom half had left school at the minimum age and half had stayed on. The two groups were matched for ability, family size and sex, and all were working class and Roman Catholic. Those who stayed on had parents with higher value scores. Particularly important was the *time* orientation and mother's as opposed to father's values. Father low and mother high was much more likely to be associated with staying on than the reverse and in many cases was as effective as when they were both high. The scores similarly predicted the length of further and higher education.

Swift (1967) related parental mobility ideologies to children's performance at 11+ and the cohort was followed up to the age of 17 by Reid (1969). Mobility ideology was operationalized in three ways: (1) *Parental social horizons* – both working and middle-class parents of children who were successful at 11+ and 16+ wanted their children to have middle-class jobs. 'Successful' working-class parents' choices were more like those of the middle class than of working-class parents of unsuccessful children, though their choices included 'lower'-middle-class jobs not considered by middle-class parents. Of course it is likely that parental choice was affected by parents' knowledge of their child's performance at school to the age of 10. (2) *Parental social class identification* – those with successful children were much more likely to see themselves as middle-class than those with unsuccessful ones (at both 11+ and 16+). 'Successful' parents who did identify with the working class were more likely to see themselves as upper- rather than lower-working-class. (3) *Fathers' mobility pessimism* – measured by responses to questions like 'It is said that Britain is a land of opportunity and that people get pretty much what they are worth. Do you think this is true?' A negative answer was seen as pessimistic. Fathers' high pessimism was generally associated with their children's success at school. Such pessimism was more common in the working class, and it operated differently within each class. So while high pessimism in the working class was associated with success, in the middle class lack of pessimism was associated with lack of success. These differences almost certainly result from intervening variables related to the social situation and class location of fathers.

Of course, the effects of latent values – like any other kind – can only be appreciated when viewed in relation to those of schools and education. As Bourdieu (1974) among others has pointed out, it is because schools are a conservative force that education continues mainly to reward those with a particular cultural heritage (see also 9.1a).

### 7.9d EDUCATIONALLY SUPPORTIVE HOME AND ENVIRONMENT

The research critically reviewed in 7.9a to c has some very broad implications. Plainly and simply it forms the basis of, and is part of, the argument that the cultural and familial settings of some children, particularly but not only middle-class, provide for, or assist, them to take advantage of the educational system. Successful children, in the educational sense, can be seen as being variously socially equipped; for example, their language, values and attitudes are similar to those of the school, they are motivated to achieve and are well supported, materially and otherwise, in their efforts. Other children, lacking these background benefits, can be seen as disadvantaged. One relatively dangerous assumption to be avoided in this approach is that schools and education are passive – their success dependent upon what they receive in terms of appropriately equipped pupils. This might result in teachers being unaware and inactive in respect of their practice and institutions, accepting institutionalized constraints (see also 6.5). As we have seen, early research was concerned with poverty and material conditions and it has to be remembered that while it may be out of fashion to explore such factors they remain both real and relative aspects of peoples' lives in the 1980s. It may not be over-cynical to claim that factors like poverty, overcrowding, slums, and so on, became unpopular because, while their cure was obvious, society was unwilling to undertake it – much easier, one could argue, for society to concentrate research and effort on fairly nebulous factors which are difficult enough to describe and investigate let alone act upon.

It is also true, however, that the imprecision of predictions about educational outcomes based on any or all of these familial or cultural factors is likely to stem from one or more of the following:

- the lack of anything approaching complete knowledge of any real family social situations;
- an inability to identify, investigate or to measure the factors involved;
- a failure to appreciate the complex inter-relationships, compensations and contradictions, between factors.

All of these call not only for more, and more sophisticated research, but also for changes in thinking and in the application of both to practice.

### 7.9e CULTURAL DEFICIT OR DIFFERENCE?

Despite the cautions dealt with so far, the sort of evidence we have reviewed has given rise among some teachers and educators to the opinion that the unsuccessful in school are culturally deficient; that, for example, working-class and minority groups' culture are deficient in that they produce children who are incapable of, or handicapped in, becoming educated. As has been suggested, cultures are 'produced', exist in relation to given social situations and cannot be viewed as deficient with respect to those situations. To use a very extreme example, think about the likely features of the culture of the poor unemployed in a slum ghetto and then that of a rich middle-class academic ghetto in a residential college. While both are well related to their circumstances, neither would be much use in the other. They are clearly different but the differences are only really apparent and become crucial when they enter a common arena where one is recognized and rewarded more than the other – adults in court or children in school. If, in such arenas, the first culture is seen as deficient, it smacks of middle-class imperialism.

Refusing to recognize cultures as deficient but accepting that they are different is no mere tinkering around with words because of the implications. First, deficiency implies inferiority and consequently lack of respect or understanding. After reading this book readers might like to ponder on whether the fact that working-class parents have lower aspirations than middle-class parents for children of the same ability is due to cultural deficiency or whether it is not rather due to reasonable expectations arising from both social classes' knowledge of the social system in which they live. In other words, both are realistic and understandable in terms of cultural differences related to differing location in the social structure. Second, deficiency can imply educational responses aimed at making up what is assumed to be lacking, or, more extremely and disastrously, can lead to the acceptance that such a lack indicates the relative ineducability of such children and consequently the avoidance of serious concern. On the other hand, recognizing cultural differences could entail attempting to accommodate these in a real and meaningful sense in the organization, teaching and curriculum of schools and, indeed, in society at large. Nevertheless, given that schooling and examinations represent and reflect in large measure the dominant culture of our society, and are strongly related to occupation and hence lifestyle (see 8.2) there can be no doubt about the relative disadvantage of those whose cultural and familial background varies markedly from that traditionally rewarded.

## 7.10 Educational ecology, expenditure and resources

Explanations of differing educational attainment which depend on concepts of cultural differences tend to assume that educational provision is similar for, and in, all parts of our society. Here we question this assumption by examining the variation in the provision of education and educational outcomes, together with the relationship of these to the environment – what can be termed educational ecology. As we shall see it is easy to illustrate variation, relatively easy to relate such variation to social factors, but difficult to demonstrate a causal relationship between provision and/or resources and educational outcomes. Given the basic inequalities in our society and the decentralized nature of its educational system (for example, 104 LEAs in England and Wales alone), variation might be expected as inherent. It is then perhaps surprising that greater attention has not been paid to it. Our consideration here concentrates on social class, although similar analysis has been undertaken in respect of sex (Byrne 1975, 1978). Briefly, this revealed that the allocation of educational resources was biased in a variety of ways towards boys and that this can be seen as a factor in the different achievement of the sexes.

While there was some earlier interest in the subject, for our purposes we can start with the 1960s, when government interest in education was at its height. Four in five secondary schools in slum areas were revealed to be materially inadequate (*Half our Future* 1963) and inner city primary schools needed positive help (*Children and their Primary Schools* 1967 and see 7.9a). Wide variation in selective secondary school provision existed between LEAs and regions, and this did not reflect differences in the ability of children, according to standardized tests, or the availability of private schools (Douglas 1964). Provision was related to educational attainment, for example, working-class children in the south, with its superior selective school provision, had higher reading scores than those in the north; 4 per cent more received selective education, more were likely to stay on at school, and at each level of measured ability they obtained slightly higher grades in public examinations (Douglas et al 1968). So where one lived affected the type of school attended, which, together with variation within the type of school, affected educational experience and outcome.

The idea that the educational opportunity provided for children and their ability to take it up depended upon non-educational, environmental factors was explored using available official data by Taylor and Ayres (1969) who contrasted the north and south of England – 'the education split', as Taylor (1971) termed it. The contrasts may be summarized as follows: *Environmental factors of the family*: the north had higher rates of adult mortality, sickness and injury and, therefore, more one-parent families and those with chronically sick parents. There were fewer doctors and dentists in relation to population than in the south, and babies and children had poorer health. Its houses were older, more overcrowded, more often lacking in basic amenities and surrounded by greater dereliction. The south (with the exception of the south-west) had higher family incomes than the north. Standards of adult education varied similarly: in Tyneside 37 mothers in every thousand had received sixth-form education, but in Greater London the figure was 136; in Featherstone (Yorkshire) only 17 in every thousand mothers had left education at age 17 to 19, whereas in Hampstead, London, the number was 170. *Social structure and career opportunities*: the north had a higher proportion of semi- and unskilled and a lower proportion of professional and managerial workers than the south. It had higher rates of unemployment and a greater dependency on single industries. Job opportunities and high incomes were more limited in the north, leading to migration of the skilled and ambitious to the south. These factors were seen as important in affecting parental and child attitudes towards extended education. *LEA income and provision*: a measure of the wealth of an LEA is its rate income per child – computed by dividing the amount of money raised by a penny on the rates by the number of children. Comparison showed the poverty of the north mirrored by the prosperity of the south. Most northern LEAs were below and most southern ones above the national average. Despite government attempts to help the poor LEAs by support grants, Taylor and Ayres maintained that they lacked the resources to provide an average educational service, and yet in terms of need, they should have provided a higher level. The same LEAs tended to have more than their fair share of old schools because school building policy had been for 'roofs overheads' and these areas had had shrinking school populations. Consequently, the paucity of school buildings was related to old and overcrowded homes. *Educational outcomes*: in the north a smaller percentage than the national average stayed at school beyond the minimum age, while in the south the percentage was higher. The percentage of school leavers with 2 or more GCE A levels in the north was just short of the national average, in the south above. A smaller percentage of those in the north entered university and a slightly higher one went to colleges of education. In the north, university students were more likely to attend technological universities (reflecting their A level GCE choices) and less likely to go to Oxford or Cambridge than those in the south. Similar findings are also documented by Pratt et al (1973), and much the same remains true today. Such work once more leads us to see that the social structure is mirrored in the educational system.

## 7.10a SOCIAL CLASS VARIATION

There have been relatively few attempts to relate educational expenditure directly to social class, though an analysis of the 1973 GHS and DES data does just that (Le Grand 1982). From data on the social class use of educational services and service unit costs, it was estimated that classes 1 and II (20 per cent of the population) received 24 per cent of the expenditure, while classes V and VI (22 per cent of the population) received but 20 per cent. Calculating expenditure per person showed that those in social classes 1 and II received 40 per cent more than those in V and VI, even when the figures were standardized for age and sex. Such class bias in a public service expenditure may be surprising and disturbing, though a similar and perhaps even more alarming situation occurs in the NHS (Le Grand 1978). The education figures are likely to under-estimate the differences because they treat each unit of cost as equal. For example, secondary schooling was not separated into grammar, comprehensive and secondary modern, yet grammar schools were more expensive and attended by a higher proportion of middle-class children (see 6.2).

## 7.10b LEA VARIATION

Mainly because of its availability, data on educational variation between LEAs has received a great deal of attention (see also 6.2). As will be seen, such data has considerable limitations, and consequently poses problems in limiting explanations. Frequently published data concerns expenditure per pupil and pupil/teacher ratios. The expenditure per primary pupil in 1982/3 in England varied from £1,444 (ILEA) to £601 (Somerset) and that per secondary pupil from £1,633 (ILEA) to £828 (Wakefield) (CIPFA 1984). Primary and secondary school pupil/teacher ratios varied respectively from 18.5 and 14.7 for ILEA to 23.3 and 17.2 for Wiltshire. However, there is no apparent direct relationship between this range and educational outcome. For example, the two LEAs with the highest percentage of school leavers with five or more O levels or two or more A levels (average for 1980/3) were Harrow and Barnet, the two with the lowest, Newham and Knowsley (Hansard 1985b). Yet all these four LEAs had 'high' secondary pupil expenditures – Newham £1,215, Harrow £1,192, Barnet £1,127, and Knowsley £1,071. While, as we have seen in 7.2b, such differences are clearly related to the social composition of LEAs, there is a whole series of factors related to LEA expenditure and its role in educational achievement. Before looking at some of the specific research it is necessary to outline the main limitations of the data. First, there is some discussion as to whether the data is collected on strictly comparable bases. Second, it is clear that costs vary, for example, cost of employing teachers are related to turnover since they are paid on incremental scales; sparsely populated areas incur high costs in respect of travel and/or those related to small schools; London in particular, but inner cities in general, have higher property and services costs (London teachers are paid a weighting) and face particular problems. Third, expenditure changes from year to year and this may be related to rising or falling numbers and to policy decisions.

The work of Byrne et al (1975) takes us away from the mainly descriptive analysis we have so far dealt with. They propose a 'socio-spatial model of educational attainment', based on Weber's ideas of class (see also 8.5b). Social classes are viewed as relationships between groups that are differently placed in terms of rewards in society; relationships between them are those of control and domination via power, varying from direct control to the manipulation of symbols, concepts and ideas. Rewards are spatially distributed, and can be viewed as reflecting the distribution of income in society – which is broadly defined to include the provision and range of public services (including education). Their argument is that educational attainment is a product of the distribution of power and resources in society rather than the distribution of intelligence. They identify as the most important factors social class background; local environmental factors; and LEA policy, resources and provisions, which they analyze in respect of educational attainment. Their statistical analysis of official data, cautiously presented, indicates an interaction between these factors. They argue that differences in 'school system inputs' are important in explaining social class differences in attainment and that 'there is a systematic relationship between the class background of an area and the educational resources available. In general, the higher the social class composition of an area, the better the provision.'

Somewhat contrasting findings arise from the study of primary school expenditure and socio-economic factors by Howick and Hassani (1979), who argue that overall 'the result suggests that spending does tend to be higher in areas suffering from adverse conditions . . . associated with inner city deprivation rather than traditional working class areas'. However, they do not claim that this indicates positive discrimination or say whether such spending compensates for the adverse conditions, or whether it is the result of higher costs. They conclude that need and political affiliation are related in London LEAs, and to a lesser extent in Metropolitan districts, but not at all in Shire counties. Very similar findings were made for LEA secondary school expenditure, 'only in London is there convincing evidence that educationally disadvantaged pupils are likely to receive slightly higher expenditure' (Howick and Hassani 1980).

The influence of local politics on LEA expenditure was explored by Boaden (1971), who found that in the 1960s Labour-controlled LEAs had higher levels of spending, which were not accounted for by their higher proportions of working-class residents. Hence, this would appear to reflect a policy priority in respect of education. However, Howick and Hassani viewed the changed political scene of the 1970s and found this relationship to have weakened considerably.

It is clear, however, that LEA policy on items over which they have discretion shows wide variation and may have critical consequences. A good example is the Educational Maintenance Allowance, introduced in 1944 to enable, or help, children of poor parents to stay on at school. By 1971 the average EMA was £72 – the equivalent to half that originally recommended ranging from £123 in East Sussex to £18 in Burton-on-Trent; the payments were received by nearly 17 per cent of those over school leaving age in West Suffolk and 0.4 per cent in Reading; and they had been heard of by only a third of parents of 15–18 year olds (Townsend 1979). The total cost of awards was £1.4 million, compared with £16 million then spent by the LEAs on boarding children in independent and direct grant schools (Reddin 1972). A pilot scheme for nationally financed EMAs, comparable to supplementary benefit payments, was put forward by Labour in 1978, but abandoned by the Conservative Government in 1979. Williams (1980) commented, 'We will not, therefore, know how many boys or girls capable of more advanced education have been precluded by financial considerations, but the figure almost certainly runs into tens of thousands.'

A further example with dramatic differences is LEA expenditure on books and other equipment which is regularly surveyed. In 1982/3 the average expenditure in England and Wales per pupil on such items was £37 in secondary and £21 in primary schools. Secondary school per pupil expenditure ranged from £86 in ILEA and £55 in Waltham Forest (London) to £16 in Wakefield and £12 in Leeds. Primary school per pupil expenditure ranged from £47 in ILEA and £35 in Waltham Forest to £9 in Leeds and £8 in Merton (London) (CIPFA 1984).

An important but less well-researched approach looks at provision and expenditure within, rather than between, LEAs. King (1974) surveyed an anonymous LEA in the south of England and found that schools serving working-class areas had lower attainments than middle-class ones, but more favourable pupil/teacher ratios, greater CSE examination opportunities, and more stable staffs. A study of the London Borough of Newham in the 1970s found 'significant disparities of provision, and points to important relatedness between these and social circumstances' (Tunley et al 1979). Indices of deprivation from census data were applied to the catchment areas of schools and related to teacher 'quality' measures (based on teacher/pupil ratios and the number of senior posts) and expenditure measures, to test whether the poorest children attended the poorest schools. No such relationship was found in data for 1973/4, but there was a change in this direction in 1976/7. The authors argue that if resourcing is a vital element, then some use of a social index of schools' catchment areas would assist in sustaining a balance. They also draw attention to the implications of allocating school finance according to the age-structure of pupils, since those with the largest sixth forms and resources are attended by advantaged rather than disadvantaged children. However LEAs are constrained, of course, by a national framework in which school resources are age-biased, and sixth forms are expensive.

7.10c WHO REALLY GETS WHAT?

Our considerations so far have illustrated variation in educational provision and suggested something of its role in educational attainment and its potential in explaining social class differences. At the same time we have seen a lack of clarity and some inconsistencies in the evidence. Much of this arises from the use of crude variables, officially produced for purposes other than educational research. On the one hand, studies have used areal census measures of social class/disadvantage rather than those relating to pupils' parents. On the other hand, they have treated educational expenditure as being the global property of an LEA or school rather than that of particular groups of pupils. A further assumption is that resources come from LEAs, whereas in fact some schools receive additional resources from PTAs and parents. Since ability and willingness to so contribute clearly varies, such resourcing constitutes a further and currently growing source of inequality. Hence it is almost impossible to see who receives what, and where. To get nearer to this we should need much more sophisticated studies, especially investigations into the resources received by different types of pupil within schools. At present we are more informed by assumptions than knowledge. It may be, for example, that the deployment of staff, facilities and curriculum means that resources/costs per secondary school pupil decline with ability down to but not including, the remedial level, and follow the status hierarchy of the curriculum (4.5), which in turn reflects social class, sex and ethnic group differences; but this has yet to be explored on any scale.

There are some marked similarities between poverty (7.9a) and educational resources. So it is important to appreciate that the way in which people perceive resources, and indeed opportunities, is vital to how they are used and to outcomes. People similarly located may well vary from feeling relatively deprived to more than satisfied. Such reactions have to be seen in a cultural context which is dynamic and which shapes expectations. In the past teachers taught, and pupils learned, writing using slates but few would attempt it without paper today – while some might see a classroom as under-resourced because of the lack of a microcomputer! There are those (but very few of them teachers) who would use such arguments, together with the lack of a clear educational improvement subsequent to increased resources, to claim that resources are relatively unimportant. However, this would be to ignore the fact that, to date, British efforts at equalization or positive discrimination have been small-scale, under-financed, short-term and piecemeal. To tackle educational disadvantage in a meaningful way would require real positive discrimination in a sustained programme ranging across the whole of schooling, well coordinated and properly evaluated. A twist has been given to the situation in the 1980s where there is general agreement that educational expenditure has been cut – in some cases drastically – at the same time as demands have grown, to the dismay of many teachers, pupils and parents.

## 7.11 Schools and Classrooms

A third distinctive potential avenue for the explanation of differential educational performance lies within the arenas of direct, educational activity. Here it would be appropriate to illustrate how the organization and institutions of schools and classrooms, together with the interaction of staff and pupils, come together to differentiate pupils in terms of their ability, their performance, and along lines of social stratification. This is fully covered in 3–6, and not rehearsed here. However, it is important to appreciate that schools and classrooms do not simply receive and process input from outside – whether these be culturally differentiated pupils of varying educability, a structured curriculum, examinations, a system of education or resources to work with. They play an active as well as an interactive role in respect of all of these. While school and classroom are typically viewed as assisting in the production of socially unequal educational attainment, this is far from inevitable – as some prove. In many ways their position and influence put them in the prime position to affect it, not change, the educational life chances and styles of those who pass through them.

## 7.12 Models of educational attainment

It is useful to review the contents of this part of the book through the development of a series of models. We started with a look at the relationship between social stratification and educational attainment (7.1 to 7.6), recognizing social class as the fundamental form. Here we concentrate on class and, consequently, can start with the simple, oft-quoted and descriptive model:

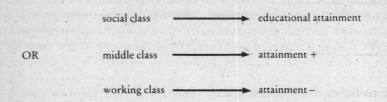

It is obvious, however, that class is in itself no explanation. Our initial approach to explanation was in terms of socio-cultural variables (7.9), those aspects of class which can be seen as related to educational attainment, hence:

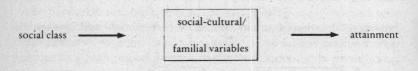

Much work in this area suggests either that the classes are related to differing socio-cultural/familial variables (7.9bii) or that such variables operate in differing ways in each class (7.9c). So a better model would be:

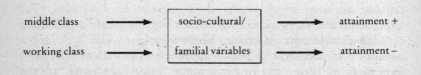

In 7.10 we saw the importance of the socio-economic-material environment and educational resources and policy, adding a further dimension:

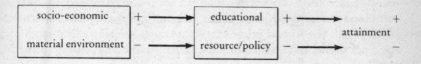

Finally, in 7.11 we recognized once more the important role of school and classroom in the whole process, so our final model is complex:

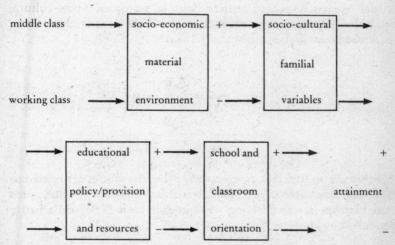

This model helps to clarify the approaches involved, although it remains an over-simplification in a number of directions. The approaches are not as self-contained as it suggests, and most contain or allow for elements of others. There is no particular logic in the order of presentation, and like the approaches themselves there is no indication of their relative importance. Most important, all the approaches display a lack of clear demonstration of the *direct* relation they have with attainment. Rather, and together, they present an identification of the promising avenues for a proper understanding and explanation. In particular, a serious short-coming of the field is the lack of an understanding of the relative importance of the environmental and socio-cultural/familial factors as opposed to school-based ones. To answer that, we should need research which combined the type of large-scale, longitudinal survey used in the NCDS with the sort of school factor analysis we viewed in 4.9. So any final model or conclusion must remain somewhat tentative and open.

# 8

# Education, Occupation and Mobility

## 8.1 Life after school

Here we trace the consequences of educational experience and achievement in their most obvious form, in life after school. While education appears to be about a whole variety of things in life – according to some people, it's about everything – a very important factor is that of occupational preparation. A common, traditional selling line of teachers is to tell pupils that they should work hard and get on in school in order to get a job which pays well, has security, offers prospects and is generally worthwhile. Apart from the fact that it is true, it is a strange sales line. It could mean that the intrinsic appeal of the curriculum is so limited that it needs the additional motivation of long-term gains to be at all palatable; or that the message has elements of moral deferred gratification in it – who foregoes present pleasure in order to succeed at school will be rewarded in occupational life. Massive unemployment in the 1980s has probably only modified this sales line, see 8.2b. Parents and pupils often have a similar faith (positive or negative) in the educational system, while politicians have supported immense budgets in the belief that the long-term health of the economy and politics depends on education.

The importance of occupation in our society goes far beyond the type of job a person does. As I concluded in a review of data on social differences:

We can state that middle-class people [those who have non-manual jobs], in comparison with the working class [those with manual jobs], enjoy better health, live longer, live in superior homes with more amenities, have more money to spend, work shorter hours, receive different and longer education, and are educationally most successful, marry later in life, rear fewer children, attend church more frequently, belong to clubs more often, have different tastes in the media and the arts, are politically more involved – to mention only a few examples (Reid 1981).

In other words, occupation and hence to some extent education is about life chances and lifestyle. This must be viewed in a cultural value set which clearly suggests that the middle-class (non-manual) way of life is superior to, and more desirable than, the working-class one. Although this, being a value judgement, is open to debate, it appears to be at the base of many assumptions within education and people's attitudes towards it. We can also expect that variations within the classes are as great as those between them; within the working class skilled jobs and in the middle class professional jobs are likely to be the most highly sought after. This is one way in which the belief in the importance of education for occupational placement is constantly witnessed, and its importance is seen too in ideas of democracy, equality and opportunity. A cosy, and for society useful, view of our society is that jobs, lifestyles and so on are open (available) to all providing they are capable and/or have the qualifications. In this way education becomes a major legitimizer not only in the sense that this person has job A because he/she has X qualifications but also in that, since all have access to education, so too they all have access to all occupations. The over-simple assumptions here will already be clear to readers and are again examined below with regard to the role(s) of education in relation to occupation.

Our first concern is to establish the extent and nature, mainly in quantitative terms, of the relationship between educational qualification, occupation and income, and to explore something of the explanation of that relationship. Our second concern is related to the first and to the content of 7. Since, as has been seen, there exists a relationship between parental social class and children's educational performance, the other side of this relationship is now explored. What is the role of education in affecting the relationship between parents' and child's occupation, and what is its role in job-changing in adult life?

## 8.2 Education, occupation and income

As has been suggested, an important, though by no means the only, role of education is to equip a person for an occupational role in society. In other words the educational system can be seen as providing suitable candidates for the occupational structure of society. While such relationships may seem obvious to most readers, it is necessary to establish their existence and to explore something of their nature and extent. The first step is to look at the available data.

### 8.2a EDUCATION AND OCCUPATION

Clearly everybody accepts that some occupations are open only to people who have particular educational qualifications, especially, for example, the professions (doctors, lawyers, accountants, and so on). However, our present concern is with the complete and general picture. Potentially, the broadest view of the relationship between education and occupation is from the census. However, the last data published was from the census of 1961 (*Education Tables* 1966 and Reid 1977a, 1981), the data for 1971 was never published and questions on education were dropped from the 1981 census. In any case, the 1961 data merely related length of education to occupation and showed in general terms that the 'higher' the occupation, the longer the length of education. More up-to-date and useful data in respect of educational qualifications held is provided by GHSs. Data from those of 1981 and 1982 appears in Table 8.1 and shows that the higher the occupational category, the smaller the percentage of persons without formal educational qualifications and the larger with such qualifications. Generally speaking, the holders of higher educational qualifications (the top two rows) are almost exclusively employed in non-manual occupations. This pattern is starkly revealed in the figures relating to men: 90 per cent of those in

## Table 8.1

Educational qualification* and occupational category**, Great Britain 1981/2† (percentages)

|  | Occupational category* | | | | | | |
|---|---|---|---|---|---|---|---|
|  | 1 | 2 | 3 | 4 | 5 | 6 | *All* |
| **Males‡** | | | | | | | |
| 1 Degree or equivalent | 73 | 13 | 14 | 0 | 0 | 0 | 9 |
| 2 Higher education below degree | 17 | 15 | 20 | 4 | 1 | Nil | 9 |
| 3 GCE A level or equivalent | 3 | 11 | 12 | 7 | 3 | 2 | 8 |
| 4 GCE O level/CSE higher grades or equivalent | 2 | 18 | 17 | 12 | 6 | 2 | 12 |
| 5 GCE/CSE other grades/ commercial/apprenticeship | 0 | 10 | 7 | 19 | 10 | 5 | 12 |
| 6 Foreign or other | 4 | 5 | 5 | 3 | 4 | 1 | 4 |
| 7 No qualifications | 1 | 28 | 25 | 55 | 76 | 90 | 46 |
| Occupational % of sample | 6 | 18 | 17 | 40 | 15 | 4 | 100 |
| **Females‡** | | | | | | | |
| 1 Degree or equivalent | § | 6 | 6 | 1 | 0 | Nil | 4 |
| 2 Higher education below degree | § | 15 | 16 | 3 | 1 | 0 | 9 |
| 3 GCE A level or equivalent | § | 6 | 4 | 2 | 1 | 0 | 3 |
| 4 GCE O level/CSE higher grades or equivalent | § | 19 | 21 | 13 | 7 | 3 | 15 |
| 5 GCE/CSE other grades/ commercial/apprenticeship | § | 11 | 14 | 11 | 7 | 6 | 11 |
| 6 Foreign or other | § | 6 | 4 | 4 | 3 | 3 | 4 |
| 7 No qualifications | § | 37 | 36 | 66 | 81 | 87 | 54 |
| Occupational % of sample | 0.8 | 7 | 50 | 8 | 24 | 11 | 100 |

* For definition see 10.2
** For definition see 10.3; 3, 4 and 5 refer to one or more.
† Data for the two years combined.
‡ Economically active, aged 25–69, not in full-time education.
§ Very small numbers: 58, 6, 3, 0, 1, 4, 1, respectively; total 73.
N = 12,352 males; 8,623 females.

(Devised from Table 7.9(a), *General Household Survey 1982* 1984.)

professional jobs have higher education, while 90 per cent of those in unskilled manual occupations have no educational qualifications. There is also a fairly clear divide between non-manual (1–3) and manual (4–6) workers, the majority of the former having qualifications at, or above, GCE O level; the majority of the latter not having any qualifications. Note that managers and employers (2) are slightly less well-qualified than the other non-manual workers (3). A similar picture is present in the figures for women, although the number of them following professional occupations (1) is too low for conversion into percentages (see footnote to table).

In comparing the figures for males and females stark differences can be noted between the sexes in respect of both educational qualifications and occupation. The overall relevant figures are reproduced in Table 8.2. At the occupational extremes, this table shows that 6 per cent of males and 0.8 per cent of females had 'professional' occupations, and 4 per cent of males and 11 per cent of females had unskilled manual jobs. Women are more likely to have non-manual occupations (one in two are in 'other non-manual'), whereas men are more likely to be in manual occupations (two in every five were in the 'skilled manual' category). At the educational extremes, 9 per cent of males were graduates compared to 4 per cent of females, while 46 per cent of males and 54 per cent of females had no formal educational qualifications. Note, however, that the educational performance of females has improved markedly in comparison to that of males over the past two decades, see 7.3 and Table 7.6.

### Table 8.2
Differences between education and occupation of males and females*, Great Britain 1981/2† (percentages)

| Educational qualification‡ | 1 | 2 | 3 | 4 | 5 | 6 | 7 |
|---|---|---|---|---|---|---|---|
| Male | 9 | 9 | 8 | 12 | 12 | 4 | 46 |
| Female | 4 | 9 | 3 | 15 | 11 | 4 | 54 |

| Occupational category§ | 1 | 2 | 3 | 4 | 5 | 6 |
|---|---|---|---|---|---|---|
| Male | 6 | 18 | 17 | 40 | 15 | 4 |
| Female | 0.8 | 7 | 50 | 8 | 24 | 11 |

* Economically active, aged 25–69, not in full-time education.
† Data for the two years combined.
‡ For definition see Table 7.1, left-hand column.
§ For definition see 10.2.

(Derived from table 7.9(a), *General Household Survey 1982* 1984.)

Apart from confirming that there is an overall relationship between education and occupation, the data presented reveals some inconsistencies. Some one per cent of male 'professional' workers had no educational qualifications and, at the opposite end, a few (less than 0.5 per cent) of unskilled manual workers held degrees. The conclusion must be that while there is a very strong relationship between education and occupation it is not absolute. For example, not all of those with higher education qualifications have non-manual occupations, nor are these jobs undertaken exclusively by the holders of such qualifications. This situation is due to changes in the occupational structure and educational opportunities over time, the relationships between them, and to the importance of factors other than educational qualifications in getting and keeping a job.

## 8.2b EDUCATION AND UNEMPLOYMENT

The first half of the 1980s witnessed sustained and dramatic growth in unemployment, with the figures for those out of work reaching between 3 and 4 million, depending on who did the counting. This led to questioning of the assumptions concerning the relationship between education and occupation, especially as school leaver unemployment rose particularly sharply and induced government action by way of YOP and YTS schemes. Consequently, it became pertinent to review the relationship of education to unemployment as well as to employment.

The survey of Scottish school leavers entering the employment market in 1980 (Main and Raffe 1983) showed that the best qualified were most likely to secure employment (79 per cent), while less than half (45 per cent) of those without qualifications were employed. While graduate and professional unemployment received a good deal of media attention, their rates compared favourably with the less well qualified. The *Labour Force Survey 1983* revealed that proportionately more of the unemployed were without educational qualifications (52 compared with 41 per cent of the employed) and fewer had any form of higher education (6 compared with 15 per cent). Among those aged 16–19 years in the labour force, educational qualifications were even more starkly related – 44 per cent of the unemployed and 24 per cent of the employed were without qualifications. Further, direct evidence is provided by the *General Household Survey 1981* (1983). In the age group 20–9 years, those with higher education or A level GCE qualifications had an unemployment rate half that of the whole group, and they were almost four times less likely to be unemployed than those without qualifications (7 compared with 27 per cent, the overall percentage of unemployed being 14). At ages 30–9, differences were more extreme: those without qualifications had an unemployment rate 15 times higher than those with higher education. Hence we can conclude that educational qualifications provide a buffer against unemployment, a relationship which appears unaffected by YOP and YTS schemes, since employers sponsoring them used similar recruitment criteria to those used for permanent jobs (Barry and O'Connor, 1983).

It is also clear that social stratification is related to unemployment. *The Labour Force Survey 1983* showed the rounded overall rate for females to be lower than that for males (10 compared with 12 per cent) and showed dramatic differences between ethnic groups. For example, male unemployment ranged from 12 per cent for whites to 28 per cent for West Indian/Guyanese, with Indian/Pakistani/Bangladeshi at 22. It is not possible to display the precise role of education in these differences, but there is a clear relationship with social class. The risk of unemployment among unskilled manual workers is some six times higher than for non-manual workers, and they also experience longer spells of unemployment (Smith 1980).

## 8.2c EDUCATION AND INCOME

In all societies occupations are differently rewarded, and so we would expect that education is related to income via occupation. In our society there are large variations in income within the same occupation. Schoolteachers, for example, could earn between £5,442 and £13,395 in 1983; deputy heads up to £16,689 and headteachers up to £22,941. Similar differences occur in many other jobs, and it is useful and interesting to look in a general and direct way at education and income. Table 8.3 shows the median earnings in 1982 of holders of various educational qualifications by sex. Median earning is that amount which splits the whole range of earnings so that half the persons in the group earn more and half earn less than this amount. The table reveals the higher the educational qualifications the higher the earnings. Male degree holders earned 76 per cent more than males without qualifications while the figure for females was 101 per cent. Overall, there is a strong relationship between qualifications and earnings, though not a complete one – not all holders of educational qualifications earned more than those without, nor were all high income earners holders of qualifications. The table also reveals distinct differences between the sexes. At each educational level women earned less than men. Overall, women's median earnings were 67 per cent of men's, although women with higher educational qualifications had earnings somewhat closer, at 74 and 81 per cent (see right-hand column). Only part of the overall

### Table 8.3
Median weekly earnings* of males and females†‡ holding given educational qualifications§ in 1982

|  | Male | Female | Female as % of male |
|---|---|---|---|
| Degree or equivalent | 204 | 151 | 74 |
| Higher education below degree | 160 | 130 | 81 |
| GCE A level or equivalent | 139 | 94 | 68 |
| GCE O level/CSE higher grades or equivalent | 133 | 88 | 66 |
| GCE/CSE other grades/commercial/ apprenticeship | 122 | 82 | 67 |
| None | 116 | 75 | 65 |
| All | 131 | 87 | 67 |

* In pounds sterling; for definition of median see text.
† Aged 20–69, employed for 31 hours or more per week (26 hours or more for teachers/lecturers) including paid overtime.
‡ Females were younger on average than males (37 cf. 40) and worked fewer hours per week than men (38.6 cf. 43.2).
§ For definitions see 10.3
** Including foreign and other qualifications.

(Derived from table 7.15, *General Household Survey 1982* 1984.)

sex earning difference is explained by the fact that women worked less hours and were slightly younger (see footnote to table). More of the difference is accounted for by the different occupations (with different levels of income) followed by the sexes – what amounts to sex segregation in employment (see Hakim 1979, Reid 1981).

The differing age structure and deployment of men and women in the same occupation produces earning differences despite equal pay. For example, the average earnings of male teachers in maintained schools in 1983 was £9,014 and for females £7,857 (*Education Statistics for the United Kingdom 1983*). This difference reflects the male predominance in secondary as opposed to primary schools (the former having more and better paid posts of responsibility) and among head and deputy head teachers. As in the last section it can be seen that the relationship, while strong, is not complete. Blaug (1970) states that a relationship between education and income has been demonstrated in thirty countries.

It is now necessary to place both education and occupation in an historical perspective, since they, and the relationship between them, are essentially dynamic.

## 8.3 Changing educational attainments

The history of education in Britain, as elsewhere, has been one of increasing provision and attainment. A number of indicators might be used to illustrate these changes, but we concentrate on school leaving qualifications and entry into further and higher education. A long-term view of school-based achievement is difficult because of changes in the examinations, from School Leaving Certificate to GCE and CSE. Further, the access to sit examinations has been changed not only by the introduction of free secondary education in 1944 and comprehensive schools, but also by changes in the underlying philosophy – first, that secondary modern children should sit examinations and, second, that it is worth taking a few, or even one subject only, rather than entering for the full range of subjects. Given these strictures, probably the most illustrative figures for our purposes are the changes in the attainment of school leavers since the introduction of GCE and CSE. Table 8.4 shows that the percentage gaining five or more O level GCE/equivalents increased by about two and a half times (11 compared with 27 per cent) between 1954/5 and 1982/3, and that for one or more A level GCE by almost three times (6 compared with 17 per cent) over the same period. More detailed data relating to the highest achievement of UK school leavers is provided in Table 8.5. The combined effect of the introduction of CSE and the raising of the school leaving age to sixteen years (in 1972/3) was that the percentage leaving without any qualifications (67 per cent in 1963/4) fell dramatically to only 13 per cent in 1981/2. While the percentage leaving with matriculation (two A level GCE/ three H level SCE, or more) rose from 11 to 15 per cent between 1965/6 and 1981/2, it is clear that the largest increases were of those with lower level achievements – the percentage of those with one to four higher grade passes grew from 15 to 26 and those with any other grade passes from 0 to 32 per cent. Note that these figures relate only to school leavers and, consequently, do not include the sizeable number gaining such qualifications in further education establishments.

**Table 8.4**
Percentage* of school leavers† gaining A level
and five O level GCEs or equivalents

|  | 1954/5 | 1963/4 | 1974/5 | 1982/3 |
|---|---|---|---|---|
| 1 or more GCE A level | 6 | 10 | 15 | 17 |
| 5 or more GCE O level or equivalent‡ | 11 | 17 | 22 | 27 |

\* Percentages are rounded.
† England and Wales; figures for 1982/3 are for England only.
‡ Includes CSE grade 1 for 1974/5 and 1982/3; for last year higher grades only.

(Devised from Table 22, *Statistics of Education 1964*, Vol. 3; Table 22, *Statistics of Education 1975*, Vol. 2 and data from DES 1985.)

## Table 8.5

Percentage* of school leavers by highest qualification† held,
United Kingdom

|  | 1965/6 | 1970/1 | 1975/6 | 1981/2 |
|---|---|---|---|---|
| 2 or more GCE A level/<br>3 or more SCE H level | 11 | 14 | 13 | 15 |
| 1 GCE A/1 or 2 SCE H | 3 | 4 | 4 | 4 |
| 5 or more GCE/SCE O level/CSE,<br>higher grades *only* | 8 | 8 | 8 | 10 |
| 1 to 4 GCE/SCE O level/<br>CSE higher grades | 15 | 18 | 25 | 26 |
| 1 or more GCE/SCE O<br>level/CSE other grades | 63 | 10‡ | 31‡ | 32 |
| No qualifications |  | 46‡ | 19‡ | 13 |
| Number of leavers | 725 | 717 | 823 | 913 |

* Percentages are rounded.
† For definitions see 10.3.
‡ Based on data for Great Britain.

(Devised from Table 29, *Education Statistics for the United Kingdom 1984*.)

Even more dramatic has been the growth in higher education. At the turn of this century 0.8 per cent of the relevant age group in Britain attended university, and by 1962 this had increased to 4 per cent (*Higher Education* 1963). There followed a considerable expansion of higher education, with the creation of new universities and the polytechnics. By 1980/1 the age participation rate for higher education was 12.5 per cent. Between 1962 and 1981 the number of full-time higher education students in Britain rose from 190,000 to 467,000 and part-time students rose from 115,000 in 1962 to 259,000 (including nearly 70,000 Open University students) in 1978/9 (Farrant, 1981). In 1982/3 there were 273,000 home students in UK universities, 249,000 in other higher educational institutions (a 19 per cent increase from 1980/1) and 305,000 part-time higher education students (an 85 per cent increase from 1970/1) (*Social Trends 15*, 1985). It is abundantly clear from such evidence that an increasing proportion of the population is achieving educational qualifications. We are as a society becoming more and more qualified if not educated.

## 8.4 Changing structure of occupations

Over the same period there has been considerable change in the occupational structure of our society. Table 8.6 compares the structure of 1911 with that of 1971. The most notable feature is that, whereas there has been a decline in employers and proprietors of over 50 per cent (from 6.7 to 2.6 per cent) and of manual workers from almost 75 per cent to some 55 per cent of the population, the proportion of white collar workers has more than doubled (from 18.7 to 42.7 per cent). The implication is that the resulting structure contains a very much larger proportion of occupations for which educational qualifications are likely to be necessary. The second part of the table reveals that the greatest rate of growth within the

### Table 8.6
Change in the structure of occupations between 1911 and 1971 in Great Britain (percentages*)

|  | 1911 | 1971 |
|---|---|---|
| Employers and proprietors | 6.7 | 2.6 |
| White collar workers | 18.7 | 42.7 |
| Manual workers | 74.6 | 54.7 |
| **White Collar** | | |
| Managers and administrators | 3.4 | 8.6 |
| Higher professionals | 1.0 | 3.8 |
| Lesser professionals/technicians | 3.1 | 7.7 |
| Foremen and inspectors | 1.3 | 3.0 |
| Clerks | 4.5 | 14.0 |
| Salesmen and shop assistants | 5.4 | 5.6 |

* Of total occupied population.

(Derived from Table 5, price and Bain 1976.)

white collar section has been among higher professionals, clerks and lesser professionals and technicians, whereas the proportion of salesmen and shop assistants has remained relatively stable. The remaining occupations, while displaying increases, are more difficult to relate directly to education. Managers and particularly foremen and inspectors are likely to be at least as dependent on experience and skill as on educational qualifications, and maybe even more so.

## 8.5 The relationship of education and occupation

Having viewed the evidence on the relationship between education, occupation and income and on the rising level of educational attainment and the changing structure of occupations, we are now in a position to explore two basic questions. On what basis can we explain the combination of rising educational attainment and a changing occupational structure in our society? On what basis can we explain the fact that better educated people have different jobs and higher incomes than those who are less well educated or are without educational qualifications? In a real sense these two questions are one. They relate to the fundamental relationship of education to the social structure (society), and in exploring them we shall not be able to differentiate neatly between them.

In surveying the remarkable growth in the length of British male secondary schooling and examination success between 1925/6 and 1970/1 Halsey et al (1980) discuss four avenues of explanation. First, that educational standards have declined; more candidates presented themselves and the pass rate remained constant. This they do not support because A level GCE successes increased at a faster rate than O level, and because of the impossibility of testing standards over time in a sensible way – given, for example, changes in the curriculum, examinations, etc. Second, that technological change created a growing demand for highly educated personnel (discussed further below, 8.5a). While there is evidence of the growth in such jobs, it is not sufficient to account for the size of educational change, 'over-education' for available jobs being apparent. Third, that educational growth is a result of demand on the part of families and status groups for 'mobility opportunities' (the line taken by Collins 1971, which is dicussed at length below). Halsey et al show that as one level of achievement becomes saturated (say O levels) the demand spirals, assisted by employers' demands. Fourth, that the pool of ability (those capable of passing examinations) is socially defined, being related to those believed to be, and believing they are, capable and to the costs involved. Hence changes of belief or in the costs will directly affect educational achievement. They find, interestingly enough, that over the period surveyed, the proportion 'staying on' at school was inversely related to the size of the age cohorts. Marginal pupils are likely to be encouraged to stay on when numbers are low and deterred when they are high.

An important ingredient in our consideration is the attitudes and practices of employers in respect of educational qualifications. Maguire and Ashton (1981) surveyed some 350 British employing organizations and found five separate strategies in use:

1. Minimum educational level stated, highest available selected (used in educational establishments, but rarely by others).
2. Use minimal level to screen applicants, those without excluded, but selection then on non-academic criteria (used for recruiting professionals, managers and technicians).
3. Balance shifts, education used to focus on suitable level of ability, but not rigidly used if other qualities apparent (used to recruit clerks, sales and skilled workers).
4. Personal or physical attributes used and educational qualifications functionless (used to recruit operatives and skilled workers).
5. Educational criteria seen as a disqualification, since they indicate ability and ambition (only sometimes used to recruit for repetitive jobs).

The non-academic criteria identified by employers were: personality of applicant (self-presentation, attitude to work, interest in job, family background [important where long training was in-

Education, Occupation and Mobility

volved]); and the nature of the work situation (type of work group, abilities and physical attributes required).

The study also revealed employers' attitudes towards educational qualifications: some 50 per cent thought they were useful (of whom nearly half saw them as a true measure of ability and a third as an indication of attitude and application); 23 per cent saw them of some use but had reservations; while 27 per cent thought they were of no use at all (including a few who saw them only as a negative screening device). Large employers were most likely to use educational qualifications for recruitment purposes and this may be because they tended to have personnel departments with rationalized hiring practices.

The study casts several doubts on the instrumental role of employers in tightening and heightening the relationship of educational qualifications to occupation. Employers varied in their perception of qualifications; some selected school leavers before examination results were available, many displayed a preference for non-academic qualities (also found by MSC 1978 and Reid, E. 1980), or used education in a symbolic way, as a measure of other traits. As Gray et al (1983) point out, 'it could be argued that the association between qualifications and job success comes about, not because employers care for qualifications themselves, but because employers choose young people with favourable backgrounds, attitudes and behaviour, and that these young people also tend to have good educational qualifications'.

Of those who did use educational qualifications, four fifths said that these had not been raised in the past five years, and that when faced with a large number of applicants they tended to use either informal methods or to turn to official agencies (Job Centre, Careers Office). The study also revealed that employers had an indifference to the curriculum; (like Reid, E. 1980) there was little evidence of interest in vocational subjects and a preoccupation with general behaviour and attitudes. Maguire and Ashton argue that since the proportion of the population with qualifications is continuing to grow (see 8.3), any comparison over time will reveal this rise amongst employees, but this is not due to the demands of employers in general. Qualifications maybe a prerequisite for competition but they are not the cause of, or the deciding factor in, obtaining a job.

A further insight specifically related to school leavers is provided by NOP (1980) who interviewed some 200 employers with 30 or more young workers. The most important attributes they took into account when recruiting were, in descending order: interest in job; willingness to learn; appearance and personality (impression at interview); examination results (only 15 per cent saw these as the most important); references. Again, this suggests a relative lack of importance accorded to education. About a third of the employers expressed some dissatisfaction with young workers; the most common cause was a poor sense of discipline/attendance, followed more or less equally by lack of interest in work, academic standards and aptitude for the job.

We now turn our attention to appraising two sociological explanations.

## 8.5a THE TECHNICAL-FUNCTION THEORY OF EDUCATION

This was developed by Clark (1962) and is based on the structural-functionalist theory of social stratification (for details see Bendix and Lipset 1967) which can be briefly stated as follows: occupations require varying forms of skill; people with appropriate skills must be recruited for them; differential rewards exist to motivate people with appropriate skills to take up particular occupations and to keep them there; by implication the education system functions to help this process.

The technical-function theory of education contains two major propositions.

1. The skill requirement for jobs increases with technological change in industrialized society. This causes a decline in the proportion of low-skill, and an increase in highly skilled, jobs, while some jobs increase their demand of skills (for example, those affected by new industrial, scientific and information technologies).
2. Education provides people with either specific skills for jobs or general capacity for jobs, and therefore the educational requirements for jobs rise and an increasing proportion of the

population spends longer on education and achieves qualifications.

Clearly this suggests a direct and balanced relationship between
education and occupation which we have already begun to question
above and now pursue further. American studies have seriously
questioned the fit between rising educational levels and
occupational demands. During the 1940s and 1950s only 15 per cent
of the increase in the educational level of the work force could be
atributed to changes in the occupational structure (Fogler and Nam
1964). During the 1960s this percentage was seen to rise to some 25
per cent (Rodriguez 1978). It is clear that the great majority of
educational upgrading occurred within existing occupations and
that educational growth out-paced occupational change. Similarly, a
United States Department of Labor study reported that the
educational level of the work force had increased in excess of that
plausibly necessary for changing requirements due to the growth of
skills demanded by occupations. It reported 'over-education', particularly among male graduates and female high school graduates –
that is, they often worked in jobs that did not require such a high
level of education.

A further question raised is whether better educated employees
are more productive. At a simple level and provided there was
perfect competition between them (that they were inter-
changeable), the fact that, as we have seen, educated labour is paid
more highly than raw labour would mean that they were more
productive. Such higher productivity would explain their higher
income. Of course, this argument is circular, and in any case Blaug
(1972) has argued that competition is far from perfect. There is both
indirect and direct evidence to be considered.

The indirect evidence takes three forms. First, the national-
growth approach, where calculations are made about such growth
and the part played by the capital and labour in its production.
What is left unexplained by these factors is attributed to changes in
the educational levels of the work force. Obviously it can be argued
that such a claim is largely arbitrary because it leaves out a number
of other factors such as changes in technology, in organization and

in cultural values which are also likely to affect production. Second, the cross-cultural approach: generally speaking, those countries with the highest economic levels also have the highest educational levels, but this begs the question of the direction of causality. Hoselitz (1965) suggests that the very wide variation between societies of similar economic levels in the percentage of population at any given level of education indicates that these can only be explained in terms of political (as opposed to economic) demands for education. These demands can run counter to the economic needs of society. Third, time-lag approaches. It has been established that the 'take-off' stage in a society's move from an agrarian to an industrial economic base is achieved when 30 to 50 per cent of the 7- to 14-year-olds are in school. Similarly, economic developments are predicted to relate to further educational achievements. Peaslee (1969) has shown, in a study involving 37 countries, that these predictions are far from clearly supported. The establishment of secondary schools appears related to economic advances in only 12 countries. While university development is so related in 21 countries, the exceptions – America, Russia, Japan, France and Sweden, for example – rather make a mockery of the theory. Berg (1970) reviewed much of the direct evidence which related productivity to educational levels of factory workers, store clerks, technicians, secretaries, insurance salesmen, research scientists, the military and civil servants. He concluded that the evidence actually shows a negative relationship between educational level and productivity. Layard et al (1971) compared 68 British companies in the electrical industry, matched for the type of product they produced. Assuming that they operated with similar capital and labour ratio, their educational structure (broken down into graduates, professionally trained, HNC/ONC) was related to profit rates, sales per unit of capital, rates of growth of sales, higher output per unit of labour, and lower unit costs. None of these was found to be statistically related. While not actually claiming to refute the assumption that educated labour is more productive, Layard suggested that the evidence might shake our faith in the economic explanation. Berg (1970) reports a negative relationship between educational level and job satisfaction – the more educated being also the more dissatisfied. Mottaz (1984) argues that education has an indirect positive effect on job satisfaction: it leads to the valuation of intrinsic job rewards such as autonomy and involvement, but also to higher aspirations and work-associated values. Hence among workers in jobs with similar intrinsic rewards, work satisfaction is lower for the more educated.

A further question arising from the technical-function theory is whether, or to what extent, vocational skills are learned in the educational system or elsewhere. The utility and role of schooling and educational qualifications in occupational performance has been a fairly regular item for discussion through the history of education. In late nineteenth century Britain it centred on the need for the development of technical education to provide suitable recruits to keep Britain apace with the growing industrial strength of Europe. More recently, higher education was encouraged to be industrially and economically more relevant with the introduction of sandwich courses (involving industrial experience), vocationally pertinent degrees and the development of technological universities and the polytechnics. At the time of writing, secondary schooling is in the process of being affected by the government-backed and -financed Technical and Vocational Educational Initiative (TVEI), designed to equip school leavers with relevant knowledge and skill for the labour market. Although designed for all children, if past experience is anything to go by its main recipients are most likely to be those deemed less 'academically able' and/or less socially advantaged, like those who received technical schooling pre and post World War II. It will be interesting to see the effect of TVEI on the independent schools' curriculum. There is also a more sinister side to TVEI, in that it can be seen to imply that the causes of school leaver unemployment lie with the schools – their products are ill-equipped with the knowledge and skills necessary to gain employment. What is difficult to comprehend is how producing suitable recruits will create jobs for them. This would appear to be another aspect on the theme of blaming the victim: rather than tackling the underlying economic factors, education becomes a scapegoat (and, by implication, those who pass through it).

Until the present, it is clear that most manual workers have acquired their skills on the job or by casual means (Collins 1971) and in some cases by work experience together with day release/evening class further education. Work experience opportunities for secondary school pupils have been available for a minority and recent YOP/YTS schemes have typically included training and/or educational elements. It is also noteworthy that most firms which recruit graduates run subsequent training schemes for them and that vocationally specific and sandwich degrees remain in a minority and have not always been seen as being of equivalent status (or even utility) as traditional 'academic' ones.

The extent to which education imparts suitable occupational knowledge and skills for non-manual jobs is difficult to determine. Some professions show a relationship between educational level and level of professional responsibility, as Perrucci and Perrucci (1970) showed in the case of engineers in USA. The same study, however, found that 40 per cent of practising engineers in the 1950s were without college degrees, suggesting that all the necessary skills could be learned from the job. Study of management recruitment by British firms revealed that only a third had any higher education, (29 per cent with a first degree) and just under half any management training. Interestingly enough, US firms recruiting in Britain took higher proportions with educational qualifications (Jamieson 1980). This sort of evidence suggests that educational qualifications do not have the direct occupational relevance which is often assumed and is implicit in technical-functional explanations.

Collins (1971) has added a further aspect to the criticism by claiming that 'demands' of an occupation are not fixed but are the result of behaviour (or negotiation) between employer and employees. In order to gain and hold a job, an employee must display that amount of productive or other skills that the employer can or does demand of him. Both sides can be seen to refrain from giving or demanding. Employers' strategies are geared towards gaining satisfactory rather than optimum performance and they make changes only when performance falls below fairly low standards. Workers on the other hand are protected from having to give their all by trade union agreements, informal organization and standards. In the same way, ascriptive factors remain of considerable importance in industrialized society. The business élite in America is predominantly Protestant, white, male and upper-middle-class. Likewise we noted in 6.3 that the occupational élite of our society was composed, to a large extent, of the products of public schools recruited almost exclusively from the upper section of our social structure. Within a traditional technical-function framework such relationships would be viewed as a residual happening, but there is little evidence to show that any major change is taking place. One hypothesis put forward by Collins is that the prime basis of selection is the ascribed group, technical skills being a secondary consideration. Education is a mark of membership of a particular group. Hence the institution of examinations for posts in the civil service in 1870 (before which posts were bought) was a result of a struggle between the upper-middle educated classes and the traditional aristocracy.

Clearly, our considerations lead to the conclusion of a very limited explanative role for technical-function or human-capital theories of the relationship between education and occupation. We turn then to a second sociological approach.

## 8.5b CONFLICT THEORIES OF EDUCATION STRATIFICATION

Collins has developed such a theory from two of Weber's ideas (see also 7.10b). First, *status groups*: Weber argued that the basic units of society were associational groups who shared a common culture (language, taste, manners, opinion, leisure, and so on) and a sense of status equality. They distinguish themselves from other groups by way of moral (social) evaluation and exclude those who do not possess 'the in group' culture. He did not claim that such groups had distinct boundaries, but that there were three main determinates: economic situation, or class; differences in power; cultural conditions such as race, religion, area, intellectual/aesthetic culture, etc. Second, *struggle for advantage*, which Weber saw as a struggle over socially scarce goods (like wealth, power and prestige) taking place on the basis of groups rather than individuals. Those holding power in society or an organization – called here the élite –

have an interest in maintaining their advantage. This they pursue by attempting to recruit into the élite group people who are similar to those already there, and to recruit for the non-élite (or work force), wherever possible, people having respect for the élite's cultural superiority.

Education is viewed as status culture, and the main function of schools and educational institutions is the teaching of particular status cultures. Hence any failure to teach technical knowledge and specific skills is not important, since vocabulary, inflection, taste, values, manners, emphasis on sociability and athletics are not extraneous but core factors of a particular status culture. Readers will recognize that some of these factors, in a different context, were discussed in 4, 5 and 6. Education is, then, viewed as a labelling process allowing the ready identification and recruitment of a suitable élite and work force.

General evidence of the utility of the conflict theory can be seen in the following terms: that distinctions exist between status group cultures (such as evidence of social class differences, see Reid 1981); that status groups occupy different positions in the occupational structure and in organizations (as suggested by such data as in Tables 6.1 and 8.1); and that there exists a struggle for power between status groups (industrial and political strife). To show that employers use educational experience and qualifications to recruit members of different status groups for managerial and production jobs demands evidence that schools either educate pupils into élite culture or into a respect for it (as discussed in 4 and 6, where it was suggested that only the academically able and public school pupils explored the whole nature of education and that schools elicited a full response only from such pupils) and that employers use education as a means of selecting cultural attributes. In support of the latter point, Collins quotes research to show that employers see education as a screening device enabling them to choose employees with desirable (middle-class) character traits (see also 8.5 above). This was seen as particularly important in white collar jobs because such employees were visible to the public. In much the same way Berg (1970) argued that employers believed that education provides evidence of ability to get on with others, to make the most of opportunities and of greater potential for learning and promotion. At the same time he revealed that virtually no employers collected data to examine such beliefs in the light of their employees' performance. Lydall (1968) took a somewhat different line, although with similar consequences. He argued that employers are unaware of precisely what requirements they have of employees, but that experience tells them that those with given levels of education usually have what they want: in other words, that educational level predicts a higher level of performance without necessarily contributing to it. On the other hand, for students educational qualifications mean a meal ticket to the top table. This, he claims, could explain why earnings and educational level are related and why qualifications are often not directly related to jobs.

If education does function in this way – screening and selecting for employers – then its net contribution to national output might well be negative. Greater educational provision may well serve only to increase competition for certain jobs. In economic terms the educated may be seen to exploit the labour market, by being paid more than they contribute. By the same token, uneducated labour is relatively exploited – (echoes here of their respective roles in school, see 6.1).

A study of British employers (Gordon 1983) revealed: that they expected graduates to be more productive, highly able and quick to learn. They favoured graduates with applicable skills (seen as relevant knowledge of science and communication) over other graduates; they preferred in descending order graduates from Oxbridge, old civic, new civic, technological and plate glass universities, with further gaps between these and the polytechnic and college of higher education graduates. Employers saw the disadvantages of graduates in terms of their lack of industrial and commercial experience, unrealistic career expectations and lack of careful thought in career choice. The apparent contradiction between employers' choice of type of graduate and their criticism of lack of relevant experience is further borne out by Bacon et al (1979) who found graduate recruiters viewed polytechnic products as second-rate both intellectually and socially to those from university; deficits which were not seen as alleviated by the former's better knowledge and experience of industry. An earlier study revealed that degrees were regarded as important for trainee managers not on account of ability or technical skill, but because they were assumed to indicate motivation and social experience. Being a graduate of a business school was seen as important, in spite of employers' wide scepticism of the courses' utility, because it showed commitment to a career in business (Gorden and Howell 1959). Collins's own study of some 309 organizations showed that those most concerned with having normative control over employees (those concerned with financial, professional, government and public services as opposed to manufacturing, construction and trade) tended to emphasize educational qualifications most highly. This stress on education was true only for white collar workers.

Collins predicts that education is most important when two conditions are found together: the type of education most closely reflects the membership of a particular status group; the same status group controls employment. These neatly encapsulate British public schools and Oxbridge in respect to élite occupations (see Table 6.1). Similarly, Collins found that large US firms were predominantly manned by personnel recruited from private schools and Ivy League colleges. Minority group members worked in smaller businesses. Technological change affected demands for educational qualifications only in smaller, localized firms. A study of nationally prominent US businessmen found that the most highly educated were not working in rapidly developing enterprises but in financial and utility companies. Since the highly qualified businessmen tended to have social origins in the upper middle class, it appeared to indicate that education is more a correlate of their social origins than a determinant of their success.

The concept of education as 'status culture' goes some way to explaining the lack of correspondence between educational achievement and occupational placement; the relationship between education, occupation and income; and the fact that educational and occupational opportunities appear to be stratified in a rather similar way to the social stratification of society. Certainly it casts doubt upon the usefulness of seeing education and occupation as essentially linked in the purely technical sense, allowing for if not explaining the lack of direct correlation between the two. Relationships between education, occupation and income must be viewed as being strongly mediated by the social and power structure and the relations of society. Not only has this to be seen in the differing opportunities and access to education and occupation but also, as Young (1971) has pointed out, in terms of the control of knowledge. As we saw in 4.5, knowledge and education are both culturally defined and stratified. The persistence of, and reward for, high-status knowledge is not because of its necessary utility or superiority, but because of the value placed on it by dominant groups in society. Given the relationship of such groups to, and control of, the educational institutions providing such knowledge and the occupational, social and political structures that reward it, such use clearly serves their interests well.

Marxist commentators arrive at much the same conclusion (see 9.1a). For example, Bowles and Gintis (1976) put forward the thesis that schooling by reproducing in school the social relationships of economic life provides for the development of types of people attuned to work contentedly in a capitalist mode of production rather than people with technical expertise. The educational system is viewed as one form of legitimation of inequality in a capitalist society. In reviewing the relationship between education and income and the role of the educational system, they wrote:

> ... now argument suggests ... that the mental skill demands of work are sufficiently limited, the skills produced by our educational system sufficiently varied, and the possibilities for acquiring additional skills on the job sufficiently great so that skill differences among individuals who are acceptable for a given job on the basis of other criteria including sex, personality and credentials are of little economic import. ... Education reproduces inequality by justifying privilege and attributing poverty to personal failure.

Education, they argue, reproduces inequality according to what is apparently objective merit – school performance – but the justification of inequality is largely symbolic because the transmission of social and economic status is mainly by non-cognitive mechanisms. Hence different levels of education recruit from different sections of the social structure, socialize in different ways, and subsequently feed their products into different levels of the occupational structure. We have viewed the aspects of this process in 6, 7 and 8. Bowles and Gintis point out that among US whites about one third of the correlation between schooling and economic attainment can be accounted for by socio-economic background. Children from the poorest one tenth of US families had one third of the likelihood of ending up economically well-off compared with children from the wealthiest one tenth, even when their educational achievements and childhood measured ability were identical.

## 8.6 Education and social mobility

Having established a relationship between education and occupation and explored something of its explanation, we now turn our attention to social mobility. Many people change their occupations during their working life. For most this change is from employment in one place or firm to another, with little or no change in the job they do. Sociologists refer to this as *horizontal* social mobility; it is not our concern here. For others, however, the change is dramatic – for example, labourer to managing director, skilled operative to academic or the other way round.

When the change involves moving up or down across the social classes during one's working career, it is known as *intragenerational* social mobility. Finally, the most researched form of social mobility concerns the relationship between parental and child's occupation – called *intergenerational* social mobility. It remains a sociological convention to view such mobility in respect of males only.

### 8.6a APPROACHING MOBILITY

Problems arise in measuring social mobility. Has the son of a clerical worker who becomes first a teacher and then a university professor been either, or both, intra- and intergenerationally mobile? The traditional way of measuring social mobility has been to identify movement across the manual/non-manual occupational divide. This line is used because, generally speaking, non-manual occupations have more prestige and are better paid than manual (especially when income over working life is compared); non-manual occupations typically require a higher level of education, which it is assumed implies both status and a set of values; non-manual workers, including those in routine jobs, tend to identify with, and exhibit the characteristics of, the middle rather than the working class; and because it is a comparatively simple, easily collected measure which has become a sociological convention.

It should be appreciated that such measurement is crude, misses subtle mobility, as suggested above, and recognizes short-term and relatively unimportant movements, say from small shopkeeper to skilled operative and back again. A further problem in the measurement of intergenerational mobility centres upon how and when one records the occupations of father and son. Ideally it should be at the same age or stage of career of each, but studies usually fail to achieve this. It is also true that the situation is essentially dynamic: educational and occupational opportunities change over time, as do the relationships between them, together with the status and attraction of occupations. Interestingly, the literature is more concerned with upward than downward mobility (see discussion in 8.9).

There are two major sets of factors involved in social mobility.

## 8.6b STRUCTURAL FACTORS

- A growth in middle-class (non-manual) jobs and a decline in manual jobs (see Table 8.6).
- Up to the present there has been an inverse relationship between fertility and social class so that the middle classes have not reproduced themselves, hence creating vacancies for recruits from the working classes.
- Historically there has been some decline in the importance of inherited status or ascribed factors on occupational placement, and growth in the importance of achieved factors.

Such structural factors indicate that opportunities exist for upward social mobility. What they do not explain is why the opportunities are taken, or why some people are socially mobile while others are not. To understand this, consideration must be made of non-structural factors.

## 8.6c NON-STRUCTURAL FACTORS

While sociologists have recognized the importance of non-structural factors, they have not been very active in identifying or exploring them. Veblen argued that a person's own social self-esteem was based on cues received from others and that there was a general tendency for people to want to improve upon even a favourable self-esteem. Psychologists and social psychologists inform us that people vary in their need to achieve or to improve their and other people's opinions of themselves. McClelland laid the framework for what is known as n'ach (need for achievement) which can be measured by several tests. For people who score highly on these tests, the prospect of success is greater than their fear of failure, and they strive and enter competitive situations more frequently than others. Stacey (1965) (who also provides a useful review of the literature, 1969) conducted a British study in which he found that men and women who had been upwardly socially mobile had higher n'ach scores than those who were stationary, who in turn scored higher than those who were downwardly mobile. Among college of education students who were qualified to read for degrees (BEd), it was those with the highest n'ach scores who chose to do so, the low scorers opting for certificate courses (Reid and Cohen 1973). Similar measures have revealed differences related to primary school children's educational performance (Croucher and Reid 1979).

Obviously structural and non-structural factors combine to create mobility. I use the term 'gluckenspiel' (which is my own) to refer to this in relation to upward mobility. 'Gluck' consists, mainly, of being in the right place at the right time, while 'spiel' is the ability to take advantage of the 'gluck'. Most successful people's careers contain incidents of this nature. Thompson (1971) has similarly argued that there are two alternative emphases in explaining why some males are mobile and others not. The first she calls *objective* – that the barriers to mobility are greater for some parts of the working class than others. The second is *subjective* – that values and the desire for mobility may vary within the working class. She recognizes, of course, that the two may go hand-in-hand. Her English data showed that the educational aspirations of the boys' parents (subjective) were more important than the material condition of the home (objective), but that both these were overshadowed by the type of secondary school attended, grammar school boys tending to be more mobile than secondary modern boys. The importance of selective schooling is discussed at 8.7. The effect on mobility of the comprehensivization of secondary schooling remains open to speculation.

As yet, we know comparatively little of the complexity of factors surrounding mobility. Obviously we can suspect the family to be important. In reviewing studies of the upwardly mobile, Noble (1975) shows that many of their mothers had previously been downwardly mobile (the so-called 'sunken middle class'). He estimates that for some 40 per cent of those moving from the working to the middle class the move represents a return, over three generations, to a previous family social status. An earlier American study suggested that the best chances accrued to those from small families, and eldest and only children (Anderson et al 1952). Such working-class family environments could be instrumental in producing socially mobile individuals – such children might be better materially supported within limited means, and the relatively increased involvement of such children with adults possibly enhances verbal ability and n'ach.

## 8.6d A 'PERFECT' MODEL

Of course, our prime consideration is the role of education in social mobility. There appears to be some general popular agreement that education now plays a growing and important if not crucial role in occupational placement and consequently in mobility. However, an inherent danger in analyzing the role of education in most situations is to overemphasize its importance. Hence, before reviewing the specific evidence, we shall context education and mobility in a general and hypothetical model based on a number of unrealistic assumptions. For this purpose we borrow from economics the concept of 'perfect'. Simply, this is an abstraction in which intervening real-life variables – like individual differences, luck and choice – are ignored and the relationship between two factors is seen as direct. Hence, in the present case, we shall initially accept that educational qualifications are directly related to occupation, that *all* those without qualifications get type A jobs, those with one to four O levels get type B, and so on. In other words, regardless of all other factors (background situation, personality, opportunity), education determines social status or occupation – the relationship is 'perfect'. Hence our model of education and social mobility would rest on three assumptions:

i 'perfect' educational opportunity
ii 'perfect' entry into occupations via educational qualifications
iii 'perfect' promotion via educational qualifications.

Put as boldly as this, the reality of education is underlined as a social phenomenon and as but one factor in any life situation or chance. It starkly reveals, in the light of our previous considerations, the absurdity of attempting to isolate the effect of education outside its social context. The three assumptions above need to be seriously questioned if not rejected.

i *Educational opportunity*

As we have seen in 7 and throughout this book, such opportunity is very far from 'perfect'. Opportunity is affected by educational provision which varies geographically and hence socially; economically, in respect of 'public' schools; by the way in which schools operate; and in variations among pupils in respect of a complexity of factors that can be referred to under the heading of social stratification. The weight of evidence reviewed clearly points to the fact that the educational system tends to reproduce the existing social structure rather than to change it dramatically. Of course this is a general view and does not deny the experience of many individuals for whom education has provided mobility from very poor backgrounds to highly paid occupations, but these are exceptions. Even if there was perfect educational opportunity, it would be only the first step towards education being the major factor in social placement and mobiliy.

## ii *Occupational entry*

As we saw in 8.2a, the relationship between educational qualifications and occupation, while apparent, is not 'perfect'. Not all highly qualified people were engaged in 'appropriate' occupations and vice versa. The gaining and use of qualifications can be seen as commonly related to aspirations. Douglas et al (1968) showed that while 79 per cent of high-ability boys from the upper middle class were expected by their parents to enter the professions, this was true of only 39 per cent of lower-manual boys of the same ability. Maxwell (1969), in a similar Scottish study, concludes

> But with the world before them, what appears to govern the future careers of these young people? The underlying influence seems to be social class. With all the surface variations, the basic relations are those which relate social class to the use of the educational opportunities available. Pupils of high ability leave school and close the avenue to further formal qualifications, and pupils of average ability persist, and enter the professions. Intellectual ability and personal preference come into it, but the relationship between fathers' occupational class and the critical decision is very strong. Social class also tends to determine the employment chosen where choice is relatively wide. Sons tend to follow their fathers.

Occupational entry is not only affected by individual subjective factors but also by structural barriers. In 6.3 it was suggested that some occupations might be relatively closed to applicants other than those from 'public' schools and/or Oxford and Cambridge. These factors can be suspected to operate at a more general level, for example Lee (1968) suggested 'For those who pass successfully through the hurdles at 11+, 16+ and onward, there probably exists a final barrier upon entry to the labour market at which influence, breeding and background still bestow an advantage.' The main structural barrier, however, is the available stock of job opportunities. This varies considerably from area to area and over time. The south-east region has a larger proportion of non-manual occupations and higher levels of employment than other parts of Britain. In some areas the decision to enter such a job may entail moving to another part of the country; this has been true, for example, of Wales in respect of schoolteachers. Indeed, social mobility often involves some geographical mobility. The present state of unemployment, especially among the newly qualified, often means a choice between no job or one which, in different conditions, would be considered unsuitable. Similarly, if the educational system produces more people with specific qualifications than the labour market can use, the relationship between qualifications and occupation is weakened. Conversely, the recruitment to new and developing occupations – such as computing/information technology – does not await the production of people with specific educational qualifications, but uses the available stock.

Aspects of educational opportunity and occupational entry also operate together. Since there are relationships both between father's occupation and son's education and between educational achievement and occupation we can anticipate that the typical pattern will be one of similarity between father and son, particularly in respect of occupational groups as broad as social classes.

## iii *Occupational promotion*

Although evidence is more than limited, it seems probable that, however important educational qualifications may be for entry into an occupation, their importance in the process of gaining promotion is likely to be overshadowed by other factors. This is mainly due to the fact that promotion is dependent on length of service, on the job performance or on some combination of the two. Individual and personality factors are likely to become more important – how well one 'fits in', how ambitious one is, the opportunities that exist for promotion, and so on. An illuminating study in this area is that of Perrucci (1961) who examined the social origins and job positions of a large sample of American engineering graduates. He found that fathers' social class was related to sons' careers – despite the fact that all had similar qualifications. Engineers from professional homes were more frequently found in the top jobs (presidents and vice-presidents of engineering concerns) than were those from unskilled homes who more often had lower-category jobs (design and project engineers). In reviewing the careers of graduates between 1911 and 1950, Perrucci argues that the opportunities for social mobility among graduate engineers have diminished over time. In this case, as in many others reviewed in this book, the effects of education are mediated by other social factors – here, once again, social class.

## 8.7 The evidence considered

The best available British empirical evidence on social mobility is that provided by the Oxford Mobility Study, conducted in 1972. This used a national sample of some 10,000 men aged between 20 and 64 years. It is particularly valuable in giving a long-term view, though somewhat limited in respect to the contemporary scene. Few of the sample were educated in comprehensive schools, most were educated prior to the considerable expansion of higher and further education in the post Robbins (1963) era, and the survey was conducted before the dramatic rise in unemployment of the late 1970s and 1980s. As its title suggests, the main focus of the study was mobility; this appears to have placed some limitations on the educational data collected and the two topics and their inter-relationships have been separately reported. A seven-category scale of social class was used (for details see 10.2), although this was frequently simplified into three: *service* – professionals, administrators, managers and proprietors (about 14 per cent of the sample and much larger than RG class I at 5 per cent of the male population); *intermediate* – other non-manual workers, technicians and foremen; *working* – all manual workers (about 55 per cent of the sample; unlike the RG scale, this makes no differentiation between levels of skill).

In general social mobility was recognized as movement into or out of the service class, either from origin (class of father when respondent was aged 14) or between first full-time occupation and that in 1972. The analysis reveals the importance of intragenerational mobility in any consideration of intergenerational mobility. For example, of men of service-class origins aged over 35 in 1972, only 29 per cent had entered directly into that class, but nearly two thirds were there at the time of the survey; while 35 per cent initially entered the working class, only 14 per cent were there in 1972. Of men of working-class origin 76 per cent entered occupations in that class and 4 per cent service-class ones; in 1972 these percentages had changed to 54 and 17 per cent respectively. Such data clearly indicates a good deal of movement between the classes both inter- and intragenerationally. Indeed, Goldthorpe et al (1978, 1980) show that upward mobility increased over time (the younger men had better chances of gaining service-class jobs and lower risk of downward mobility). However, this is not seen as indicating that Britain has become a more open society, since the increase is mainly accounted for by changes in the economic structure over the period considered. The *relative* chances of men from different classes display little change and the conclusion reached is:

> even in the presumably very favourable context of a period of sustained economic growth and of major change in the form of the occupational structure, the general underlying processes of intergenerational class mobiliy – or immobility – have apparently been little altered and indeed have, if anything, tended in certain respects to generate still greater inequalities in class chances.

To the fairly common assumption that there has been a tightening relationship between educational qualifications and occupational placement (and hence social mobility) has been added the view that alternative avenues, not involving education, have declined. In other words there is a counter-balance between educational and other routes to social mobility (often referred to as counter-balance theory). This view has been sustained by Little and Westergaard (1964), Westergaard (1972) and Westergaard and Resler (1975). They have argued that the class differentials in education have slightly diminished during the present century, so that more working-class children are gaining qualifications. At the same time they conclude there has been a removal of alternative routes to middle-class jobs. The net result is an unchanging frequency of inter-generational social mobility with the implication of a change in the nature of the route. Their evidence of growing educational selectivity in middle-class jobs comes from studies of peoples' educational and social backgrounds. For example, Clark (1966) showed that the proportion of managers with extended education had grown over time and that there had been a slight net drop of the number of managers with working-class backgrounds. Lee (1968) disagreed, arguing that the composition of an occupation should not be confused with opportunities to enter it. He suggested that the situation has been static, that the chances of working-class persons without education entering such jobs have never been good and such chances may, in the future, diminish. Goldthorpe and Llewellyn (1977, 1980) view the Oxford data in the light of this theory, arguing that if it were true there would be a rise in the percentage of men directly entering service-type occupations and a corresponding decline in those gaining such entry during the course of their working career. In comparing men born between 1908 and 1927 with those born between 1928 and 1947 they find evidence of increased direct entry, but no apparent decline in indirect entry. Hence they conclude that while mobility chances are increasingly affected by educational achievement, this does not imply a lessening of other opportunities to enter middle-class occupations.

Heath and Ridge (1982) used the Oxford data to view the effect of type of school and qualifications on the occupational attainments of men, pre and post World War II. In the pre-war period service-class attendance at 'public' and grammar schools resulted in social repro-duction via the educational system, while working-class attendance at such schools opened up mobility in terms of occupation. This finding echoes that of Glass (1954), whose conclusion was that grammar schools were the major factor in mobility. Attendance at such a school made for a strong relationship between middle-class fathers' and sons' occupation, in that it lessened the likelihood or distance of occupational descent. For the sons of working-class fathers, it greatly increased the likelihood or distance of occupational ascent. Since middle-class sons had a greater chance of attending grammar schools than working-class ones, the net result was to modify rather than destroy the general relationship between fathers' and sons' occupations. In reworking the Glass data, Anderson (1961) concluded that sons with low educational achievements lost status in relation to their fathers less often, and sons with high achievements rose less often, than would be expected if education was the sole criterion. Perhaps surprisingly, Heath and Ridge found in the post-war era that the occupational gap between men from the service and working classes was greater than in the pre-war one. In respect of grammar school attendance, the pre-war pecking order of occupational attainment was qualified service, qualified working, unqualified service, unqualified working; but all including the latter were afforded upward intragenerational mobility. Post-war, the achievement of those from working-class origins appears depressed, and the unqualified service did somewhat better than the qualified working. In other words, in spite of educational change, economic expansion and the growing use of educational credentials, old-fashioned class bias appears to have reasserted itself. This the authors see in terms of the expansion and competition for labour favouring the marginal member of the dominant social class. This echoes Goldthorpe's pessimistic conclusion that the main function of economic growth can best be regarded not of facilitating egalitarian reform but rather of obscuring its failure.

Halsey (1978, 1979) provides a comparison of the educational achievements of those who remained in their class of origin with those who were socially mobile. There were extremely clear educational differences among those stable. In the service class, 82 per cent had gained examination success, and 30 per cent degrees; in the intermediate class the respective percentages were 27 and one, and for the working class 4.6 and 0.1 per cent. Those upwardly mobile were better qualified than those who remained in their class of origin, but not as well qualified as those who were stable in the class they joined. The downwardly mobile were less well qualified than those who remained in the class of origin but somewhat better qualified than those in the class they joined. Hence intergenerational mobility is a partial exchange of educational qualifications between the classes; it helps reconstitute the educational attributes of the classes. Halsey concludes that the unequal relative educational chances of those of different class origins have been remarkably stable over time and that the conventional assumption of a steady trend towards equality has been an optimistic myth. The expansion of educational opportunity has been taken up by those from the most advantageous class circumstances.

This relationship was also explored using GHS data (Psacharopoulos 1977). He found that males who had been intergenerationally mobile had received longer schooling than the stable, and that the distance travelled along the Hope-Goldthorpe scale (see 10.2) varied according to the level of educational qualification gained, from O level GCE through to degree. Part-time qualifications, especially at the HNC-type level, appeared particularly important for those of low-status origins.

Estimating the importance of education as against other factors in social mobility or income is, of course, problematic. A commonly used statistical technique is path analysis. The work of Psacharopoulos and Halsey (1977) suggests that only about one third of the variance in these two areas is explained by personal characteristics such as schooling, educational qualifications and family background. This leaves the majority of variance attributable to aspects of the complexity of social life, including gluckenspiel (8.6c). What is clear from these analyzes and our discussion is that the effects of education are filtered through other aspects of life and life chances before affecting occupation, income and social mobility.

## 8.8 Public views of education and mobility

Useful illustration of British people's views is provided by Harrop (1980), whose research was based partly on market research data.

Perhaps surprisingly, the public has an accurate view of the amount of social mobility and of the proportion (two thirds) of those who 'inherit' their class from parents, which accords closely with the data of Goldthorpe et al. When presented with ability, education and social background as factors for mobility, the public over-whelmingly chose ability as the most important (79 per cent of middle-class respondents and 62 per cent of working-class); education was a poor second at 15 and 25 per cent respectively. Even among those who chose education as the most important, almost 70 per cent saw the quality of education being dependent upon individual ability rather than social background. Hence the public have a very individualistic, or meritocratic, view of mobility in some contrast to that of most social scientists. The public's view, Harrop argues, allows them to have an optimistic view about the openness of society while recognizing the extent of parent-child class determination. The compatibility of these views is sustained because of the level of residential segregation of the classes and the way in which it obscures the class bias in the distribution of opportunity. Within-class interaction and comparison is much more common than that across classes so that differences in achievement are typically viewed as resulting from differences be-tween individuals rather than as a product of the social structure.

## 8.9 Educational myth and reality

Much of this book, but particularly our considerations here and in 6 and 7, challenge a number of assumptions and beliefs concerning education and its role in society. As was pointed out in 6.1, an important and continuing role for sociology is to provide evidence with which to judge the beliefs surrounding the functioning and practice of education. Much everyday education thinking entails the use of myths – combinations of fact and fiction which explain and justify; 'ideological or conceptual shorthand, obscuring the need for argument, analysis or definition' (Bell and Grant 1974). As they point out, such myths 'flourish with special luxuriance in areas of human concern where many are vitally affected, but few are well

# Education, Occupation and Mobility

informed' (like education), and much 'current mythology is class-bound, political rationalization.'

Such myth is clearly associated with much current thinking concerning, for example, the primacy of ability over social background and resources in educational success (see 7) and the relationship of qualifications to occupational placement (8.5). Here it is further demonstrated in respect of what might be termed the mobility myth. Social mobility is seen as a necessary characteristic of industrialized society, both economically – changing technology and production demand a redefinition of occupations, and culturally – democracy has a value set geared towards an open, meritocratic society. Educational qualifications can be viewed as a relatively neutral criterion for occupational entry once educational opportunity has been extended, even minimally, to the whole of society.

The assumed function of the educational system is to provide people with the qualifications and aspirations to meet society's occupational needs. Built into the system is the assumption that people will, or should, want to be upwardly mobile. Underlying such reasoning is, then, the belief that social mobility is a desirable characteristic of society and that the educational system exists to promote and facilitate it. Given these assumptions, the educational system is viewed and evaluated in terms of how it facilitates mobility rather than how it obstructs it. This is precisely how education is sold to consumers – pupils and parents alike: educational opportunity equals occupational opportunity. If approached from this stance, research, writings and thinking about the role of education in occupational placement and social mobility are likely to result in its over-emphasis and glamourization. At the same time, such an approach provides society with a useful supporting belief in the openness of society through the educational system. One effect of the evidence reviewed in this book ought to be to suggest that such views are open to serious questioning. As we have seen, educational opportunity and achievement are strongly related to ascribed social factors, and social mobility is not so great as to suggest an open society that in any way approaches meritocracy – that is, as Young (1958) stated, a society in which intelligence plus effort equals merit.

It would be equally justifiable to cast aside the mobility myth and view the educational system as obstructing social mobility, limiting

273

educational opportunity and achievement and contributing to the closedness of our society. That this has not been done on any scale again underlines the fact that the sociology of education, like education itself, operates within a set of cultural values which are tuned to the dominant interests in our society. To work from such an assumption would not, in itself, be the whole answer. Its consideration should, however, alert us to the reality that our educational system works in both directions, leading both to elements of openness and closedness in our society. As we have seen so far in this book, it does not so operate indiscriminately. In general terms, it appears to follow the biblical edict regarding the social structure: 'for the man who has something will be given more, so that he will have more than enough' (Matthew 13:12).

# 9

# Society, Education and Sociology

## 9.1 Society and education

Throughout this book we have seen many aspects of the relationship between education and society reviewed through the sociology of education. The abiding impression gained is one of an intimate relationship in which education serves a number of social purposes. Undoubtedly the best illustrated is the way in which educational outcomes tend, in general, to reflect or reproduce existing social stratification in our society, albeit with relatively small and important variations (7 and 8). Earlier, in 4, 5 and 6, we looked at the ways in which schools and schooling contribute to this. Not surprisingly, this reproduction forms the most important aspect of theories which attempt to explain how education functions – an importance which varies little whether a consensus or a conflict perspective is adopted (4.5 iii, 8). Indeed, it might be argued that a fundamental task of sociology is to explain social reproduction just as biology has to explain human reproduction. Here we look in greater detail at some of the theories which attempt to explain the role of education (see also 2). Because of their recent importance within the discipline we concentrate mainly on Marxist approaches.

## 9.1a REPRODUCTION

An initial premise of most theories in the field is that the basis of economic life 'must' be reproduced and that this involves the maintenance of class and power relationships. Bowles and Gintis (1976) argue that in the long run such maintenance depends on 'a widely accepted ideology (for definition see 4.5 iii) justifying the social order together with a set of social relationships which both validate the ideology through everyday experience and fragment the ruled into mutually indifferent, or antagonistic groups'. As we have seen (8), they see the role of education as fostering the belief that economic success is dependent on ability and qualification and in kitting out young people with qualifications, ideas and beliefs which are appropriate to the social system (capitalism) they are to be part of. Hence the major roles of education are legitimation and socialization and there are strong parallels here with Parsons' ideas on socialization and selection (3.4) and the structural views of Durkheim (6.1). In much the same fashion, Bowles and Gintis see schooling as tailoring pupils' self-concepts, aspirations and social-class identities to society's needs through the teaching of proper subordination, by rewarding docility, passivity and obedience – aspects of schooling which readers will have experienced and which are well illustrated in 4 and 5. In straightforward terms it is the *correspondence* of the form of social relationships in school and workplace, rather than the content of education and the intentions of teachers which count – 'Specifically, the relationships of authority and control between administrators and teachers, teachers and students, and students and their work replicate the hierarchical division of labour which dominates the workplace.'

This stress upon the importance of form rather than content in education is of particular interest. For example, the contrast between Oxbridge and other institutions of higher education, or between 'public' and LEA schools is certainly much greater in respect of social relationships than of the content of courses. The almost peer-like tutorial system of Oxbridge is markedly different from the lecture-based, factory-like, teaching of other forms of higher education. The social organization of 'public' schools is in some considerable contrast to that of LEA schools and the two sets of institutions are clearly socially differentiated (6.2 and 6.3). It is relatively easy to see a correspondence here which is related to origins and destinations, for example, upper middle class – public school – Oxbridge – élite occupation (see Tables 6.1 and 6.2). In these respects the central concern of most educationists with the curriculum, and in particular its content, may be seen as misplaced.

Perhaps greater emphasis should be given to effecting the social relationships in educational institutions which might enhance the education and life chances for those who are limited at present.

Bourdieu's contributions (1967, 1973, Bourdieu and Passeron 1977) draw attention to the role of cultural capital brought into, and used by, the educational system in the process of reproduction. The most important aspect of cultural capital is what he terms 'master-patterns' of language, which as a concept has strong parallels with Bernstein's concept of codes (see 7.9bi). They amount to the basic linguistic and thinking rules from which individuals shape their reality. Bourdieu likens their use to musical notation and sees different cultures, including education, as having their own master patterns. Hence, along the lines of other cultural explanations (7.9) school attainment is seen as strongly affected by the child's home culture; middle/dominant class families provide their children with cultural capital which facilitates success, in that it lines up with educational capital. The criteria on which educational success is measured combine dominant class with educational capital, and that which is examined is not *directly* taught in educational institutions.

If schooling and education both assume and reward certain types of learning or understanding, rather than directly teaching them, and the social distribution of these is biased, then Bourdieu's ideas have considerable implications for educational practice. Like many 'grand' theories, the demonstration is not particularly convincing. It is clear from the data we have reviewed that educational success is not solely the prerogative of the middle class; education produces as well as reproduces cultural capital. To maintain Bourdieu's thesis it would be necessary to demonstrate that those who succeed from outside the dominant class come from families which provided more cultural capital than the rest (and vice versa). In other words, that cultural capital, like social class (7.2), is relative rather than absolute, or so complex as to defy simple operationalization – echoes here of Bernstein's thesis.

At the same time there is every reason to accept that children are differently culturally equipped to tackle education and, as a simple example, that those of educated parents are likely to be advantaged. Hence, it is crucial to examine the extent to which sufficient explicit teaching takes place to equip *all* students to perform and/or the extent to which schools and education examine untaught or assumed skills and knowledge. Bourdieu argues that in education style dominates content, so while the mechanics of language and elements of knowledge may be explicitly taught, the essay or examination script is likely to be assessed in terms of style and innovation, which are not. His most telling example comes from higher education, in which he portrays lecture language as incantation rather than communication and argues that only those students with the appropriate cultural capital can use it with the ease and naturalness which is recognized and rewarded by staff (echoes here of teacher-talk, see 5.5). While Bourdieu clearly has a point, it appears to be overstated. Teachers and tutors, as you will have noticed, vary considerably in their presentation, explicitness and expectations. The explicit teaching of the style, language and understanding of a subject within the confines of a lecture may well be extremely difficult but probably not impossible – but this is usually attained by protracted contact with the people and media which use them. Education never takes place solely in the formal teaching and learning situations of lessons or lectures. To claim that such attainment is limited to those whose socialization in the family had suitably equipped them for it is to suggest that the process of socialization is limited to childhood – a claim which is, other than in indirect terms, incorrect. Again, however, there is a clear implication for teachers – that they should review what they teach in relation to what they expect in terms of outcome, in order to ensure the necessary explicit teaching and learning to cater properly for the cultural range and variety of people in their classes.

Althusser (1971) sees education as part of what he calls the 'ideological state apparatus', which functions to sustain the capitalist system by means other than the use of force (the police, army, government and administration). As such, education operates along with other social institutions – the family, religion, communications and media, law, politics and trade unions, and culture as in literature, art and sport – in a unified way to disseminate ruling-class ideology. While we would find it easy to instance examples of incompatible values and beliefs arising from these different sources,

278

he maintains that diversity and contradictions are 'unified beneath the ruling ideology'. He sees education as playing the dominant part, mainly because of the legal requirement for all to participate. So education teaches job-related skills and techniques along with suitable rules and attitudes. For those bound for wage labour these include 'modesty, resignation and submissiveness'; for future capitalists and managers 'cynicism, contempt, arrogance, self importance, even smooth talking and cunning'. Both directly and indirectly, education also teaches aspects of ruling ideology. These class-maintaining processes are concealed from the public and teachers, he argues, by the belief that schools are free from ideology, that teachers respect the freedom of the conscience of those they teach and that teachers and teaching are ideological neutrals.

It is difficult to view Althusser's thesis as other than abstract description of a high level which, because it lacks specificity and evidence, cannot be demonstrated. It shares with non-Marxist structuralist views a disinclination to investigate reality through the eyes of participants and an assumption that education and socialization are inevitably successful. It offers a view of state-determined social life in which individual or corporate resistance or difference have little if any place, let alone significance. At the same time it serves to remind those who need it that teachers and schools are implicitly and explicitly involved with ideology and that there is a need for this to be recognized. As we saw in 4.5, the curriculum is an obvious site but also involved are the institutions, organization and practices of school and classroom (4, 5 and 6). Of course, the ideological underpinning of education is a political matter and becomes a concern only when it conflicts with the interests of groups who hold power. Hence, in the early 1980s there has been governmental concern and action over the teaching of peace studies and forms of social science, particularly sociology and some variants of economics, presumably because these do not coincide with the government's own interests. Likewise there have been some attempts to counter 'the undesirable' by calling for balanced teaching on the question of nuclear arms, while the TVEI projects aim to encourage appropriate attitudes and interests in technical/industrial qualifications and careers. However, this area abounds in numerous unresolved assumptions – the effectiveness of teaching ideology; the pupils' and teachers' awareness, or unawareness, of ideology in education; whether 'balanced' teaching produces 'balanced' views, and so on – few of which have as yet received much attention from researchers.

With or without the views discussed above, it is easy to assume a deterministic view in which the educational system exists to serve and directly reproduce the existing social system or the interest of the dominant class(es), but difficult to demonstrate this in real terms. Such views afford little autonomy to education, or to those who inhabit the educational world, both being seen as caught up in a mechanistic process which they are powerless to resist or affect. At the same time we are all aware of the existence of contradictions, lack of correspondence and diversity within educational and social life. We turn now to views which accommodate these aspects.

## 9.1b AUTONOMY AND RESISTANCE

As we have seen, in general terms it is quite easy to criticize the direct reproduction model with respect to correspondence between the economic base and the educational system. Reynolds (1984) points to the lack of direct relationship between the curriculum and work-related requirements, the limited swing to science and technology, the continued higher status of 'pure' as opposed to applied disciplines. He traces this to the relative autonomy of the education system, based on its decentralized system of LEAs, the authority of headteachers, and the existence of liberal teachers who are education- rather than training-orientated. He further questions the extent to which education can be seen to exhibit capitalistic economic values. Not only is there almost no empirical evidence offered in most of the arguments, but it is not easy to gain from the literature a clear idea of exactly what evidence would be required to support or refute the thesis, which obviously lacks precision.

Some Marxist writers have shifted from a model of direct reproduction to one which affords relative autonomy to education. For example, Apple (1982) replaces his earlier mirror-like model of education and society with one which recognizes pupil cultures as being at odds with the dominant culture and in a position to mediate the curriculum being taught. Hence schools can be seen as sites of resistance and creative adaptation. However, he avoids any suggestion of romanticism by recognizing the unequal power distribution and comments, 'Struggle and conflict may indeed exist, but this does not mean it is successful' (see discussion at 3.4 and 4.6). Bowles and Gintis (1981) have also reformulated their early position to recognize three sites of social practice – the state, the family and capitalist production. These sites make a contradictory whole, in other words, what happens in one site is not necessarily congruent with what happens in another. For example, women and blacks have formal political equality in the state, and receive relatively equal education (a sub-site of the state), but the site of capitalist production requires both groups to occupy relatively inferior, subordinate positions. Hence, there is no correspondence between the sites, rather than directly reproducing capitalism, education may be seen to undermine it.

As we have seen (4.7), Willis (1976, 1977) has painted a stark picture of working-class pupil resistance in tracing their school culture directly to that of the shop floor – which he characterizes as being in opposition to authority but not directly challenging it. Hence the reproduction takes place through struggle. What Willis appears to under-emphasize, however, is that both anti- and pro-school cultures existed in the working-class school he studied and it is not clear whether the 'lads' and 'earholes' came from different locations within their class, or whether and to what extent they were 'produced' in and through schooling. As we have also seen, a dichotomy into pro-and anti-school cultures is too simple – not only is there a variety of cultures, but many individuals move between them and some act as bridges.

While such views are corrective of the overly deterministic reproductive views of education in society and capture something of the obvious complexity of the situation, they fall short of providing a convincing model of any particular utility. There is then a clear need not only for the development of better models or theories but in particular for extensive research, much of which needs to be undertaken from the interpretative perspective so as to investigate the understandings of those directly involved.

## 9.2 Sociology of education

### 9.2a THE STATE OF THE ART

While raising a number of important issues, the approaches outlined in 9.1a and b leave a number of questions unresolved. In particular the extent to which education is an organ of the state or dominant class, as opposed to a relatively autonomous institution and to what extent it follows its own ends, and the congruence between these ends and the perceived needs of society or its economy. Such questions will entertain sociologists, politicians and others for some time to come. At a more pragmatic level it has to be realized that the educational system, on balance, reproduces the social structure more than it produces it or changes it. Within the context of concern over equality and equal opportunity, this remains a problem for those involved in the practice of education. The fact that reproduction is neither direct or complete, and the failure to demonstrate the direct control of education by state or social class, at least provides space for those who wish to affect the process or implement change (see below).

As far as the sociology of education is concerned, our considerations here, and throughout the book, clearly point to the need to use all the sociological perspectives in a corporate, complementary manner – there being no clear indication of any superiority. In particular it is necessary to reiterate once again the need for approaches which combine structuralist and interpretative perspectives, in order to avoid, on the one hand, the reification of educational phenomena and, on the other, their trivialization. A balance must be struck between the two sides of the dilemma concerning the relationship of the individual and society (2.3); as King (1980) has neatly put it 'to regard the teachers and pupils both bound and free does not make for simple explanations, but it is the honest experience of what it is to be social.'

As outlined in 2, the sociology of education has developed a great deal in a comparatively short time. This book has illustrated much of the diversity of interest and approach within the discipline, along with many of the tensions and shortcomings it exhibits. In some senses we have recognized a divorce or lack of relationship between theory (perspective) and empirical research. In some cases this has provided a very limited explanation of social life and interrupted the development of deeper understandings. In particular, theories developed in relative isolation from observation, or those unavailable for verification or refutation by empirical research, are likely to remain sterile for sociologists and educationalists alike. Some of the research is small-scale and hence limited in respect to generalization, some very large-scale but lacking in the detail necessary to provide the basis for a proper understanding or the development of strategies to affect practice or outcome. All research takes place within a fairly rapidly changing social and educational reality, presenting what amounts to a still frame of what is essentially a moving picture. So some of our knowledge is based on types of school and their organization which are no longer the norm – though overall much the same processes and outcomes of schooling appear to be sustained (see, for example, 6).

The discipline lacks the tradition of replication – for the rewards lie with 'new' research – and this adds to the relatively piecemeal state of empirical knowledge. The severe cutbacks in higher education and research funding has not so much brought about a decline in the quantity of research being undertaken as it has redirected it into lower-budget, one-person, and limited research. Almost regardless of shifts in the predominant perspectives within the discipline, these factors have resulted in most research being of the interpretative type. The discipline often has to rely on knowledge and data collected by outside bodies for different purposes, for example, census data relating to occupied males in a school's catchment area, rather than parental occupation and education data to indicate the social background of pupils.

There is also some variation in the terminology used and the operationalization of variables. An obvious example is 'social class' which is in almost constant use, but rarely explicitly defined or accurately measured. Sometimes data from different sources is presented together without distinction; sometimes the definition seems to shift from context to context. This is related to the further divorce between conceptualization and operationalization. In social

283

class the first is normally complex and multi-dimensional, the second typically based on occupation. Finally, there is the continued tension between those for whom the sociological study of education is academic, and those for whom it serves to inform their practice of, or in, education. While far from being mutually exclusive, there are clear differences of interest and priorities.

While for some the concerns outlined here amount to distractions from the utility of the sociology of education, many can be viewed more positively. Divergence of interests, perspectives, methodology and the like are the essential dynamics of scientific endeavour and the advancement of knowledge. The dialectic involved – thesis (idea) and anti-thesis (opposite) holds the hope, if not the promise, of synthesis (new idea). A uniform, mono-perspective approach would clearly have severe limitations with respect to a set of phenomena as complex as that which makes up social and educational life.

At the same time, there are signs that the calls upon the discipline made by Hargreaves (1978) and myself (Reid 1978b) are receiving some attention. Hargreaves saw the need for a much greater discourse between structuralist and interpretative sociology, in that they produce problems for each other. At the general level, for instance, interpretative sociology of education ought to help correct the tendency of structuralism to 'over-simplify, under-estimate or ignore the complexity of the detailed operation of the relevant factors in actual social settings'. Clearly the converse can also be easily argued. I called for new levels of co-operation and co-ordination within the discipline. Instead of continuing with small-scale, single-perspective studies, what is called for are larger-scale, multi-perspective approaches on a systematic basis which address educational problems. A co-ordinated attack on a specific area, say the classroom, by a group of sociologists would be likely to be a great improvement upon the present rather fragmented studies. Such an approach using the full range of available theory and methodology could well make significant contributions to both sociology and education. As readers will appreciate from the contents of this book the discipline has some way to go in these directions. In the meantime, they, like textbooks, will have to build their own bridges!

Despite the discipline's present diversity, the pressures of the working environments of sociologists of education and the severe distractions imposed by cutbacks in higher education (Reid et al 1983), there should be real hope that, having survived, the discipline will move towards a future in which it will be empirical rather than speculative, more analytical than critical, and concerned with examining value judgements rather than making them. Theory will not be formal abstraction, but related in a meaningful way to the activities it attempts to explain in ways which acknowledge the complexity of the educational process and respect their basic humanity (after King 1980).

In drawing attention to these concerns and to the fact that the discipline is a developing one the purpose is not, of course, to overemphasize its limitations and problems. Precisely the same concerns abound in all disciplines, including the so-called 'pure' sciences. They do, however, have to be borne in mind by all who approach and use the discipline – not only to assist understanding and appreciation, but also because a critical audience is a contribution to any discipline.

## 9.2b AVOIDING PESSIMISM

As we have seen in numerous places in this book, the general view of sociologists of education is divorced from that which many like to hold of schools, schooling and education. It is a long way from a meritocratic and individualistic view, and moves towards a relatively deterministic, social one. While this is an important and necessary corrective (see also 2) it can give rise to pessimism and unfortunate defensiveness of existing practice. An overly deterministic view of, say, the relationship between social stratification and educational outcomes may see teachers, pupils and educational system either as innocent bystanders, helpless in the flow of societal forces, or even as conspiratorial partners in the crime of perpetuating inequality and subscribing to the maintenance of the existing social structure. Teachers might be drawn towards sets of expectations for their pupils solely based on their ascribed attributes and regard their own practice as relatively unimportant. In many ways there are parallels here with the pessimism engendered by the psychometric view that educational performance is determined by innate ability. Such views linger on and contribute to the terrifying prospect of a combination of sociological and psychometric determinism. What prognosis then for the ethnic minority, female child with a low measured IQ from a disadvantaged unskilled/manual class home background? Further contributions to pessimism might well include: the present state of educational knowledge (including sociology); the limited success of change exhibited in our educational history; the containment/cuts in educational expenditure and the pressurizing involvement and direction of central and local government in the early to mid 1980s.

Readers of this book will be able to avoid much of this pessimism, especially that arising from the misunderstanding and misuse of the sociology of education. They will have recognized that there are intra- as well as intergroup variations in educational outcomes and some autonomy and variation among schools and teachers. Most particularly, they should appreciate the necessity of basing their understanding of schooling and education on a positive and broad appreciation of its social context gained via sociology.

## 9.2c WHAT'S ON OFFER?

As pointed out in 2, the sociology of education has an educative rather than a prescriptive role in education. By analogy, the discipline is less like a doctor writing a prescription than the chemist holding a stock of ingredients. Teachers and others in education are less like patients waiting to receive a prescription than doctors wanting access to the chemist's stock in order to make up the right prescription to fit their diagnosis. Like all analogies these have limitations. Clearly, the discipline also critically monitors the educational system and provides an independent body of knowledge along with new, differing and challenging perspectives for it and for educational practice. It is sustained as a subject through interaction with teachers and their professional education (2.5), while its vitality and utility could be enhanced by fuller involvement (Reid 1975, 1978).

Without rehearsing the contents of this volume, here, we can identify some aspects of the discipline's contribution. First, there are the direct insights into practice afforded by the many empirical studies reviewed above. These serve not only to inform but, and more importantly, to provide the basis for comparison and evaluation. Second, there are the less direct but nevertheless useful insights gained from the consideration of general theories – as illustrated in 9.1. Over and above all, however, its contribution is in providing a unique conceptual framework, language and knowledge of education.

There are several further aspects worthy of consideration. The exploration and demonstration of the nature of the relationships of teachers, pupils and schooling with society, and the social definitions and functions of education are capable not only of broadening discussion, strategy and practice but also of facilitating it. However much teachers and others may wish to see the activities of classroom and school as apolitical, ideologically neutral and isolated from life beyond their doors, the reality is inescapably different. The sociology of education provides the vehicle for analysis. On the one hand, for example, it is likely to lead to a realization that many of the problems faced by teachers are corporate ones, best tackled by groups rather than the individual, or politically rather than educationally. On the other hand, it provides a knowledge base and language to explore and impart the tacit knowledge of the classroom that teachers rely on. Both have important roles to play in the enhancing of educational practice and teacher education. Readers will be able to expand and add to these examples and appreciate their implications for all the many parties involved with education.

Finally, while the vital importance of the discipline to any proper understanding of schooling and education has been shown and illustrated, it remains clear that we have some way to go to a full understanding. The recognition of the complexity of schooling, education and society should encourage and challenge us to strive towards further knowledge and understanding rather than retreating to simplistic explanations or defending what we have. What we have viewed in this book is a contribution towards a goal identified some time ago, in which education, like other areas of social life, calls for: 'We must fashion rationalists . . . who are concerned with clarity of thought; but they must be rationalists of a new kind who know that things, whether human or physical, are irreducibly complex and who are yet able to look unfalteringly into the face of this complexity.' Durkheim (1938, 1977).

# 10

# Appendices

## 10.1 Key to abbreviations and acronyms

| | |
|---|---|
| APU | Assessment of Performance Unit |
| ATCDE | Association of Teachers in Colleges and Departments of Education |
| BEC | Business Education Council |
| BEd | Bachelor of Education |
| BERA | British Educational Research Association |
| CATE | Council for the Accreditation of Teacher Education |
| CIPFA | Chartered Institute of Public Finance and Accountancy |
| CES | Centre for Educational Sociology |
| CRC | Community Relations Council |
| CRE | Commission for Racial Equality |
| CSE | Certificate of Secondary Education |
| CSO | Central Statistical Office |
| DES | Department of Education and Science |
| DOE | Department of Employment |
| EOC | Equal Opportunities Commission |
| EPA | Educational Priority Area |
| ESN | Educationally Subnormal |
| GB | Great Britain |
| GBA | Association of Governing Bodies of Public Schools |
| GBBSA | Association of Governing Bodies of Girls' Public Schools |
| GCE | General Certificate of Education |
| HMC | Head Masters' Association |
| HMI | Her Majesty's Inspectors (of education) |
| HMSO | Her Majesty's Stationery Office |
| HNC | Higher National Certificate |
| HND | Higher National Diploma |
| ILEA | Inner London Education Authority |
| ISIS | Independent Schools' Information Service |
| LEA | Local Education Authority |
| MSC | Manpower Services Commission |
| NCB | National Children's Bureau |
| NCDS | National Child Development Survey |
| NHS | National Health Service |

289

| | |
|---|---|
| NFER | National Foundation for Educational Research |
| NOP | National Opinion Polls Market Research Ltd |
| ONC | Ordinary National Certificate |
| OND | Ordinary National Diploma |
| OPCS | Office of Population Censuses and Surveys |
| PGCE | Postgraduate Certificate in Education |
| PTA | Parent-Teacher association |
| RG | Registrar General |
| SC | School Certificate |
| SCE | Scottish Certificate of Education |
| SCOTBEC | Scottish Business Education Council |
| SCOTEC | Scottish Technical Education Council |
| SLC | Scottish Leaving Certificate |
| SUPE | Scottish Universities Preliminary Examination |
| SRHE | Society for Research into Higher Education |
| SSC | Scottish School Certificate |
| TEC | Technical Education Council |
| TVEI | Technical and Vocational Educational Initiative |
| UCCA | Universities' Central Council on Admissions |
| UGC | Universities' Grant Commission |
| VRQ | Verbal Reasoning Quotient |
| YOP | Youth Opportunities Programme |
| YTS | Youth Training Scheme |

## 10.2 Key to social class classifications

Social class, as used in empirical research, refers to the grouping of people into categories on the basis of their occupation, or in the case of children that of their parent(s), typically father or head of household. In this book three classifications are referred to as follows:

*Tables 7.1, 7.2 and 7.5* use the Registrar General's social class classification devised for census purposes which is based on occupation and employment status (for example, foremen or managers are allocated to classes II or III if their basic occupation is IV or V).

| Social class | Descriptive definition | Examples of occupations included |
|---|---|---|
| I | Professional, etc. | Accountant, architect, chemist, company secretary, doctor, engineer, judge, lawyer, optician, scientist, solicitor, surveyor, university teacher |

## Appendices

| | | |
|---|---|---|
| II | Intermediate | Aircraft pilot or engineer, chiropodist, farmer, laboratory assistant or technician, manager, proprietor, publican, MP, nurse, police or fire-brigade officer, schoolteacher |
| III(nm) | Skilled non-manual | Auctioneer, cashier, clerical worker, commercial traveller, draftsman, estate agent, sales representative, secretary, shop assistant, typist, telephone supervisor |
| III(m) | Skilled Manual | Baker, bus driver, butcher, brick layer, carpenter, cook, electrician, hairdresser, miner (underground), policeman, fireman, railway engine driver/guard, upholsterer |
| IV | Partly skilled | Agricultural worker, barman, bus conductor, fisherman, hospital orderly, machine sewer, packer, postman, groundsman, street vendor, telephone operator |
| V | Unskilled | Charwoman, chimney-sweep, kitchenhand, labourer, lorry driver's mate, office cleaner, railway porter, van guard, window cleaner |

*Tables 7.3, 8.1 and 8.2* use a similar Registrar General's scale based on socio-economic groups.

| Socio-Economic Class | Descriptive Definition |
|---|---|
| 1 | Professional |
| 2 | Employers and managers |
| 3 | Intermediate and junior non-manual |
| 4 | Skilled manual (with own account non-professional) |
| 5 | Semi-skilled manual and personal service |
| 6 | Unskilled manual |

## The Sociology of School and Education

Full details of both RG's scales are contained in *Classification of Occupations 1970*.

In tables and text the term working or manual class refers to classes III(m), IV and V, or 4, 5 and 6: the term middle or non-manual class to classes I, II and III(nm), or 1, 2 and 3.

In 8, reference is made to the Hope-Goldthorpe scale which is based on a modified set of OPCS groups of occupations, ordered in relation to their ranking on the criteria of social standing by a sample of the public. These were subsequently collapsed into the following categories:

| Categories | Descriptive definition |
|---|---|
| I | All higher grade professionals, self-employed or salaried higher-grade administrators/officals in central/local government and public/private enterprises (including company directors), managers in large industrial establishments, large proprietors |
| II | Lower-grade professionals/administrators/officials, higher-grade technicians, managers in small business/industrial/service establishments, supervisors of non-manual workers |
| III | Routine non-manual, mainly clerical, sales and rank-and-file employees in services |
| IV | Small proprietors, including farmers/smallholders/self-employed artisans/own-account workers other than professional |
| V | Lower-grade technicians (whose work is to some extent manual), supervisors of manual workers |
| VI | Skilled manual wage-workers, all industries |
| VII | All manual wage-workers in semi- and unskilled grades, agricultural workers |

These categories were then further collapsed into three classes:

| | |
|---|---|
| Service class | categories I and II |
| Intermediate class | categories III, IV and V |
| Working class | categories VI and VII |

Full details of this scale can be found in Goldthorpe and Hope 1974.

## 10.3 Key to educational qualifications

There is a considerable range of qualifications, with some changes over time. The following outlines the terms used in tables and text and defines their equivalents.

*16+ examinations* are presently of two main types: O level GCE/SCE and CSE. Each of these has five grades of pass: A–E and 1–5 respectively. Until 1975 GCE/SCE O levels were pass/fail only. CSE grade 1 is equivalent to an O level pass (grades A–C). A distinction is drawn between:

> *Higher grades* GCE/SCE O level grades A, B and C and CSE grade 1.
>
> *Other grades* GCE/SCE O level grades D and E and CSE grades 2–5.

*Higher education* (HE) is that above GCE A/SCE H level and ONC/OND level.

*Advanced further education* includes the majority of full- and part-time students in the public sector of HE (polytechnics, colleges and institutes of HE and technical and further education colleges) reading for degrees, HNC/HND/BEC/TEC qualifications and those awarded by professional institutions.

EQUIVALENTS

*Degree*: university and other diplomas/certificates, etc., of degree standard.

*HE below degree*: non-graduate teaching qualifications; HNC/HND; BEC/TEC, SCOTBEC/TEC, higher; nursing qualifications; other qualifications above A level GCE/Higher SCE but below degree.

*A level*: School Certificate, SSC, SLC, SUPE, higher; ONC/OND; BEC/TEC, SCOTBEC/TEC, national/general/ordinary level; City and Guilds, advanced/final level.

*O level higher grades* SC, SSC, SLC, SUPE, lower/ordinary level; City and Guilds craft/ordinary level.

# 11

# Bibliography and Author Index

All these sources are followed by page references which show where they are discussed or mentioned in the text. Works are referenced, wherever possible by author(s)/editor(s) and otherwise by title. Reproduction of a source in a listed reader is cross-referenced. A key to abbreviations is at 10.1.

Acland, H. (1980) 'Research as stage management: the case of the Plowden Committee' in Blumer 1980. 217

*A Language for Life* (1975) (The Bullock Report). DES. London: HMSO.

Alexander, R. J. and Wormald, E. (1979) *Professional Studies for Teaching*, London: SRHE. 40

Althusser, L. (1971) *Lenin and Philosophy and other Essays.* London: New Left Books. 75, 278

Anderson, C. A. (1961) 'A skeptical note on the relation of vertical mobility to education', *American Journal of Sociology.* 66(6). 270

Anderson, C. A., Brown, J. C. and Bowman, M. J. (1952) 'Intelligence and occupational mobility', *Journal of Political Economy*, 60(3). 252

Apple, M. (1980) 'Analysing determinations: understanding and evaluating the production of social outcomes in school', *Curriculum Inquiry*, 10(2). 75, 76

Apple, M. (1982) *Cultrual and Economic Reproduction in Education.* London: Routledge and Kegan Paul. 280

Apple, M. (1982) *Education and Power.* London: Routledge and Kegan Paul. 280

*APU Mathematical Development Primary Survey. Report No. 1.* (1980) London: HMSO. 186

*Aspects of Secondary Education in England* (1979). DES. London: HMSO. 186

Atkinson, P. A. and Delamont, S. (1977) 'Mock-ups and cock-ups – the stage-management of guided discovery instruction' in Woods and Hammersley 1977, and Hammersley and Woods 1976, 1984b. 115

Bacon, C., Benton, D. and Gruneberg, M. M. (1979) 'Employers' opinions of university and polytechnic graduates', *Vocational Aspect of Education*, 31(80). 257

Bagley, C., Bart, M. and Wong, J. (1979) 'Antecedents of scholastic success in West Indian ten-year-olds in London' in Verma and Bagley 1979. 202

# Bibliography and Author Index

Ball, S. J. (1980) 'Initial encounters in the classroom and the process of establishment' in Woods 1980, Hammersley and Woods 1984a. 97, 118, 124

Ball, S. J. (1981) *Beachside Comprehensive*. Cambridge University Press. 83, 101, 136, 156, 158, 160

Ball, S. J. and Lacey, C. (1980) 'Subject disciplines as the opportunity for group action: a measured critique of subject subcultures' in Woods 1980b, Hammersley and Woods, 1984b. 89

Banks, O. (1968, 1971 and 1976) *The Sociology of Education*. London: Batsford. 36, 57, 63

Banks, O. and Finlayson, D. (1973) *Success and Failure in the Secondary School*. London: Methuen. 219

Barker Lunn, J. C. (1970) *Streaming in the Primary School*. Slough: NFER. 155, 156, 159, 217

Barker Lunn, J. C. (1972) 'Length of infant school and academic performance', *Educational Research*, 14(2). 196

Barker Lunn, J. C. (1982) 'Junior schools and their organisational policies', *Educational Research*, 24(4). 141, 154

Barnes, D. (1976) *From Communication to Curriculum*. London: Penguin. 114, 115, 116

Barnes, J. (1975) *Educational Priority*, Vol. 3. London: HMSO. 190

Barry, J. and O'Connor, D. (1983) 'Costs and benefits of sponsoring the unemployed', *Employment Gazette*, March. 241

Barton, L. and Meighan, R. (1978) *Sociological Interpretations of Schooling and Classrooms: a Reappraisal*. Driffield: Nafferton. 303, 308, 312

Barton, L. and Meighan, R. (1979) *Schools, Pupils and Deviance*. Driffield: Nafferton. 307, 309

Barton, L., Meighan, R. and Walker, S. (1981) *Schooling, Ideology and the Curriculum*. Lewes: Falmer Press. 296

Barton, L. and Walker, S. (1981) *Schools, Teachers and Teaching*. Lewes: Falmer Press. 313

Barton, L. and Walker, S. (1984) *Social Crisis and Education*. London: Croom Helm. 309

Bealing, D. (1972) 'The organisation of junior school classrooms', *Educational Research*, 14(3). 154

Becker, H. S. (1952) 'Social class variation in pupil-teacher relationships', *Journal of Educational Sociology*, 25(8) in Cosin et al 1971, Hammersley and Woods 1984b. 101

Bell, R., Fowler, G. and Little, K. (1973) *Education in Great Britain and Northern Ireland*. London: Routledge and Kegan Paul with Open University Press. 311

Bell, R. and Grant, N. (1974) *A Mythology of British Education*. London: Panther Books. 272

Belotti, E. G. (1975) *Little Girls*. London: Writers' and Readers' Publishing Cooperative. 57

Bendix, R. and Lipset, S. M. (1967) *Class, Status and Power*. London: Routledge and Kegan Paul. 250

Berg, I. (1970 and 1973) *Education and Jobs*. London: Penguin. 252, 256

Berg, L. (1968) *Risinghill: Death of a Comprehensive*. London: Penguin. 137

# The Sociology of School and Education

Bernstein, B. (1969) 'A critique of the concept of compensatory education', paper given at the Teachers' College, Columbia University, in Bernstein 1971/3. 211

Bernstein, B. (1970) 'Education cannot compensate for society', *New Society*, 26 February in Cosin et al 1971. 90

Bernstein, B. (1971) 'A socio-linguistic approach to socialisation: with some reference to educability' in Hymes and Gumperz 1971 and Bernstein 1971/3. 205, 208

Bernstein, B. (1971/73) *Class, Codes and Control*, Vol. 1. London: Routledge and Kegan Paul/Paladin. 205, 208, 295, 296

Bernstein, B. (1974) 'Sociology and the sociology of education' in Rex 1974 and Bernstein 1975. 26, 37

Bernstein, B. (1975) *Class, Codes and Control*, Vol. 3. London: Routledge and Kegan Paul. 75

Beynon, J. (1984) '"Sussing out" teachers: pupils as data gatherers', in Hammersley and Woods 1984a. 117

Blackburn, R. (1972) *Ideology in Social Science*. London: Fontana. 313

Blaug, M. (1970) *An Introduction to the Economics of Education*. London: Penguin. 243

Blaug, M. (1972) 'The correlation between education and earnings: What does it signify?', *Higher Education*, 1(1). 251

Blishen, E. (1973) 'Why some secondary school teachers are disliked', *Where*, 86. 98

Blumer, H. (1965) 'Sociological implications of the thought of G. H. Mead', *American Journal of Sociology*, 71(4) in Cosin et al 1971. 31

Blumer, M. I. A. (1980) *Social Research and Royal Commissions*. London: Allen and Unwin. 294

Boaden, M. (1971) *Urban Policy Making. Influences on County Boroughs in England and Wales*. Cambridge University Press. 228

Booth, T. and Stratham, J. (1982) *The Nature of Special Education*. London: Croom Helm. 312

Bourdieu, P. (1967) 'Systems of education and systems of thought' in Young 1971, Dale et al 1976. 277

Bourdieu, P. (1971) 'The thinkable and the unthinkable', *The Times Literary Supplement*, 15 October. 75

Bourdieu, P. (1973) 'Cultural reproduction and social reproduction' in Brown 1973, Karabel and Halsey 1977. 75, 277

Bourdieu, P. (1974) 'The school as a conservative force: scholastic and cultural inequalities' in Eggleston 1974, Dale et al 1976. 220

Bourdieu, P. and Passeron, J. C. (1977) *Reproduction in Education, Society and Culture*. London: Sage. 277

Bowles, S. and Gintis, H. (1976) *Schooling in Capitalist Society*. London: Routledge and Kegan Paul. 56, 75, 259, 275

Bowles, S. and Gintis, H. (1981) 'Contradiction and reproduction in educational theory' in Barton, et al 1981 and Dale et al 1981a. 281

Briggs, D. (1971) 'The influence of handwriting on assessment', *Educational Research*, 13(2). 170

Briggs, D. (1980) 'A study of the influence of handwriting upon grades using examination scripts', *Educational Review*, 2(2). 170

# Bibliography and Author Index

Brittan, E. M. (1976) 'Multiracial Education 2 – teacher opinion on aspects of school life', *Educational Research*, 18(3). 107

Brockington, F. and Stein, Z. (1963) 'Admission, achievement and social class', *Universities Quarterly*, 18(1). 184

Broderick, D. (1973) *Image of the Black in Children's Literature*. New York: Bowker. 72

Brooks, D. and Singh, K. (1978) *Aspirations versus opportunities: Asian and white school leavers in the Midlands*. Walsall CRC and Leicester CRC. 190

Brophy, J. E. and Good, T. L. (1974) *Teacher-Student Relationships*. New York: Holt, Rinehart and Winston. 162, 170

Brown, C. (1984) *Black and White Britain*. London: Heinemann. 192

Brown, R. (1973) *Knowledge, Education and Cultural Change*. London: Tavistock. 37, 296, 299

Brynner, J., Cashdan, A. and Commings, B. (1972) *Attitudes, Learning Problems*. Course E281, Unit 15, Appendix B. Milton Keynes: Open University Press. 168

Bull, R. and Stevens, J. (1979) 'The effects of attractiveness of writer and penmanship on essay grades', *Journal of Occupational Therapy*, 52(1). 170

Burgess, R. G. (1977) 'Sociology of education, courses for the intending teacher: an empirical study, *Research in Education*, 17. 40

Burgess, R. G. (1983) *Experiencing Comprehensive Education*. London: Methuen. 121

Burnhill, P. (1981) 'The relationship between examination performance and social class', *CES Collaborative Research Newsletter*, 8. 178, 179

Burt, C. (1961) 'The gifted child', *British Journal of Statistical Psychology*, 14(2). 148

Butler, D. and Kavanagh, D. (1984) *The British General Election of 1983*. London: Macmillan. 142

Bynner, J. M. (1972) *Parents' Attitudes to Education*. OPCS, Social Surveys Division. London: HMSO. 168, 216

Byrne, D. S., Williamson, W. and Fletcher, B. (1975) *The Poverty of Education*. Oxford: Martin Robertson. 227

Byrne, E. M. 'Inequality in education – discriminal resource allocation in school's, *Education Review*, 27(3). 71, 223

Byren, E. M. (1978) *Women and Education*. London: Tavistock, 71, 223


*Cambridge University Reporter* (1985) Vol. CXVI, Special No. 7. 146, 147

Capello, F. S., Dei, M. and Rossi, M. (1982) *L'Immobilta Sociale*. Bologna: Il Muuno. 304

Carrington, B. (1981) 'Schooling an underclass: the implications of ethnic differences in attainment', *Durham and Newcastle Research Review*, 11 (47). 107

Cashden, A. and Grugeon, E. (1972) *Language in Education*. London: Routledge and Kegan Paul. 309

Chanan, G. (1973) *Towards a Science of Teaching*. Slough: NFER. 313

Chanan, G. and Delamont, S. (1975) *Frontiers of Classroom Research*. Slough: NFER. 313

*Children and their Primary Schools*. (1967) (The Plowden Report) DES. London: HMSO. 90, 204, 214, 223

# The Sociology of School and Education

Children's Rights Workshop (1976) *Sexism in Children's Books: Facts, Figures and Guidelines*. London: Writers' and Readers' Publishing Cooperative. 306

CIPFA (1984) *Education Statistics 1982–83 Actuals*. London: CIPFA. 226, 229

Clark, B. R. (1962) *Educating the Expert Society*. San Francisco: Chandler. 250

Clark, D. G. (1966) *The Industrial Manager – his Background and Career Pattern*. London: Business Publications. 296

*Classification of Occupations 1970*. OPCS. London: HMSO. 292

Coard, B. (1971) *How the West Indian Child is Made Educationally Subnormal in the British Educational System*. London: New Beacon. 156

Cohen, P. S. (1968) *Modern Social Theory*. London: Heinemann. 29

Coleman, J. S. (1961) *Adolescent Society*. Glencoe: Free Press. 81

Coleman, J. S. (1965a) *Adolescents and their Schools*. New York: Basic Books. 81

Coleman, J. S. (1965b) *Education and Political Development*. Princeton University Press. 304

Coleman, J. S., Coser, L. A. and Powell, W. W. (1966) *Equality of Educational Opportunity*. Washington: US Government Printing Office. 90

*College Admissions 10; The Behavioural Sciences and Education*. (1963) New York: College Entrance Examination Board. 301

Collins, R. (1971) 'Functional and conflict theories of educational stratification', *American Sociological Review*, 36(6) in Karabel and Halsey 1977. 135, 248, 254

Command 8836 (1983) *Teacher Quality*. London: HMSO. 41

*Comprehensive Education* (1978) Report of DES Conference. London: HMSO. 143

*Consultative Committee on the Primary School* (1931) (The Hadow Report) Board of Education. London: HMSO. 153

Cornbleth, C. (1984) 'Beyond the hidden curriculum', *Journal of Curriculum Studies*, 16(1). 76

Cortis, G. and Grayson, A. (1978) 'Primary school pupils' perception of student teachers' performance', *Educational Review*, 30(2). 100

Coser, L. A. (1956) *The Functions of Social Conflict*. Glencoe: Free Press. 30

Cosin, B. R., Dale, I. R., Esland, G. M. and Swift, D. F. (1971) *School and Society*. London: Routledge and Kegan Paul; Open University Press. 295, 296

Craft, M. (1974) 'Talent, family values and education in Ireland' in Eggleston 1974. 219

Craft, M. and Craft, A. (1983) 'The participation of ethnic minority pupils in further and higher education', *Educational Research*, 18(3). 191, 193

Croucher, A. and Reid, I. (1979) 'Internalised achievement responsibility as a factor in primary school children's achievement', *Educational Studies*, 5(2). 252

Dahlke, H. O. (1958) *Values in Culture and Classroom*. New York: Harper and Row. 59, 63

Dahrendorf, R. (1959) *Class and Class Conflict in Industrial Society*. London: Routledge and Kegan Paul. 29, 30

Dale, R. (1977) 'The structural context of teaching', Course E202 Unit 5, *Schooling and Society*, Block 1, Schooling and Capitalism. Milton Keynes: The Open University Press. 66

Dale, R. (1981) 'Control, accountability and William Tynedale' in Dale et al 1981b. 137

# Bibliography and Author Index

Dale, R., Esland, G., Fergusson, R. and MacDonald, M. (1981a) *Schooling and the National Interest*. Lewes: Falmer Press in association with the Open University Press. 313

Dale, R., Esland, G., Fergusson, R. and MacDonald, M. (1981b) *Politics, Patriarchy and Practice*, Vol. 2. Lewes: Falmer Press in association with the Open University Press. 298

Dale, R., Esland, G. and MacDonald, M. (1976) *Schooling and Capitalism*. London: Routledge and Kegan Paul. 296

Daniels, J. C. (1961) 'The effects of streaming in primary schools', *British Journal of Educational Psychology*, 31(1). 154

Darby, J. (1973) 'Divisiveness in education', *The Northern Teacher*, 8(1). 44

Darby, J. (1977) 'Educational provision in Northern Ireland', *The Northern Teacher*, 12(4). 44

Davie, R., Butler, M. and Goldstein, H. (1972) *From Birth to Seven*. London: Longman. 176, 177, 216

Davies, B. (1973) 'On the contribution of organisational analysis to the study of educational institutions' in Brown 1973. 57

Davies, B. (1981) 'Schools as organisations and the organisation of schooling', *Educational Analysis*, 3(1). 57

Davies, L. (1984) *Pupil Power*. Lewes: Falmer Press. 84, 97, 106, 164

Davies, L. and Meighan, R. (1975) 'A review of schooling and sex roles', *Educational Review*, 27(3). 106

Deem, R. (1978) *Women and Schooling*. London: Routledge and Kegan Paul. 71, 301

Delamont, S. (1976) *Interaction in the Classroom*. London: Methuen. 84, 100, 122

Delamont, S. and Hamilton, D. (1974) 'Classroom research – a cautionary tale', *Research in Education*, 11, in Stubbs and Delamont 1976. 94

Denscombe, M. (1980) 'Pupil strategies and the open classroom' in Woods 1980a. 123, 130

DES Circular 11/67 (1967) *School Building in Educational Priority Areas*. London: HMSO. 204

DES Circular 3/84 (1984) *Initial Teacher Training: Approval of Courses*. London: HMSO. 41

Douglas, J. D. (1971, 1974) *Understanding Everyday Life: Toward the Reconstruction of Sociological Knowledge*. London: Routledge and Kegan Paul. 33

Douglas, J. W. B. (1964) *The Home and the School*. London: MacGibbon and Kee. 106, 155, 157, 178, 181, 223

Douglas, J. W. B., Ross, J. M. and Simpson, H. R. (1968) *All Our Future*. London: Peter Davies. 106, 146, 181, 224, 265

Driver, G. (1977) 'Cultural competence, social power and school achievement', *New Community*, 5(4). 158

Driver, G. (1980) *Beyond Underachievement*. London: CRE. 192

Driver, G. (1986) 'How West Indians do better at school (especially the girls)', *New Society*, 27 January. 192

Driver, G. and Ballard, R. (1979) 'Comparing performance in multi-racial schools: South Asian pupils at 16+', *New Community*, 8(1). 190

# The Sociology of School and Education

Durkheim, E. (1897, 1952) *Suicide*. London: Routledge and Kegan Paul. 132

Durkheim, E. (1911, 1956) *Education and Sociology*. New York: the Free Press. 69, 134, 135, 136

Durkheim, E. (1938, 1977) *The Evolution of Educational Thought*. London: Routledge and Kegan Paul. 287

*Education: A Framework for Expansion*. (1972) DES. London: HMSO. 176

*Education for All*. (1985) Command 9453 (The Swann Report). Report of Committee of Inquiry into the Education of Children from Ethnic Minority Groups. London: HMSO. 168, 189, 191, 193, 302, 306

*Education Statistics for the United Kingdom 1983*. (1984) London: HMSO. 243

*Education Statistics for the United Kingdom 1984*. (1985) London: HMSO. 143, 144, 146, 148, 188, 245

*Education Statistics For the United Kingdom 1985* (1985). 43

*Education Tables (10% sample)*. (1966) Census 1961, England and Wales, OPCS. London: HMSO. 237

Edwards, A. D. (1976) *Language in Culture and Class*. London: Heinemann. 209

Edwards, A. E. and Furlong, V. J. (1978) *The Language of Teaching*. London: Heinemann. 112, 114

Edwards, E. G. and Roberts, I. J. (1980) 'British higher education: long-term trends in student enrolment', *Higher Education Review*, 12(1). 194

Edwards, J. R. (1979) 'Judgements and confidence reactions to disadvantaged speech' in Giles and St Clair 1979. 170

Edwards, V. K. (1978) 'Language attitudes and underperformance in West Indian children', *Educational Review*, 30(1). 169, 213

Edwards, V. K. (1979) *The West Indian Language Issue in British Schools*. London: Routledge and Kegan Paul. 213

Eggleston, J. (1974) *Contemporary Research in the Sociology of Education*. London: Methuen. 296, 298

Eggleston, J. (1979) *Teacher Decision-Making in the Classroom*. London: Routledge and Kegan Paul. 303

Essen, J. and Ghodsian, M. (1977) 'Sixteen-year olds in households in receipt of supplementary benefit and family income supplement', *Supplementary Benefits Commission 1977*. 203

Essen, J. and Ghodsian, M. (1979) 'The children of immigrants: school performance', *New Community*, 8(3). 190

Essen, J., Fogelman, K. and Tibbenham, A. (1979) 'Some non-academic correlates of ability grouping in secondary schools', *Educational Studies*, 5(1). 160

Etzioni, A. (1962) *Readings on Modern Organisations*. New York: Holt, Rinehart and Winston. 302

Evans, K. (1974a) 'The spatial organisation of infants' schools', *Journal of Architectural Research*, 3(7). 65

Evans, K. (1974b) 'The head and his territory', *New Society*, 24 October. 65

Farrant, J. H. (1981) 'Trends in admissions', in Fulton 1981. 183, 245

# Bibliography and Author Index

Feuer, L.S. (1969) *Marx and Engels: Basic Writings on Politics and Philosophy*. London: Fontana. 34

*15–18*. (1960) (The Crowther Report) Central Advisory Council for Education, Ministry of Education. London: HMSO. 143

Finlayson, D. S. (1971) 'Parental aspirations and the educational achievements of children', *Educational Research*, 14(1). 216

Fletcher, C. and Thompson, N. (1980) *Issues in Community Education*. Lewes: Falmer Press. 64

Floud, J. E. and Scott, W. (1961) 'Recruitment to teaching in England and Wales', in Halsey et al 1961, 86

Fogelman, K. (1983) *Growing Up in Great Britain*. London: Macmillan for NCB. 301

Fogelman, K. R. and Goldstein, H. (1976) 'Social factors associated with changes in attainment between 7 and 11 years of age', *Educational Studies*, 2(2). 177

Fogelman, K., Essen, J. and Tibbenham, A. (1978a) 'Ability grouping in secondary schools and attainment', *Educational Studies*, 4(3). 159

Fogelman, K. R., Goldstein, H., Essen, J. and Ghodsian, M. (1978b) 'Patterns of attainment', *Educational Studies*, 4(1). 178

Fogelman, K. and Gorbach, P. (1978) 'Age of starting school and attainment at school', *Educational Research*, 21(1). 196

Fogler, J. K. and Nam, C. B. (1964) 'Trends in education in relation to the occupational structure', *Sociology of Education*, 38(1). 251

Ford, J. (1969) *Social Class and the Comprehensive School*. London: Routledge and Kegan Paul. 157

French, J. (1980) 'Gender and the classroom', *New Society*, 7 March. 165

Friendenburg, E. Z. (1963) 'The school as a social environment', *College Admissions 10*, 1963. 52

Fuller, M. (1980) 'Black girls in a London comprehensive school' in Deem 1980, Hammersley and Woods 1984a. 84

Fulton, O. (1981) *Access to Higher Education*. Surrey: SRHE. 300

Furlong, V. (1976) 'Interaction sets in the classroom: towards a study of pupil knowledge' in Stubbs and Delamont 1976, Hammersley and Woods 1984a. 84, 97

Furlong, V. (1977) 'Anancy goes to school: a case study of pupils' knowledge of their teachers' in Woods and Hammersley 1977. 97


Gallup Polls (1973) *Report No. 157*. London: Social Surveys (Gallup Polls) Ltd. 149

Galton, M., Simon, B. and Croll, P. (1980) *Inside the Primary School*. London: Routledge and Kegan Paul. 112

Gannaway, H. (1976) 'Making sense of school' in Stubbs and Delamont 1976, Hammersley and Woods 1984a. 99, 100

Garfinkel, H. (1967) *Studies in Ethnomethodology*. New York: Prentice Hall. 33

Garwood, S. G. (1976) 'First name stereotypes as a factor in self-concept and school achievement', *Journal of Educational Psychology*, 68(4). 170

Garwood, S. G. and McDavid, J. W. (1975) 'Ethnic factors in stereotypes of given names', *Resources in Education*. Atlanta: Georgia State University. 170

*General Household Survey 1972*. (1975) OPCS. London: HMSO. 144, 176

*General Household Survey 1976.* (1978) OPCS. London: HMSO. 144

*General Household Survey 1978.* (1980) OPCS. London: HMSO. 144

*General Household Survey 1981.* (1983) OPCS. London: HMSO. 241

*General Household Survey 1982.* (1984) OPCS. London: HMSO. 178, 180, 238, 239, 242

Ghodsian, M., Gorbach, P. and Richardson, K. (1983) 'Parents' and pupils' appreciation of education and school' in Fogelman 1983. 51

Giglioli, P. P. (1972) *Language and Social Context.* London: Penguin. 305

Giles, H. and Powesland, P. F. (1975) *Speech Style and Social Evaluation.* London: Academic Press. 169

Giles, H. and St Clair, R. N. (1979) *Language and Social Psychology.* Oxford: Blackwell. 204, 300

Glass, D. V. (1954) *Social Mobility in Britain.* London: Routledge and Kegan Paul. 270

Glennerster, H. and Pryke, R. (1973) 'The contribution of the public schools and Oxbridge' in Urry and Wakefield 1973. 147

Goffman, E. (1962) 'The characteristics of total institutions' in Etzioni 1962. 149

Goldthorpe, J. H. and Hope, K. (1974) *The Social Grading of Occupations: A New Approach and Scale.* Oxford: Clarendon Press. 292

Goldthorpe, J. and Llewellyn, C. (1977) 'Class mobility in modern Britain', *Sociology,* 11(2). 269

Goldthorpe, J. H., Llewllyn, C. and Payne, C. (1978) 'Trends in class mobility', *Sociology,* 12(3). 268

Goldthorpe, J. H., Llewllyn, C. and Payne, C. (1980) *Social Mobility and Class Structure in Modern Britain.* Oxford: Clarendon Press. 268, 269

Goodacre, E. J. (1967) *Reading in Infant Classes,* Slough: NFER. 164

Goodacre, E. J. (1968) *Teachers and Their Pupils' Home Backgrounds.* Slough: NFER. 164

Gorbutt, D. (1972) 'The new sociology of education', *Education for Teaching,* 89, in Reid and Wormald, 1974. 40

Gordon, A. (1983) 'Attitudes of employers to the recruitment of graduates', *Educational Studies,* 9(1). 257

Gorden, R. A. and Howell, J. E. (1959) *Higher Education for Business.* New York: Columbia University Press. 258

Gouldner, A. W. (1956) 'Explorations in applied social science', *Social Problems,* 3(3). 24

Gouldner, A. W. (1973) *For Sociology.* London: Penguin. 38

Grace, G. (1978) *Teachers, Ideology and Control.* London: Routledge and Kegan Paul. 89

Gray, J. (1981a) 'School effectiveness research: key issues', *Educational Research,* 24(1). 92

Gray, J. (1981b) 'A competitive edge: examination results and the probable limits of secondary school effectiveness', *Educational Review,* 33(1). 93

Gray, J., McPherson, A. and Raffe, D. (1983) *Reconstructions of Secondary Education: Theory, Myth and Practice in Scotland Since the War.* London: Routledge and Kegan Paul. 249

Greer, B. (1968) 'Teaching' in Sills 1968. 54

Green, P. A. (1985) 'Multi-ethnic teaching and the pupils' self-concepts', *Education for All*, Annex B, Chapter 2, (1985). 166

Hakim, C. (1979) *Occupational Segregation*. DOE Research Paper No. 9. London: HMSO. 243

*Half our Future*. (1963) (The Newsom Report) Ministry of Education. London: HMSO. 223

Halsey, A. H. (1972) *Educational Priority. EPA Problems and Policies*. Vol. 1. London: HMSO. 217

Halsey, A. H. (1977) 'Towards meritocracy? The case of Britain' in Karabel and Halsey 1977. 271

Halsey, A. H. (1978) *Change in British Society*. London: Oxford University Press. 270

Halsey, A. H. (1979) 'Social mobility and education' in Rubinstein 1979. 270

Halsey, A. H., Floud, J. E. and Anderson, C. A. (1961) *Education Economy and Society*. New York: Free Press. 301, 307

Halsey, A. H., Heath, A. F. and Ridge, J. M. (1980) *Origins and Destinations*. Oxford: Clarendon Press. 145, 247

Hammersley, M. (1977) 'Teacher perspectives', Course E202, Unit 9, *Schooling and Society*. Milton Keynes: Open University Press. 122

Hammersley, M. and Woods, P. (1976) *The Process of Schooling*. London: Routledge and Kegan Paul. 294, 305, 308, 309, 313

Hammersley, M. and Woods, P. (1984a) *Life in School*. Milton Keynes: Open University Press. 295, 296, 301

Hammersley, M. and Woods, P. (1984b) *Classrooms and Staffrooms*. Milton Keynes: Open University Press. 294, 295, 303, 305

*Hansard* (1984) 15 January, Cols. 88–90. 143

*Hansard* (1985) a 22 January Cols. - 146. b 12 February, Cols. 126–29. 220

Harai, H. and McDavid, J. W. (1973) 'Name stereotypes and teacher expectations', *Journal of Educational Psychology*, 65(2). 170

Harary, F. (1966) 'Merton revisited: a new classification for deviant behaviour', *American Sociological Review*, 31(5). 78

Hardy, C. (1977) 'Architects and the hidden curriculum', *Times Educational Supplement*, 22 July. 64

Hargreaves, A. (1978) 'The signficance of classroom coping strategies' in Barton and Meighan 1978, Purvis and Hales, 1983, Hammersley and Woods 1984b. 118

Hargreaves, A. (1979) 'Strategies, decisions and control: interaction in a middle school classroom' in Eggleston 1979. 124

Hargreaves, D. H. (1967) *Social Relations in a Secondary School*. London: Routledge and Kegan Paul. 83, 136, 156

Hargreaves, D. H. (1972) *Interpersonal Relationships and Education*. London: Routledge and Kegan Paul. 88, 123

Hargreaves, D. H. (1977) 'The process of typification in classroom interaction: models and methods', *British Journal of Educational Psychology*, 47(3). 102

Hargreaves, D. H. (1978) 'Whatever happened to symbolic interactionism?' in Barton and Meighan 1978. 284

# The Sociology of School and Education

Hargreaves, D. H. (1980) 'The occupational culture of teachers' in Woods 1980b. 87

Hargreaves, D. H., Hestor, S. K. and Mellor, F. J. (1975) *Deviance in Classrooms*. London: Routledge and Kegan Paul. 102, 108

Hartley, D. (1978) 'Teachers' definitions of boys and girls: some comparisons', *Research in Education*, 20. 106

Harrop, M. (1981) 'Popular conceptions of mobility', *Sociology*, 14(1). 271

Harvey, D. and Slatin, G. (1976) 'The relationship between child's SES and teacher expectation: a test of the middle-class bias hypothesis', *Social Forces*, 54(1). 168

Havinghurst, R. J. and Neugarten, B. L. (1967) *Society and Education*. Boston: Allyn and Bacon. 62

Heath, A. and Clifford, P. (1980) 'The seventy thousand hours that Rutter left out', *Oxford Review of Education*, 6(1). 92

Heath, A. and Ridge, J. (1982) 'Schools, examinations and occupational attainment' in Capello, Dei and Rossi 1982 and Purvis and Hales 1983. 269

Hebb, D. O. (1949) *Organisation of Behaviour*. New York: Wiley. 200

*Higher Education*. (1963) (The Robbins Report) Command 2154. London: HMSO. 25, 86, 182, 245

Holly, D. (1973) *Beyond Curriculum*. London: Hart-Davies MacGibbon. 121

Holt, J. (1982) *How Children Fail*. London: Penguin. 123

Hopper, E. (1971) *Readings in the Theory of Educational Systems*. London: Hutchinson. 134

Hoselitz, B. F. (1965) 'Investment in education and its political impact' in Coleman 1965b. 252

*Household Composition Tables (10% Sample)* (1975) Census 1971, England and Wales, OPCS. London: HMSO. 183

Howick, C. and Hassani, H. (1979) 'Education spending: primary', *CES Review*, 5. 227

Howick, C. and Hassani, H. (1980) 'Education spending: secondary', *CES Review*, 8. 228

Hymes, D. and Gumperz, J. J. (1971) *Directions in Social Linguistics*. New York: Holt, Rinehart and Winston. 205, 296

Illich, I. (1971) *Deschooling Society*. London: Penguin. 74

Ingleby, J. D. and Cooper, E. (1974) 'How teachers perceive first year school children: sex and ethnic differences', *Sociology*, 8(3). 106, 165

Jackson, B. (1964) *Streaming: An Educational System in Miniature*. London: Routledge and Kegan Paul. 153, 154

Jackson, B. (1979) *Starting School*. London : Croom Helm. 57

Jackson, B. and Marsden, D. (1962/66) *Education and the Working Class*. London: Routledge and Kegan Paul. 78, 137

Jackson, P. (1968) *Life in Classrooms*. Eastbourne: Holt, Rinehart and Winston. 49, 68

Jamieson, I. (1980) 'Capitalism and culture', *Sociology*, 14(2). 254

# Bibliography and Author Index

Jencks, C., Smith, M., Acland, H., Bane, M. J., Cohen, D., Gintis, H., Heyns, B. and Michelson, B. (1972) *Inequality: A Reassessment of the Effect of Family and Schooling in America*. New York: Basic Books. 90

Jensen, A. R. (1973) *Educability and Group Differences*. London: Methuen. 198

Jensen, A. R. (1973) *Educational Differences*. London: Methuen. 198

Joiner, D. (1971) 'Office territory', *New Society*, 7 October. 66

Kalton, G. (1966) *The Public Schools*. London: Longman. 146

Kamin, L. (1974) *The Science and Politics of IQ*. New York: Wiley. 201

Karabel, J. and Halsey, J. H. (1977) *Power and Ideology in Education*. New York: Oxford University Press. 296, 298, 303

Keddie, N. (1971) 'Classroom knowledge' in Young 1971, Hammersley and Woods 1984b. 60, 101, 108

Kelsall, R. K. (1963) 'Survey of all graduates', *Sociological Review Monograph*, 7. 184

Khan, V. (1979) *Minority Families in Britain*. London: Macmillan. 57

Kimberley, A. E. (1986) 'Attitudes to sex education with junior school-aged children'. Unpublished PhD thesis, University of Bradford. 114

King, R. (1969) *Values and Involvement in a Grammar School*. London: Routledge and Kegan Paul. 136, 157

King, R. (1974) 'Social class, educational attainment and provision', LEA case study. *Policy and Politics*, 2(3). 229

King, R. (1977) *Education*, 2nd edition. London: Longman. 89

King, R. (1978) *All Things Bright and Beautiful?* London: Wiley and Sons. 105, 107, 115, 163

King, R. (1980) 'Weberian perspectives and the study of education', *British Journal of Sociology of Education*, 1(1). 282, 285

King, R. (1983) *The Sociology of School Organisation*. London: Methuen. 57

Kluckhohn, F. R. and Strodbeck, F. L. (1961) *Variations in Value Orientations*. Illinois: Row Peterson. 218

Kozol, J. (1968) *Death at an Early Age*. London: Penguin. 115

*Labour Force Survey 1983* (1986) OPCS, Series LFS, No. 5. London: HMSO. 240, 241

Labov, W. (1969) 'The logic of non-standard English', *Georgetown Monographs on Language and Linguistics*, 22 in Giglioli 1972. 169, 209

Lacey, C. (1970) *Hightown Grammar*. Manchester University Press. 83, 136, 156, 157

Lacey, C. (1977) *The Socialisation of Teachers*. London: Methuen. 87, 89

Lambart, A. M. (1976) 'The sisterhood' in Hammersley and Woods 1976. 84

Lambert, R. with Milam, S. (1968) *The Hothouse Society*. London: Weidenfeld and Nicolson. 84

Lawson, J. and Silver, H. (1973) *A Social History of Education in England*. London: Routledge and Kegan Paul. 56

Layard, P. R. G., Sagan, J. D., Ager, M. E. and Jones, D. J. (1971) *Qualified Manpower and Economic Performance*. London: Penguin. 252

Lee, D. J. (1968) 'Class differentials in educational opportunity and promotion from the ranks', *Sociology*, 2(2). 266, 269

Le Grand, J. (1978) 'The distribution of public expenditure: the case of health care', *Economica*, 45. 225

Le Grand, J. (1982) 'The distribution of public expenditure on education', *Economica*, 49. 225

Levitas, M. (1974) *Marxist Perspectives in the Sociology of Education*. London: Routledge and Kegan Paul. 53

Little, A. (1975) 'The educational achievement of ethnic minority children in London schools' in Verma and Bagley 1975. 138

Little, A. (1981) 'Education and race relations in the United Kingdom' in Nisbet and Hoyle 1981. 189

Little, A. and Westergaard, J. (1964) 'The trend of class differentials in educational opportunity in England and Wales', *British Journal of Sociology*, 15(4). 269

Lobban, G. (1976) 'Sex roles in reading schemes' in Children's Rights Workshop 1976. 71

Lydall, H. (1968) *The Structure of Earnings*. London: Oxford University Press. 257

McCready, D. (1972) *Guide to Social Science Courses*. London: ATCDE. 40

McDonald, J. and Thomson, A. (1975) 'Boy beats girl', *Times Educational Supplement*, 25 July. 71

McLeish, J. (1970) *Students' Attitudes and College Environments*. Cambridge Institute of Education. 38

McNamara, D. R. (1972) 'Sociology of education and the education of teachers', *British Journal of Educational Studies*, 20(2), in Reid and Wormald, 1974. 40

Mabey, C. (1981) 'Black British literacy', *Education Research*, 23(2). 190

Mackintosh, N. J. and Massie-Taylor, C. G. N. (1985) 'The IQ Question', Annex D in *Education for All* 1985. 201

Maguire, M. J. and Ashton, D. N. (1981 Analysis, 3(2). 248

Main, B. and Raffe, D. (1983) 'The transition from school to work', *British Educational Research Journal*, 9(1). 240

Mannheim, K. and Stewart, W. A. C. (1962) *An Introduction to the Sociology of Education*. London: Routledge and Kegan Paul. 36

Marsden, D. (1971) *Politicians, Comprehensives and Equality*, Fabian Society Tract 411. London: Gollancz. 150

Masters, P. L. and Hockey, S. W. (1963) 'Natural reserves of ability – some evidence from independent schools', *Times Educational Supplement*, 17 May. 146

Maxwell, J. (1969) *Sixteen Years On*. London University Press. 265

Maxwell, J. (1977) *Reading Progress from 8–15*. Slough: NFER. 186

Measor, L. and Woods, P. (1984) 'Cultivating the middle ground: teachers and school ethos', *Research in Education*, 31. 130

Meighan, R. (1977) 'Pupils' perceptions of the classroom techniques of postgraduate student teachers', *British Journal of Teacher Education*, 3(2). 100

Meighan, R. (1981) *A Sociology of Educating*. London: Holt, Rinehart and Winston. 100

# Bibliography and Author Index

Mennell, S. (1974) *Sociological Theory: Uses and Unities*. London: Nelson. 33

Mercer, N. (1981) 'Making sense of school', *New Society*, 19 October. 114

Merton, R. K. (1957) *Social Theory and Social Action*. Glencoe: Free Press. 77, 80, 133

Meyenn, R. J. (1980) 'Schoolgirls' peer groups', in Woods 1980a. 84

Midwinter, E. (1972) *Social Environment and the Urban School*. London: Ward Lock. 73

Midwinter, E. (1977) *Education for Sale*. London: Allen and Unwin. 217

Millstein, B. (1972) *Women's Studies–Women in History*. New York Board of Education. 71

Mottaz, C. (1984) 'Education and work satisfaction', *Human Relations*, 37(11). 253

MSC (1978) *Young People and Work*, Manpower Studies No. 19781. London: HMSO. 249

Murdock, G. and Phelps, G. (1972) 'Youth culture and the school revisited', *British Journal of Sociology*, 23(4). 82

Murdock, G. and Phelps, G. (1973) *Mass Media and the Secondary School*. London: Schools Council Publications, Macmillan. 84

Musgrave, P. W. (1968) *Society and Education in England since 1800*. London: Methuen. 56

Musgrave, P. W. (1970) *Sociology, History and Education*. London: Methuen. 56


Nash, R. (1972) 'History as she is taught', *New Society*, 3 August. 72

Nash, R. (1973) *Classrooms Observed*. London: Routledge and Kegan Paul. 102, 164

Nash, R. (1974) 'Pupils' expectations of their teachers', *Research in Education*, 12 in Stubbs and Delamont 1976. 96

Newson, J. and Newson E. (1963, 1968, 1976, 1977) *Infant Care in an Urban Community*; *Four Years Old in an Urban Community*; *Seven Years Old in an Urban Community*; *Perspectives on School at Seven Years Old*. London: Allen and Unwin. 57

Nisbet, S. and Hoyle, E. (1981) *World Yearbook of Education*. London: Kogan Page. 306

Noble, T. (1975, 1981) *Modern Britain: Structure and Change*. London: Batsford. 263

*NOP Review No. 23* (1980) London: NOP. 149, 250


*Organisation of Secondary Education* (1965). Circular 10/65, DES. London: HMSO. 150

Ottaway, A. K. C. (1953) *Education and Society*. London: Routledge and Kegan Paul. 36

*Oxford University Gazette* (1984). Supplement (1) to No. 3966. 146


Pallister, R. and Wilson, J. (1970) 'Parents' attitudes to education', *Educational Research*, 13(1). 51

Parsons, T. (1942) 'Age and sex in the social structure of the United States', *American Sociological Review*, 29(4). 81

Parsons, T. (1949) *Essays in Sociological Theory*. New York: Free Press. 29

Parsons, T. (1951) *The Social System*. New York: Free Press. 29

Parsons, T. (1959) 'The school class as a social system', *Harvard Educational Review,* 29(4), in Halsey et al 1961. 50, 59

Partridge, J. (1966/68) *Life in a Secondary Modern School.* London: Gollancz/ Penguin. 157

Peaslee, A. L. (1969) 'Education's role in development', *Economic Development and Cultural Change,* 17. 252

Perrucci, R. (1961) 'The significance of intragenerational mobility: some methodological and theoretical notes, together with a case study of engineers', *American Sociological Review,* 26(1). 267

Perrucci, C. C. and Perrucci, R. (1970) 'Social origins, educational contexts and career mobility', *American Sociological Review,* 35(3). 254

Pollard, A. (1979) 'Negotiating deviance and "getting done" in primary school classrooms' in Barton and Meighan 1979. 84, 123, 125, 126

Pollard, A. (1980) 'Teacher interests and changing situations of survival threats in primary school classrooms' in Woods 1980b. 121, 130

Pollard, A. (1982) 'A model of classroom coping strategies', *British Journal of Sociology of Education,* 3(1). 121

Pollard, A. (1984) 'Goodies, jokers and gangs' in Hammersley and Woods 1984a. 131

Pratt, D. J., Burgess, T., Allemano, R. and Locke, M. (1973) *Your Local Education.* London: Penguin. 225

Preece, P. F. W. (1979) 'Fifteen taus and rhos', *Research Intelligence,* (BERA) August. 92

Price, R. and Bain, G. S. (1976) 'Union growth revisited: 1948–1974 in perspective', *British Journal of Industrial Relations,* 14(3). 246

*Primary Education in England. A survey by HM Inspectors of Schools* (1978), DES. London: HMSO. 154, 186

Pscharopoulos, G. (1977) 'Family background, education and achievement: a path model of earnings determinants in the UK and some alternatives', *British Journal of Sociology,* 28(3). 271

*Public Schools Commission* (1968), DES. London: HMSO. 145, 158

Pumfrey, P. D. (1975) 'Season of birth, special educational treatment and selection procedures within an LEA', *Research in Education,* 14. 196

Purvis, J. and Hales, M. (1983) *Achievement and Inequality in Education.* London: Routledge and Kegan Paul. 303, 304, 313

Ratcliffe, R. (1971) 'The adolescent and authority', *Youth in Society,* 58. 98

Rayner, J. and Harden, J. (1973) *Equality and City Schools,* Vol. 2. London: Routledge and Kegan Paul. 74

Rayner, J. and Harris, E. (1977) *Schooling and the City,* Vol. 2. London: Ward Lock. 74

Reddin, M. (1972) 'Which LEAs help children stay on at school?' *Where,* 72. 228

Reid, E. (1980) 'Employers' use of educational qualifications', *Education Policy Bulletin,* 8(1). 249

Reid, I. (1969) 'An analysis of social factors in children's educational experience between 11 and 17 years of age in two LEA areas'. Unpublished MA Thesis, University of Liverpool. 184, 219

# Bibliography and Author Index

Reid, I. (1975) 'Some reflections on sociology in colleges of education', *Educational Studies*, 1(1). 36, 286

Reid, I. (1977a) *Social Class Differences in Britain*. London: Open Books; 2nd Edition 1981. 35, 36, 237

Reid, I. (1977b) 'Some views of Sunday School teachers', *Learning for Living*, 17(2). 54

Reid, I. (1978a) *Sociological Perspectives on School and Education*. London: Open Books. 56, 286

Reid, I. (1978b) 'Past and present trends in the sociology of education – a plea for a return to educational sociology' in Barton and Meighan 1978. 36, 284, 286

Reid, I. (1980) 'Teachers and social class', *Westminster Studies in Education*, 3. 86

Reid, I. (1981) *Social Class Differences in Britain*. 2nd Edition, Oxford: Blackwell. 35, 133, 176, 184, 192, 236, 243, 256

Reid, I. (1986a) 'Who's afraid of social class?' *New Education*, 8(1). 193

Reid, I. (1986b) 'Hoops, roundabouts and swings in teacher education: a critical review of CATE criteria', *Journal of Further and Higher Education*, 10(2). 41

Reid, I., Brennen, J., Waton, A. and Deem, R. (1984) 'The cuts in British higher education', *British Journal of Sociology of Education*, 5(2). 285

Reid, I. and Cohen, L. (1973) 'Achievement orientation, intellectual achievement responsibility and choice between degree and certificate courses in colleges of education', *British Journal of Educational Psychology*, 42(1). 262

Reid, I. and Rushton, J. (1985) *Teachers, Computers and the Classroom*. Manchester University Press. 73

Reid, I. and Wormald, E. (1974) *Sociology and Teacher Education*. London: ATCDE. 36, 40, 302, 306, 310

Reid, I. and Wormald, E. (1982) *Sex Differences in Britain*. Oxford: Blackwell. 164

Reid, M. I., Clunies-Ross, L. R., Goacher, B. and Vile, C. (1981) 'Mixed ability teaching: problems and possibilities', *Educational Research*, 24(1). 161

Reid, W. (1972) *The Universities and the Sixth-Form Curriculum*. London: Schools Council Research Studies. 69

Rex, J. (1974) *Approaches to Sociology*. London: Routledge and Kegan Paul. 296

Reynolds, D. (1976) 'The delinquent school' in Hammersley and Woods 1976. 37, 91

Reynolds, D. (1984) 'Relative autonomy reconstructed' in Barton and Walker 1984. 280

Reynolds, D., Jones, D. and St Ledger, S. (1976) 'Schools do make a difference'. *New Society*, 29 July. 91

Reynolds, D. and Sullivan, M. (1979) 'Bringing schools back in' in Barton and Meighan 1979. 90

Rist, R. C. (1970) 'Student, social class and teacher expectation', *Harvard Educational Review*, 40(3). 59

Roberts, K., Noble, M. and Duggan, J. (1983) 'Young, black and out of work' in Troyna and Smith 1983. 192

Robinson, P. (1977) *Education and Poverty*. London: Methuen. 204

Rodriguez, O. (1978) 'Occupational shifts and educational upgrading in the American labour force between 1950 and 1970' *Sociology of Education*, 51(1). 251

Rogers, R. (1980) 'The myth of "independent" schools', *New Statesman*, 4 Jan. 144

Rosen, H. (1972) 'The language of textbooks' in Cashdan and Grugeon 1972. 115

Rubinstein, D. (1979) *Education and Equality*. London: Penguin. 303

Rutter, M., Maughan, R., Mortimore, P. and Ouston, J. (1979) *Fifteen Thousand Hours*. London: Open Books. 91, 182


Sampson, A. (1982) *The Changing Anatomy of Britain*. London: Hodder and Stoughton.

Schuard, H. (1981) 'Mathematics and the ten-year-old', *Times Educational Supplement*, 27 March.

Searle, P. M. A. and Stibbs, A. (1985) The participation of ethnic minority students in post-graduate teaching training. *Collected Original Resources in Education*. 10, 2

*Secondary Education* (1938) (The Spens Report). Board of Education London: HMSO. 25

Sharp, R. and Green, A. (1975) *Education and Social Control*. London: Routledge and Kegan Paul. 37, 110, 156

Sharpe, S. (1976) *Just like a Girl*. London: Penguin. 57, 138

Shipman, M. D. (1968 and 1975) *Sociology of the School*. London: Longman. 56

Shipman, M. D. (1971) *Education and Modernisation*. London: Faber and Faber. 56

Shipman, M. D. (1974) 'Reflections on early courses' in Reid and Wormold 1974. 37

Sills, D. L. (1968) *International Encyclopedia of Social Science*. New York: Macmillan. 302

Silver, H. (1973) *Equal Opportunity in Education*. London: Methuen. 141

Sinclair, J. M. and Coulthard, R. M. (1974) *Towards an Analysis of Discourse: The English Used by Teachers and Pupils*. London: Oxford University Press. 113

Smith, D. J. (1977) *Racial Disadvantage in Britain*. London: Penguin. 204

Smith, D. J. (1980) 'Unemployment and racial minority groups', *Employment Gazette*, 88(6). 241

*Social Trends 15* (1985) CSO. London: HMSO. 140, 144, 187, 245

Soloff, S. (1973) 'The effect of non-content factors on the grading of essays', *Graduate Research in Education and Related Disciplines*, 6(2). 170

*Special Educational Needs* (1978) (The Warnock Report). The report of the Committee of Enquiry into the education of handicapped children and young people. London: HMSO. 139

Spencer, H. (1861) *Education: Intellectual, Moral, and Physical*. London: Manwaring. 36

Spender, D. (1980) *Man Made Language*. London: Routledge and Kegan Paul. 165

Squibb, P. (1973) Education and class. *Educational Research*, 15(3). 214

Stacey, B. (1965) 'Achievement motivation and intergenerational mobiliy', *Life Sciences*, 4(B). 262

Stacey, B. (1969) 'Achievement motivation, occupational choice and intergenerational mobiliy', *Human Relations*, 22(3). 262

Stanworth, M. (1983) *Gender and Schooling*. London: Hutchinson with the Exploration in Feminism Collective. 98, 106

# Bibliography and Author Index

Stanworth, P. and Giddens, A. (1974) *Elites and Power in British Society*. Cambridge University Press. 313

*Statistical Bulletin 6/84* (1984). DES. London: HMSO. 43

*Statistical Bulletin 13/84* (1984). DES. London: HMSO. 185

*Statistics of Education 1961*: Supplement (1962) Ministry of Education. London: HMSO. 181

*Statistics of Education 1964*, Vol. 3 (1966) DES. London: HMSO. 244

*Statistics of Education 1970*, Vol. 4 (1972) DES. London: HMSO. 36

*Statistics of Education 1975*, Vol. 4 (1976) DES. London: HMSO. 36

*Statistics of Education 1975*, Vol. 2 (1977) DES. London: HMSO. 244

*Statistics of Education 1982*, (1984) DES. London: HMSO. 187

*Statistics of School Leavers, CSE and GCE, England 1984* (1985) DES. London: HMSO. 147

Stebbins, R. A. (1980) 'The role of humour in teaching' in Woods 1980b. 130

Stewart, O. F. (1978) 'The role of ethnicity in teachers' accounts of their interaction with pupils in multicultural classrooms'. Unpublished MSc, University of Aston, quoted in *Education for All* (1985). 107

Stone, M. (1981) *The Education of the Black Child in Britain*. London: Fontana. 98

Stones, E. (1979) 'The colour of conceptual learning' in Verma and Bagley 1979. 202

Stubbs, M. (1976) 'Keeping in touch: some functions of teacher talk' in Stubbs and Delamont 1976. 122

Stubbs, M. (1983) *Language, Schools and Classrooms*. London: Methuen. 206, 208

Stubbs, M. and Delamont, S. (1976) *Explorations in Classroom Observation*. London: Wiley and Sons. 299, 301, 307, 311, 312

Sugarman, B. M. (1966) 'Social class and values as related to achievement in school', *Sociology*, 14(3). 219

Sugarman, B. M. (1967) 'Involvement in youth culture; academic achievement and conformity on school', *British Journal of Sociology*, 18(2). 81

Supplementary Benefits Commission, *Annual Report 1976* (1977). London: HMSO. 300

Sutherland, M. (1973) 'Education in Northern Ireland' in Bell, et al 1973. 44

Swift, D. F. (1967) 'Social class, mobility ideology and 11+', *British Journal of Sociology*, 17(2). 219


Taylor, F. (1974) *Race, School and Community*. Slough: NFER. 212

Taylor, G. (1971) 'North and south: the education split', *New Society* 4 March. 224

Taylor, G. and Ayres, N. (1969) *Born and Bred Unequal*. London: Longman. 224

Taylor, M. T. (1976) 'Teachers' perceptions of their pupils', *Research in Education*, 18. 102

Taylor, P. H. (1962) 'Children's evaluations of the characteristics of the good teacher', *British Journal of Educational Psychology*, 32(3).

*The Times House of Commons* (1964/84) London: Times Newspapers. 142

Thompson, B. L. (1975) 'Secondary school pupils' attitudes to school and teachers', *Educational Research*, 18(1). 98

Thompson, D. (1971) 'Season of birth and success in the secondary school', *Educational Research*, 14(1). 196

Thompson, P. G. (1971) 'Some factors in upward social mobility in England', *Sociology and Social Research*, 55(2). 252

Tibbenham, A., Essen, J. and Fogelman, K. (1978) 'Ability grouping and school characteristics', *British Journal of Educational Studies*, 26(1). 191

Tizard, B., Mortimore, J. and Burchell, B. (1981) *Involving Parents in Nursery and Infant School*. London: Grant McIntyre. 217

Tomlinson, S. (1980) 'The educational performance of ethnic minority children', *New Community*, 8(3). 191

Tomlinson, S. (1982) *A Sociology of Special Education*. London: Routledge and Kegan Paul. 139

Townsend, H. E. R. and Brittan, E. M. (1972) *Organisation in Multi-racial Schools*. Slough: NFER. 107

Townsend, P. (1979) *Poverty in the United Kingdom*. London: Penguin. 202, 208

Troyna, B. S. (1978) 'Race and streaming: a case study', *Educational Review*, 30(1). 83, 156, 158, 213

Troyna, B. (1984) 'Fact or artefact? The educational under-achievement of black pupils', *British Journal of Sociology of Education*, 5(2). 192

Troyna, B. and Smith, D. (1983) *Racism, School and the Labour Market*. Leicester: National Youth Bureau. 309

Trudgill, P. (1975) *Accent, Dialect and the School*. London: Edward Arnold. 169, 204

Tuckwell, P. (1982) 'Pleasing teacher' in Booth and Stratham 1982. 123

Tunley, P., Travers, T. and Pratt, J. (1979) *Depriving the Deprived*. London: Kogan Page. 229

Turner, G. (1983) *The Social World of the Comprehensive School*. London: Croom Helm. 129

UCCA (1984) *Statistical Supplement to the Twenty-first Report* Cheltenham: UCCA. 146

UCCA (1985) *Twenty-second Report 1983–4*. Cheltenham: UCCA. 183

UCCA (1985) *Statistical Supplement to the Twenty-second Report 1983–4*. Cheltenham: UCCA. 183

*University Statistics 1980* (1982). Vol. 1, Students and Staff. Cheltenham: Universities' Statistical Record. 188

Urry, J. and Wakefield, J. (1973) *Power in Britain*. London: Heinemann. 302

Van Den Berghe, P. L. (1963) 'Dialectic and functionalism: towards a theoretical synthesis', *American Sociological Review*, 28(5) in Wallace 1969. 30

Vaughan, M. and Archer, M. S. (1971) *Social Conflict and Educational Change in England and France*. Cambridge University Press. 56

Verma, G. and Bagley, C. (1975) *Race and Education across Cultures*. London: Heinemann.

Verma, G. K. and Bagley, C. (1979) *Race, Education and Identity*. London: Macmillan. 294, 311

Vulliamy, G. (1978) 'Culture, class and school music' in Barton and Meighan 1978. 72

# Bibliography and Author Index

Wakeford, J. (1969) *The Cloistered Elite*. London: Macmillan. 78

Walker, R. and Adelman, C. (1975) 'Interaction analysis in informal classrooms: a critical comment on the Flanders system', *British Journal of Educational Psychology*, 45 (1). 112

Walker, R. and Adelman, C. (1976) 'Strawberries' in Stubbs and Delamont 1976. 95, 113, 129

Walker, R. and Goodson, I. (1977) 'Humour in the classroom' in Woods and Hammersley 1977. 129

Wallace, W. L. (1969) *Sociological Theory*. London: Heinemann. 27, 312

Waller, W. (1932) (1965) *The Sociology of Teaching*. New York: Wiley. 21, 53, 58, 81

Wanzel, J. G. (1970) 'On the containment of education', *Interchange*, 1(4). 64

Ward, M. (1979) *Mathematics and the ten-year-old*. Schools Council Working Paper, 61. London: Evans/Methuen.186

Watson, J. L. (1977) *Between Two Cultures*. Oxford: Blackwell. 57

Wedge, P. and Prosser, H. (1973) *Born to Fail*? London: Arrow. 203

Weeks, D. R. (1972) *A Glossary of Sociological Concepts*. Milton Keynes: Open University Press. 46

Westergaard, J. (1972) 'The myth of classlessness' in Blackburn 1972. 269

Westergaard, J. and Resler, H. (1975) *Class in a Capitalist Society*. London: Heinemann. 269

*West Indian Children in our Schools*. (1981) (The Rampton Report) Interim report of the education of children from ethnic minority groups. London: HMSO. 190

Whincup, J. (1983) 'The teachers' underlife: a defence of participant observation'. Unpublished MSc dissertation, University of Bradford. 89

*Whitaker's Almanac 1984* (1984) (116th Edition) London: Whitaker. 142

Whitely, R. (1974) 'The city and industry: the directors of large companies, their characteristics and connections' in Stanworth and Giddens 1974. 142

*Who's Who* (1984) London: A. and C. Black. 142

Williams, S. (1980) 'Stumbling over the sixth-form step', *Guardian*, 26 Feb. 228

Willims, J. D. and Cuttance, P. (1985) 'School effects in Scottish schools', *British Journal of Sociology of Education*, 6(3). 93

Willis, P. (1976) 'The class significance of school counter culture' in Hammersley and Woods, 1976, Dale et al 1981a Purvis and Hales 1983. 76, 281

Willis, P. (1977) *Learning to Labour*. Farnborough: Saxon House. 76, 79, 83, 89, 158, 281

Woods, P. (1975) 'Showing them up in secondary school' in Chanan and Delamont 1975. 129

Woods, P. (1976) 'Having a laugh: an antidote to schooling' in Hammersley and Woods 1976. 130

Woods, P. (1977) *The Pupils' Experience*. Course E202, Unit 11, Block II. Milton Keynes: Open University Press. 78, 80, 119

Woods, P. (1979) *The Divided School*. London: Routledge and Kegan Paul. 78, 80, 89, 107, 119

Woods, P. (1980a) *Pupil Strategies*. London: Croom Helm. 299, 306

Woods, P. (1980b) *Teachers' Strategies*. London: Croom Helm. 295, 303, 308, 310

Woods, P. (1981) 'Strategies, commitment and identity: making and breaking the teacher role' in Barton and Walker 1981. 122

Woods, P. (1983) *Sociology and the School*. London: Routledge and Kegan Paul. 123, 127

Woods, P. and Hammersley, M. (1977) *School Experience*. London: Croom Helm. 294, 301, 312

Wragg, E. C. (1973) 'A study of student teachers in the classroom' in Chanan 1973. 112

Wright, C. (1985) 'Learning environment or battleground?', *Multi-cultural Teaching*, 4(1). 166

Wright, C. (1985) 'Who succeeds at school – and who decides?', *Multi-cultural Teaching*, 4(1). 166

Wright Mills, C. (1959) *The Sociological Imagination*. London: Oxford University Press. 38


Young, M. (1958) *The Rise of the Meritocracy*. London: Thames and Hudson. 273

Young, M. and Willmott, P. (1975) *The Symmetrical Family*. London: Penguin. 57

Young, M. F. D. (1971) *Knowledge and Control*. London: Cassell and Collier. 69, 259, 296, 305

Young, T. R. and Beardsley, P. (1968) 'The sociology of classroom teaching – microfunctional analysis', *Journal of Educational Thought*, 33(2). 61

# Index

*Figures in italics refer to tables*

# Index

# Index